YOUTH ACTIVISM IN AN ERA OF
EDUCATION INEQUALITY

QUALITATIVE STUDIES IN PSYCHOLOGY

This series showcases the power and possibility of qualitative work in psychology. Books feature detailed and vivid accounts of qualitative psychology research using a variety of methods, including participant observation and field work, discursive and textual analyses, and critical cultural history. They probe vital issues of theory, implementation, interpretation, representation, and ethics that qualitative workers confront. The series mission is to enlarge and refine the repertoire of qualitative approaches to psychology.

GENERAL EDITORS

Michelle Fine and Jeanne Marecek

Everyday Courage: The Lives and Stories of Urban Teenagers
Niobe Way

Negotiating Consent in Psychotherapy
Patrick O'Neill

Flirting with Danger: Young Women's Reflections on Sexuality and Domination
Lynn M. Phillips

Voted Out: The Psychological Consequences of Anti-Gay Politics
Glenda M. Russell

Inner-City Kids: Adolescents Confront Life and Violence in an Urban Community
Alice McIntyre

From Subjects to Subjectivities: A Handbook of Interpretive and Participatory Methods
Edited by Deborah L. Tolman and Mary Brydon-Miller

Growing Up Girl: Psychosocial Explorations of Gender and Class
Valerie Walkerdine, Helen Lucey, and June Melody

Voicing Chicana Feminisms: Young Women Speak Out on Sexuality and Identity
Aida Hurtado

Situating Sadness: Women and Depression in Social Context
Edited by Janet M. Stoppard and Linda M. McMullen

Living Outside Mental Illness: Qualitative Studies of Recovery in Schizophrenia
Larry Davidson

Autism and the Myth of the Person Alone
Douglas Biklen
With Sue Rubin, Tito Rajarshi Mukhopadhyay, Lucy Blackman, Larry Bissonnette, Alberto Frugone, Richard Attfield, and Jamie Burke

American Karma: Race, Culture, and Identity in the Indian Diaspora
Sunil Bhatia

Muslim American Youth: Understanding Hyphenated Identities through Multiple Methods
Selcuk R. Sirin and Michelle Fine

Pride in the Projects: Teens Building Identities in Urban Contexts
Nancy L. Deutsch

Corridor Cultures: Mapping Student Resistance at an Urban High School
Maryann Dickar

Gay Men Becoming Dads: Transitions to Adoptive Fatherhood
Abbie E. Goldberg

Living with Brain Injury: Narrative, Community, and Women's Renegotiation of Identity
Eric Stewart

Violent Accounts: Understanding the Psychology of Perpetrators through South Africa's Truth and Reconciliation Commission
Robert N. Kraft

Youth Activism in an Era of Education Inequality
Ben Kirshner

Youth Activism in an Era of Education Inequality

Ben Kirshner

NEW YORK UNIVERSITY PRESS

New York and London

NEW YORK UNIVERSITY PRESS
New York and London
www.nyupress.org

References to Internet websites (URLs) were accurate at the time of writing.
Neither the author nor New York University Press is responsible for URLs
that may have expired or changed since the manuscript was prepared.

ISBN: 978-1-4798-6131-6 (hardback)
ISBN: 978-1-4798-9805-3 (paperback)

For Library of Congress Cataloging-in-Publication data, please contact
the Library of Congress.

New York University Press books are printed on acid-free paper,
and their binding materials are chosen for strength and durability.
We strive to use environmentally responsible suppliers and materials
to the greatest extent possible in publishing our books.

Manufactured in the United States of America

10 9 8 7 6 5 4 3 2 1

Also available as an ebook

To my parents, Louis and Kathryn.

CONTENTS

ACKNOWLEDGMENTS

This book bears my name on its cover but it grows out of a series of projects that have each been fundamentally collaborative. Ideas always have social origins. And good ideas about youth activism depend on examples of imaginative, dedicated people working together to improve the world. In this brief acknowledgment I want to honor the contributions of many of the people who contributed to the research and writing of this book.

Over the past ten years I've spent time with and learned from politically engaged youth and young adults in California and Colorado who fight to expand opportunities and access for young people of color. I owe a giant thank you to all these people for granting my request to spend time in their organizations and classrooms and document their work. In Oakland and San Francisco, this includes young people and staff from Youth Engaged in Leadership and Learning, Kids First, and Teens Restoring the Urban Environment. During my research in the Bay Area several people in the youth development field played a key role in helping me define my questions and gain access to organizations, including: Yolanda Anyon, McCrae Parker, Taj James, Kim Miyoshi, Ken Ikeda, and Tom Ahn. I benefited from the guidance of expert scholars and mentors at Stanford University, including Na'ilah Nasir, Milbrey McLaughlin, Ray McDermott, and William Damon. Colleagues in the John W. Gardner Center, Jennifer O'Donoghue, Karen Strobel, and María Fernandez, pushed my thinking and writing.

After moving to Colorado, several people helped me navigate the landscape of youth organizations and community organizing, including Soyun Park, DeQuan Mack, Brian Barhaugh, Candi CdeBaca, Michael Simmons, Shanita Lewis, Shontel Lewis, Pam Martinez, Brad Jupp, Ricky Escobedo, Jorge Merida, and Araceli Lerma. In addition, I am indebted to the members of the Tracing Transitions participatory research team for their collaborative work to understand and speak out

about high school closure. I thank all the students from Jefferson High School for telling their stories and sharing their perspectives. I also owe a tremendous debt to the students and teachers who participated in the Critical Civic Inquiry project, which took place at multiple schools and with hundreds of students. Shelley Zion and Carlos Hipolito-Delgado initiated the idea of developing Critical Civic Inquiry in a way that would be sustainable and impactful.

I have sought out the constructive criticism of several scholars on various parts of this manuscript. Although I take sole responsibility for the perspectives and analyses presented here, I want to thank the following people (in alphabetical order) for their feedback on earlier drafts of chapters: Matt Diemer, Rubén Donato, Erik Dutilly, Shawn Ginwright, Hava Gordon, Andrew Greene, Nosakhere Griffin-EL, Rashida Govan, Kris Gutiérrez, Carlos Hipolito-Delgado, Buzzy Jackson, Susan Jurow, Soo Ah Kwon, Peter Levine, Dan Liston, Pam Martinez, Mike McDevitt, Elizabeth Mendoza, Kevin O'Connor, William Perez, Bill Penuel, Joe Polman, Kristen Pozzoboni, Rod Watts, Kevin Welner, and Shelley Zion.

Several graduate students also played essential roles in data collection and analysis for work presented in this book. Kristen Pozzoboni helped to design and facilitate the Tracing Transitions project and worked with me to analyze data. We coauthored three manuscripts about the project, one of which was adapted for this book's discussion of activism against school closures. Matthew Gaertner led the quantitative analysis of achievement data from the Tracing Transitions project and coauthored one manuscript. For the Critical Civic Inquiry (CCI) project, Carrie Allen, Erin Allaman, Josie Chang-Order, Elizabeth Mendoza, Emily Price, Rita Tracy, and Adam York helped Shelley Zion, Carlos Hipolito-Delgado, and me to design the CCI project, as well as to code and analyze data. Elizabeth Mendoza was the lead ethnographer for data collected at Roosevelt High, discussed in chapter 1.

I want to thank the Spencer Foundation for providing a grant that supported the Tracing Transitions project and a major grant that enabled us to develop and implement the Critical Civic Inquiry project. This funding was essential to our ability to carry out our work. In addition, the Carson Foundation and the University of Colorado provided grants that enabled us to provide stipends to youth researchers and other necessary materials for the Tracing Transitions project. My ethnography of youth activism in the Bay Area was supported in part by the John W. Gardner Center for Youth and Their Communities, based at Stanford University, where I was a graduate research assistant. The Atlantic Philanthropies provided funds that supported research about student organizing to end the school to prison pipeline.

I could not have written this book without the support of my family. Thank you, Buzzy and Jackson, for your love and inspiration.

Introduction

It was 1993 and I needed a job. I had heard about a program called Youth in Action, located in a meeting space rented from a church in San Francisco's Mission District, which offered full-time positions for youth workers. I was attracted to the energy, youthfulness, and diversity of its staff, its emphasis on cultivating youths' strengths, and its focus on improving the city's public spaces. They hired me to supervise and mentor middle school youth working on environmental conservation projects around the city. On any Saturday you could see young people wearing blue pants, white T-shirts, and yellow hard hats picking up trash in Dolores Park, gathering recyclables on Ocean Beach, or planting shrubs in Golden Gate Park. It wasn't just manual labor: all the crews explored the ecology and sociology of San Francisco's neighborhoods through our "urbanology" curriculum. Two media crews—journalism and videography—produced stories about issues that mattered to youth. Youth in Action anticipated several of the innovations in youth work that proliferated in the United States in the 1990s, including service learning, digital media, and positive youth development.

A few years into my work in the Mission District I walked around the corner, to the offices of Youth Making a Change (YMAC) on 22nd Street, and encountered something different. They had T-shirts too, but theirs said things like, "Jobs Stop Violence." Instead of cleaning up parks the teenagers in YMAC were leading city campaigns to fund programs for children and organizing against state initiatives that would increase prison spending at the expense of schools. The staff seemed to treat the youth there differently—as people whose ideas about politics and social change mattered, as people with a sense of political agency. YMAC's approach to youth work challenged my assumptions. Youth could be treated more like partners than recipients of help. They were analyzing complex systems and strategizing about how to change them.

Several years later, as a graduate student studying education and youth development, it dawned on me that the kinds of activism I had seen at YMAC were not getting adequate attention from academic researchers. Studies of civic development tended to privilege skills and habits that maintain civil society rather than those that seek its transformation.[1] Although research had begun to emphasize the strengths of urban youth rather than just their deficits, few were documenting an emergent ecology of youth activism that focused on social justice and change. Organizing groups were springing up throughout California in response to a series of state referenda that affected poor and low-income youth of color and immigrant youth, such as Proposition 187 (1994), which barred undocumented immigrants from public education and health care; Proposition 209 (1996), which prohibited the state from considering race, sex, or ethnicity in public education; and Proposition 21 (2000), which increased penalties for crimes committed by youth.[2] The Bay Area, in particular, became a vibrant place for an approach to youth engagement that emphasized political empowerment, partnership, and social justice.[3] Thousands of youth participated in a series of walkouts in the late 1990s to protest the underfunding of education in California and the state's overinvestment in incarceration. Two organizers in the emerging youth movement described it this way:

> For young people, the fight . . . against the rising public investment in punishment and prison is a fight for their lives. The cry is for schools and parks, not prisons; books, not bars; more teachers, counselors and nurses in their schools, not more police officers.[4]

Flash forward from the mid-1990s to Oakland, California, in 2003, where I studied firsthand this emerging activism: Denise, an African American high school student, recounted to me what it was like to speak to the Oakland School Board in support of greater student participation in school governance. "Oh my god, I'm being listened to," she remembered. "I'm about to really bring it! . . . I'm not even going to shut up. I'm finally being listened to!" With supporters filling the first five rows of the meeting room, Denise and her colleagues from a group called

Kids First had taken to the microphone and reported results of more than 900 surveys showing that students wanted input into issues such as school safety and teacher quality. They submitted a "student power resolution" that called for stronger student councils that would work on "real issues—not just planning proms." At the conclusion of the presentation, the school board president stated that he would vote for the resolution and asked that his colleagues do the same. Two weeks later, however, the Oakland school board lost its decision-making authority to a state-appointed administrator when it was reported that the school district faced a deficit in the tens of millions of dollars. Kids First's student leadership resolution did not become policy and Oakland would not have an elected school board accountable to its residents. Organizers went back to the drawing board and reformulated their campaign to create a place for students in improving urban schools.

Activism by groups such as YMAC and Kids First offers examples of youth of color building political power in a context of inequality and exclusion.[5] Oakland students, for example, experienced education inequity every day in schools plagued by longtime permanent subs, undemanding classes, and deteriorating infrastructure. Young people's experiences of inequity were compounded by their typical experience of exclusion from public decision making. Since the early twentieth century American human service institutions—schools, youth programs, and social work—have tended to operate on the basis of perceptions of youth as either dangerous or vulnerable.[6] This pattern continues today, particularly for youth of color, who are more likely to be targets of remediation than partners in decision making. Denise's excitement about "finally being listened to" was emblematic of the scarcity of opportunities for youth to be at the table when important decisions about their schools and neighborhoods are made.

Denise's actions at the school board meeting confronted these problems. And, of course, she was not on her own. She had found her way to an organization that blended a youth development paradigm with a community organizing one. People there discussed inequality as a socially produced problem rather than part of the natural order. Denise and her peers talked about their shared experiences in Oakland's schools, envisioned alternatives, and turned that vision into sustained public work. Such experiences benefited Denise, whose sense of personal agency was fortified by her new repertoire of political skills. But just as important, her participation was good for the Oakland schools because of the way she and her peers introduced new ideas, during that brief moment before the state takeover, into a struggling system. Kids First persisted with its campaign, which has since earned acclaim for its successes. Its example signals how greater youth participation in the public square would enrich and enliven American democracy.

The interdependent relationship between youths' political engagement, their development, and societal health is the central focus of this book. Youth and societal institutions are strengthened when young people, particularly those most disadvantaged by education inequity, turn their critical gaze to education systems and participate in efforts to improve them. The book's case studies of youth organizing and student activism analyze what these experiences mean for young people and why they are good for a socially just democracy. This research is motivated by questions about the relationship between youth activism, human development, and democratic renewal: What is youth activism and how does it contribute to youth development? How might collective movements of young people expand educational opportunity in the United States and resuscitate participatory democracy?

The practical need for such research is stark. The long-standing practice in American schools has been to treat high school students as dependent recipients of services.[7] This status, while providing important legal protections, reinforces social constructions of youth as immature and restricts them to limited forms of participation.[8] How might schools become places where student voice is part of the fabric of institutional decision making? What kinds of learning ecologies are necessary to support youths' engagement in public work with their teachers?

Similarly, although youth development programs have adopted rhetoric that emphasizes young people's assets and strengths, youth-adult partnerships are still the exception rather than the norm.[9] Youth-adult partnerships call for a more radical engagement with youth as *people*, by building sustained intergenerational collectives that deliberate and act together around an issue of shared concern.[10] This book pushes and extends the asset-based approach by providing evidence about young people as partners in decision making rather than just targets of remediation. Rich examples, grounded in the exigencies of practice, are provided that generate tools and strategies. What roles do organizers play? How do young people, who are typically novices in the political realm, learn the necessary skills for participation?

Values and Evidence

The argument for engaging young people as partners in public work, rather than objects of policy, is rooted in a set of normative values. Youth should not be treated as "citizens of the future"; they are citizens now who experience, interpret, and sometimes resist the policies that organize their everyday lives.[11] They deserve to be heard about the institutions and policies that influence their lives, as enshrined in the UN Convention on the Rights of the Child.[12] These values shaped my approach to this research. I acknowledge having an agenda in the sense that I want to highlight the conditions under which youth develop and exercise their collective political agency. I draw on the view of Paolo Freire and others in the community organizing tradition that people who experience the sharp edges of systemic failures ought to be leaders in collective efforts to understand and dismantle them. As a white male from an upper middle-class background, I acknowledge my outsider status in this struggle and engage in ongoing reflection about how my racial privilege shapes my approach to this work. I aspire to provide insight that comes from careful empirical analysis and solidarity with young people's claims to voice and dignity.

The empirical claims in this book draw on evidence from ten years of research in settings—both in and out of school—where youth of color interpreted and took action to solve complex problems ranging from inadequate schools to media bias to barriers to college. The book presents findings from three research studies carried out between 2003 and 2012.[13]

The first study, an ethnography of youth activism, focused on groups in the San Francisco Bay Area where high school youth worked with young adults to develop campaigns to address issues relevant to youths' everyday experiences. One group was motivated by Oakland's dropout rate and wanted to expand opportunities for student voice and leadership in the schools. Another organized a campaign—Don't Believe the Hype—which called for West Oakland's youth to be portrayed with dignity and accuracy by local media. The third organized a conference to educate young people about how the upcoming Iraq war (this was in 2003) would affect their Southeast San Francisco neighborhood.

The second study, called Tracing Transitions, was a participatory action research project carried out with students whose high school had been shut down. Our goal was to document student perspectives about the closure and find out how displaced students fared in transitions to new schools. Because this was action research, when the study was over youth researchers shared their findings and recommendations with national and local policy makers, including testifying at a federal congressional hearing on urban education.

The third study differed from the first two by focusing on school classrooms as contexts for young people to engage in critique and collective agency. The project, called Critical Civic Inquiry, co-led with Shelley Zion and Carlos Hipolito-Delgado, worked with secondary school teachers to provide opportunities for their students to discuss, investigate, and take action to dismantle educational barriers such as unsafe school climates or inadequate facilities. We investigated sociopolitical learning among students and the conditions in schools that supported or frustrated action civics projects.

Some Context: Youth Activism in an Era of Education Inequality

Youth activism is fueled by a series of contradictions that implicate American society as a whole. The first is a structural contradiction: low-income youth of color are exhorted to work hard and fulfill their responsibilities to go to college, but for many this is a remote possibility, either because of failing schools, economic barriers to higher education, or citizenship laws that block children of immigrants from legal employment or financial aid.[14] This structural contradiction is accompanied by a developmental contradiction: most youth are developmentally ready to participate under conditions of support, but lack opportunities to do so. Think of this as a lack of fit between paternalistic societal institutions and young people's rapidly growing cognitive capacities and desire for personal agency. Both structural and developmental contradictions are shaped and twisted by the persistence of racial caste in an allegedly color-blind world.

Structural Contradictions

In 2009 President Barack Obama, during his State of the Union speech, asked "every American to commit to at least one year or more of higher education or career training." In an update of John F. Kennedy's plea to "ask not what your country can do for you, but what you can do for your country," Obama presented educational attainment as a national duty:

> [W]hatever the training may be, every American will need to get more than a high school diploma. . . . And dropping out of high school is no longer an option. It's not just quitting on yourself, it's quitting on your country—and this country needs and values the talents of every American.[15]

Obama's speech was an example of a broader discourse about closing the achievement gap, which has become increasingly pronounced since the advent of No Child Left Behind in 2002. It is a discourse that tells students that they can get ahead if they work hard. It exhorts them to graduate from high school and seek postsecondary education. It has a moral flavor, in the sense that it implies that students who do not contribute to boosting their school's scores or who do not stay in school are letting others down.

You can see this achievement discourse in the kinds of messages communicated to students in the widely celebrated "No Excuses" schools, such as the Knowledge Is Power Program (KIPP).[16] The No Excuses phrase emerged from an effort to highlight the successes of charter schools in high poverty neighborhoods and identify the characteristics that made them effective.[17] Echoing Obama's call, No Excuses schools build a culture of college going by adorning hallways with college pennants, using call and response phrases ("when I say '[name of school],' you say 'college'"), and identifying student cohorts not by their grade level but by the year in which they will graduate college (e.g., "Class of 2021"). Students and teachers are told to make no excuses for failure.

So what's the problem? Hard work is a virtue; achievement is good. But simultaneous with the drumbeat of "study hard" and "go to college" is a set of structural barriers that make education achievement for kids in neighborhoods of concentrated poverty accessible to only the most exceptional children and schools. Here I mean exceptional in the sense of *unusual or uncommon*. Consider the metaphor of a public park, a big one, with all sorts of trails and paths, as a stand-in for the education system. Imagine that getting from kindergarten through high school and into postsecondary education is like finding your way from one end of the park to the other. Children from all types of backgrounds must walk through that park—it requires desire, effort, and endurance. But children of the affluent enter a park with well-maintained paths, clear signs, and detailed maps. Paid guides provide supplementary training in bird watching, orienteering, and stargazing. Students are encouraged to veer off the path and use a compass to get through dense forests. They sweat when it is hot, just like the others, but they have ample water, food, and sunscreen to cushion hardship.

You can guess where I'm going with this. Children from poor neighborhoods enter a different park. The path that leads to higher education and sustainable livelihoods is not well marked. There are numerous forks and diversions with little guidance about where they lead. The bridges built in prior decades to carry people across rivers are falling apart. On hot days children must use ingenuity and craft to find water, and even then it may not be safe to drink. Their families provide guidance and emotional support, but certain paths are unfamiliar, so they are unsure where to proceed at forks in the road. And, at risk of pushing this metaphor too far, those who are most resilient, who make it over hills and streams, graduate from high school only to be confronted by massive boulders blocking their path in the form of insurmountable tuition costs or admissions standards they haven't met.

Worse yet, it all seems so natural. The eroding path and the foreboding trees have been like that for so long it just feels like the way things are. And some kids really do seem to try harder than others. Why can't everyone be like the ones whose grit propelled them past hazards and stretches of barren land? No excuses!

Alas, we need a critical geographer to save us from this metaphor and point out all the ways that a supposedly "natural" space has been shaped by human interests and power, related to decisions about how to structure the intersecting pathways, the money spent to maintain them, and which neighborhood gets which choice piece of land on which to locate them. Lois Weis and Michelle Fine, for example, are two education scholars who applied this kind of critical lens to the education system and they concluded that young people in high poverty neighborhoods move through "circuits of dispossession" in their everyday lives. The term "dispossession" signals the active role played by entities (public or private) to take away resources from certain classes of people.

One type is dispossession by *categorical denial*. People who arrive in the United States as children have the right, because of the Plyler v. Doe Supreme Court case, to attend public schools without having to reveal their citizenship status. But this relative sanctuary ends in late adolescence where, in many states, they are not eligible for in-state tuition rates or federal aid, not to mention legal privileges such as driver's licenses and work permits. Consider how this must feel for undocumented young people who have embraced the achievement discourse but then find that it is not available to them.[18]

A second type of dispossession, harder to solve through changes in the law, stems from the "cumulative, cross sector disinvestment" that has eroded public institutions serving poor communities of color.[19] One of the most powerful studies documenting this disinvestment, connected to changes in tax law, took place as part of the filings for Williams v. California in 2000. The opening paragraph of the complaint summarizes the widespread gaps in resources and opportunities to learn for children and youth in California, including a lack of "trained teachers, necessary educational supplies, classrooms, even seats in classrooms, and facilities that meet basic health and safety standards."[20] Philadelphia is another city that suffers from the erosion of support for public schools. After the state-appointed school board closed twenty-four of Philadelphia's schools at the end of the 2012–13 school year because of lack of funds, parents, teachers, and students prepared to start school without sports teams, nurses, lunchroom monitors, and librarians. An organization called Philly Student Union curated tweets on the first day back at school under the header "The Worst of #Philly1stDay":

My 11 yr old reads 3–5 books/week. Number she'll be checking out from school library this year? 0. No librarian. Sad reader.

Water's on at Masterman but my 5th grader was advised not to risk drinking it—"white and foamy."

NE High has one counselor for 3,000 students. "I'm losing my mind," says principal.

Straight A student. Can't take the honors classes I signed up for because there aren't any teachers to teach them.

Philadelphia offers an egregious case of inadequate support for public schools in multiple cities in the United States.[21]

Part of the reason that school closures and underfunded schools are tolerated stems from the increasing segregation of those schools from the broader population. Urban schools designated for turnaround status are highly segregated institutions where Latino and African American students are more likely than white students to be in class with other kids in poverty.[22] Segregation has been increasing in districts that were released from court-ordered desegregation, and African American students attend on average more racially isolated schools than in 1970.[23] As public schools have cut back on enrichment activities such as art and music programs, there has been a corresponding increase in affluent families' investment in their children's cognitive enrichment.

High-income families are increasingly focusing their resources—their money, time and knowledge of what it takes to be successful in school— on their children's cognitive development and educational success. They are doing this because educational success is much more important than it used to be, even for the rich.[24]

Families—whether rich or poor—recognize the diminishing safety net and an erosion of sustainable career options for those without higher education.

Dispossession can also be seen in policing practices, such as New York City's Stop and Frisk policy, which make routine movements through public spaces unsafe for youth of color.[25] It is seen in Trayvon Martin's tragic shooting walking home after buying Skittles, for which his killer was exonerated because of Stand Your Ground laws. And, in 2014, a police officer's shooting of Michael Brown brought the crisis of extrajudicial violence against African American males into the open, even if it was not new.[26]

Racial profiling is also rampant in schools, where ample evidence has documented that Latino and African American students are more likely to be referred to police for nonviolent infractions. A national database analyzed by the National Council on Crime and Delinquency, for example, reported that among youth with no prior detentions who were charged with the same offenses, African Americans were six times more likely than whites to be incarcerated and Latino youth were three times more likely.[27] To return to the park metaphor, watch out: If you are a Latino or black young person walking on the main path, you are more likely than white counterparts to get stopped and have your backpack checked for illegal substances. And if you do happen to break one of the rules along the way, you're more likely to get kicked off the path altogether.

These examples of dispossession amount to a *structural contradiction* facing youth of color in working-class and poor neighborhoods. They are exhorted to stay on that path and to make no excuses when they get fatigued or take a wrong turn; many adopt this high standard and judge themselves or their peers deficient against it. But certain diversions and barriers make it out of reach for all but the most gritty and resilient youth. This structural contradiction goes hand in hand with a developmental contradiction, in which teenage youth are ready for mature roles in their communities but tend to be excluded from civic participation.

Developmental Contradictions

Going back to early twentieth-century debates between G. Stanley Hall and Margaret Mead, two narratives about teenagers have competed for attention.[28] The first, driven by the discipline of psychology and reinforced by the mass media, has promoted an image of adolescence as impulsive, emotional, and irrational. This "tribe apart" narrative emphasizes the strangeness of teenagers as a separate subgroup within American society. Early in the formation of the discipline G. Stanley Hall argued for a distinct stage of adolescence that he described as "emotionally unstable." This narrative resurfaces today in breathless reports about the immaturity of the teen brain. An NPR story referred to teenagers as "an alien species," TIME described them as "a famously reckless species," and the *New York Times* titled its article "Why Teenagers Act Crazy."[29]

These examples show that despite important advances in brain research, the "tribe apart" narrative persists, so much so that it has assumed a taken-for-granted quality, one that does not require logical argument or rigorous evidence.

Framing teenagers as a tribe apart has destructive consequences for their opportunities for participation in the public square.[30] Policy makers fail to recognize teens' local knowledge, hard-won skills, or capacity for mature roles. Sometimes this takes the form of punitive policies such as zero tolerance in schools.[31] But even benevolent approaches that try to "help" youth can be counterproductive when they treat youth as passive or vulnerable objects of intervention rather than capable contributors.[32]

Beginning, however, with anthropologist Mead's critique of Hall, a more critical and contextual perspective has fought for attention. This second narrative argues that behaviors and pathologies psychologists attribute to youth—in fact, the notion of an "adolescent stage"—is socially constructed and culturally variable.[33] This narrative recognizes the ways that young people live up (or down) to the roles and behaviors adults expect of them. Referring to youth as "alien," "emotional," or "immature" creates the very object it then ridicules. Mead critiqued Hall's stance in her book, *Coming of Age in Samoa*, first published in 1928, where she described a Samoan adolescent experience featuring little of the storm and stress typical of American teens. Mead argued that teenagers in the United States developed a separate youth culture in large part because they rarely had the chance to be part of mature community practices.[34] Contemporary scholars such as Barbara Rogoff refer to this phenomenon as "age segregation," in which, "instead of routinely helping adults, children are often involved in specialized child-focused exercises to assemble skills for later entry in mature activities."[35]

By making context more central in adolescent research, contemporary scholars have begun to document the many ways that youth of color in the United States defy pervasive stereotypes about them. Many working-class and poor youth of color contribute to their family sustenance or livelihoods. Children, for example, take care of younger sisters and brothers.[36] Teenagers who can find work contribute their paychecks to pay for their families' basic necessities, such as food and electricity.[37] Children from immigrant families translate for parents during high stakes encounters with doctors or lawyers.[38] Contrary to assertions by public figures about the lack of work habits among the urban poor,[39] evidence shows that low-income youth often play more adult-like roles in their families than their middle-class counterparts. This body of research offers a useful corrective to biologically reductive accounts of adolescence or those studies that isolate the young person from her social context.

Research about mature roles played by youth is accompanied by a new focus on *positive youth development* (PYD), which aims to reframe the enterprise of adolescence as the cultivation of strengths and purpose rather than the avoidance of risk or delinquency.[40] The PYD program of research has yielded important findings about the kinds of emerging capacities that teenagers have for strategic thinking, taking the perspective of others, and managing biases. Brain research supports this approach, particularly in terms of the affordances of the prefrontal cortex for a "developing executive" that is capable of thinking scientifically and analytically.[41]

But the institutions that organize young people's movement through adolescence are out of step with these capabilities. This is the *developmental contradiction*. Similar to findings by Jacqueline Eccles and Robert Roeser about the lack of "stage-environment fit" between the competitive, impersonal structures of middle schools and early adolescent development, there is a lack of fit between societal institutions and young people's need to participate and matter. Even within schools where student voice is supported, such opportunities are often limited to high achieving students.[42] These trends converge in a country divided by age segregation. The United States is one of only two countries that have not signed on to the UN Convention on the Rights of the Child, which asserts children's rights to express their views and be heard in policy matters.

Youth activism is fueled by this kind of developmental contradiction. A poignant example of this can be seen in students' responses to the closure of Jefferson High School, which was closed by its school district because of persistently low test scores and declining enrollment.[43] The district called the closure a "rescue mission" to enable the school's population of African American and Latino students to attend other district schools. At an early community forum a school board member defended her vote to close the school by saying, "You seem to think we're doing this to you. But we're not. We're doing it *for* you." But the effort to couch the decision in benevolent terms did not resonate with students, who answered that they were "not down with the shut down." They organized rallies, spoke at school board meetings, and engaged media outlets in the effort to try to keep their neighborhood school open. They voiced a message popular among youth organizing groups that was first coined by disability rights activists: "Nothing for us, without us!" One student explained, "It was just like they decided to close it and there was nothing that the community could have done or said." The Jefferson fight emerged because students wanted to participate but felt excluded from the decision-making process.

The Persistence of Race

These two contradictions—one structural, the other developmental— are twisted by the persistence of a racial caste system in the United States; twisted because it can be difficult to get a handle on the ways that racial hierarchies operate in the contemporary United States. The social movements of the mid-twentieth century arose in a context of explicit legal apartheid against African Americans and Mexican Americans in the system known as Jim Crow. Dr. Martin Luther King's dream that his children "not be judged by the color of their skin, but by the content of their character," was revolutionary in a context where racism was enshrined in state policy and law. Social movements could be mobilized around a relatively specific and tangible set of statutory goals: voting rights, fair housing, and antidiscrimination in employment.

In 2014 the legal apparatus of racism has changed. But the dismantling of legal apartheid that followed from the civil rights movement has been followed by a severe retrenchment of those interests seeking to maintain a racial caste system in the United States. This can be confusing, because few advocates of racist policies espouse racist language. Supreme Court Chief Justice John Roberts famously said, in striking down desegregation policies in school assignments, "The way to stop discrimination on the basis of race is to stop discriminating on the basis of race." Roberts's formulation enshrines *color blindness* as the morally right response to America's racist history. But in extolling not seeing as a virtue, it hides the ways in which racial ideologies intersect with structural and developmental barriers to participation.

Sociologist Eduardo Bonilla-Silva attributes contemporary inequality to "racism without racists," because the kinds of structural dispossession discussed above land disproportionately on people of color: inadequate schools, restrictions on voting rights, mass incarceration and its attendant disenfranchisement from the vote, and immigration deportations. The persistence of a racial caste system is hidden or obscured by the ideology of color blindness and the insistence that the United States is a meritocracy.

Age-based exclusion from decision making is also amplified for youth of color. There is a well-documented gap in opportunities for civic education, which means that most poor youth and youth of color are not getting the chance to learn and develop democracy in their schools.[44] Urban schools with fewer financial resources are less likely to have student councils.[45] Affluent and white youth can count on the political clout of their parents to represent their interests; youth from marginalized backgrounds do not have the same power.[46]

Understanding the contemporary moment as one of "racism without racists" is crucial to understanding activism among youth of color. Doing so helps to explain why organizations and classrooms that catalyze youth activism often spend time investigating and framing the root causes of educational dispossession. Educators create spaces where young people can reconcile everyday experiences of discrimination with dominant discourses of meritocracy and color blindness.[47] Americans of all hues have a tendency to *psychologize* racism—to conceive of it as a property that belongs to a few bad people. Social justice educators, however, encourage young people to view racism as emerging in a system of relations, enacted in institutions and policy, and legitimated via racial ideologies.[48] Part of the work of educational settings is to make visible taken-for-granted discourses about race in American society. In this context, social science research has an important role to play documenting and making visible various forms of racial discrimination. In contrast to Kenneth and Mamie Clarke's doll experiments cited in the 1954 Brown v. Board of Education decision, which focused on the personality development of African American children, today's research documents the presence of systemic biases that might otherwise be hidden from view or ignored, such as in disproportionate referrals to police for drug possession or racial microaggressions.[49]

In many ways contemporary ideologies of color blindness and meritocracy make today's activist work more challenging. The legal basis for depriving people of rights based on skin color is no longer viable in the United States. That legal battle, rooted in Enlightenment logics of equality and fraternity, took two hundred years to win but it was finally achieved. Yet we see new proxies for skin color that lead to similar kinds of deprivation, based on stand your ground laws, mandatory minimum sentencing laws, immigration laws, anti–school integration laws, voting eligibility laws, and public housing policies.

Youth activism represents a logical response to these contradictions and challenges: *You're not creating ongoing systems for me to participate and share my views? Then I'll find a way by walking out of school or showing up at school board meetings with scores of my peers. You want me to achieve? I do too. Let's figure out a way to make college more affordable and get police out of schools.*

Youth organizing campaigns tend to be guided by these twin goals: expanded participation and expanded opportunity. It's also true that many young people—and their organizations—seek more radical or revolutionary social transformation. But the language and objectives of the campaigns tend to focus on access, participation, and opportunity. They are a combustible mix of imaginative and practical, best described, borrowing from language and literacy scholar Kris Gutiérrez, as "social dreaming."[50] Social dreams, in this sense, are dreams for the future that are yoked to a strong collective identity.[51] They focus on creating a better future for oneself, one's peers, and one's family; they are rooted in a strong sense of interdependence with others.

A Sociocultural Perspective on Activism

The emerging literature about youth activism reflects different disciplinary traditions and foci. Shawn Ginwright's *Black Youth Rising* offers a case study of Leadership Excellence, an organization in Oakland, California. Ginwright, a sociologist of education, combines historical analysis of changes in black urban life with ethnography to identify what it takes to promote "radical healing" for youth suffering from racism and trauma. Hava Gordon, also a sociologist, published a comparative study of activism among middle-class white youth in Oregon and working-class black and Latino youth in Oakland, California. Gordon's book, called *We Fight to Win*, looks at how the social production of age-based subordination intersects with race, class, and gender. Soo Ah Kwon, drawing on ethnic studies and critical feminist theory, examines the contradictions facing progressive youth organizing groups in a capitalist state. Her book, *Uncivil Youth*, highlights the political accomplishments of Asian and Pacific Islander youth while also documenting the ways that youth foundations and nonprofits, including those aiming to empower youth, perpetuate "kid-fixing" discourses about youth of color. Several other books, although not focused centrally on youth activism, contribute to a growing interest by scholars in the role that young people can play in democratic renewal and equity-oriented school reform.[52] In developing this book's central arguments I happily claim kinship with this cohort of scholars who write about youth participation and activism; we all take an approach that emphasizes young people's agency in the face of deep-seated, structural racism and inequality.

This book, rooted in sociocultural and critical approaches to human development, departs from other books in a few ways. It examines a broad range of settings for youth activism, including community organizations, school classrooms, and geographically distributed social movements. Some of these settings utilize youth organizing strategies; others draw on participatory action research or student voice. This diversity of approaches allows for recognition of their shared features while also highlighting the ways in which institutional contexts enable and constrain varied types of activism. This comparative element will contribute to the generalizability of claims about developmental outcomes of youth activism and the kinds of settings that foster it.

This book is also distinct in its sociocultural lens, which examines individual development in relation to the broader ecologies that either nurture or inhibit youth engagement. Sociocultural theory enables close analysis of the interplay between human development and societal change.[53] Prior civic engagement research has often kept these two sets of questions separate by focusing on either how youth change through their participation or the kinds of social structures and policies that shape youth participation. Sociocultural theory, on the other hand, examines how individuals change in the context of diverse and dynamic cultural practices. This approach attends to how young people are simultaneously becoming part of existing practices and transforming those practices through their participation. This dual focus is particularly suited to the study of civic engagement and activism, which are by definition contextual and culture-bound.

Scholars taking this approach have a rigorous bar for what counts as evidence of learning and development. Rather than focus solely on cognitive change in a young person, such as deeper understanding or changed attitudes, sociocultural theory examines shifts in relationships between people. Learning and development are social processes. This calls for attention to how adults in positions of power, such as principals or politicians, position youth in social interaction.[54] Just as important, the sociocultural approach examines how youth defy deficit-based frames and author powerful identities through their roles and actions in public spaces.

Lastly, sociocultural theory offers tools for analyzing constitutive features of a learning ecology, including people, practices, and the linguistic and technological tools that mediate people's intentional activity. This focus on learning ecologies enables analysis of the kinds of opportunity structures that facilitate people's democratic participation. Such work can generate practical implications for educators in and out of school.

Organization of the Book

The first section of the book focuses on activism as a vehicle for youth development and a more just and equitable democracy. Chapter 1, "Critique and Collective Agency in Youth Development," argues that we need to expand current assumptions about positive youth development to include greater attention to sociopolitical development. I support this argument with a case study of a high school where emerging bilingual students in a sheltered English class developed a Critical Civic Inquiry project to raise awareness about racism and xenophobia at their school. The case shows what it means for youth to develop as sociopolitical actors, both in terms of their capacity to think critically about systems and to exercise political agency.

Chapter 2, "Millennial Youth and the Fight for Opportunity," shifts from a focus on individual people's development to societal change. This chapter presents two cases, based primarily on analysis of newspaper articles and other secondary sources, where millennial youth defied the steady consolidation of political power in the hands of the few and developed successful campaigns for human rights and education opportunity. The first case focuses on DREAM Activism, an intergenerational movement for immigrant rights and opportunity. The second focuses on a statewide campaign to end the school to jail track in Colorado led by Padres & Jóvenes Unidos. Both cases show how organizing in response to issues that affect the everyday lives and future aspirations of young people can mobilize young people to develop political power.

Chapter 3, " 'Not Down with the Shutdown': Student Activism against School Closure," discusses what ensued for young people whose interests were not represented adequately in a school closure decision. The chapter chronicles what young people wanted from their school and why they objected to the decision to close it. The chapter offers an object lesson in why stronger opportunities for student voice and participation are needed in the struggle for educational equity.

Part II of the book transitions away from evidence of the impact of youth participation toward analysis of the kinds of learning ecologies that foster it. Chapter 4, "Teaching without Teaching," is based on ethnographic research about youth activism in the San Francisco Bay Area. Early in my fieldwork I was intrigued by a puzzling observation: youth participants, most of whom were novice activists, played key roles implementing complex social action campaigns, but I did not see any teaching. How did youth learn to carry out campaigns? This chapter describes the kinds of guidance provided by young adults in youth organizing groups and critiques naïve conceptions of youth voice.

Chapter 5, "Schools as Sites of Struggle: Critical Civic Inquiry," focuses on schools as contexts for sociopolitical development. Can the kinds of learning environments common in youth organizing and participatory action research take root *inside* school classrooms? This question is important for developing new forms of democratic education in schools and theorizing sociopolitical learning processes. The chapter draws on research from the Critical Civic Inquiry project to explore this question.

The concluding chapter highlights themes that cut across the prior empirical chapters and identifies implications for settings that foster youths' political participation. I articulate specific examples of how community programs and schools can develop a partnership approach that contributes to democratic renewal and human development.

Throughout the book I use pseudonyms to refer to people, schools, and school districts.

* * *

Income inequality has become a familiar term in American political discourse. It limits social mobility and has a damaging effect on U.S. democracy. Education inequality is its close sibling. People are more and more aware that public education has not delivered on its promise of providing equal opportunity. These are deep and persistent problems that youth activism will not solve alone. But new youth movements, some intentionally cultivated in educational settings, others formed in response to unwelcome policies, point a way forward. They provide hope in a time of dispossession; not just hope, but strategies for expanding educational opportunity and sustaining a more participatory democracy.

PART I

How Activism Contributes to Human Development and Democratic Renewal

1

Critique and Collective Agency in Youth Development

On May 5, 2010, Luis and Gabriela, two ninth graders, showed up at school expecting to see colors from the Mexican flag adorning their classmates' gear, just as they had seen students wearing green on St. Patrick's Day six weeks earlier. It was Cinco de Mayo, a day that commemorates the Mexican army's victory over French forces in 1862, and, in the United States, has become a day when people honor and celebrate Mexican cultural traditions. Luis, born in the United States to parents from Mexico, wore the Mexican flag behind his T-shirt, in his words, "to honor my parents' country." Gabriela, born in Mexico, was less familiar with the holiday, but felt a sense of connection to her peers who celebrated it.

The school, Roosevelt High, had for most of its history been majority white, but had experienced a demographic shift during the housing boom of the early 2000s.[1] The combination of Latino settlement in certain neighborhoods and a change in school boundaries to include a nearby high school meant that by 2010 the school had become roughly 60 percent Latino and 40 percent Anglo, with those identified as Latino including recent immigrants from Mexico and Central America as well as Hispanic families with many generations of U.S. citizenship. Teachers and administrators at Roosevelt High were still overwhelmingly English-speaking and white.

When Luis and Gabriela entered the building on May 5, instead of a celebration of culture, they encountered hostility and harassment. Luis described it later in an interview:[2]

> I go upstairs, and you see all these whites with American flags, and you're going, "Whoa! What a drag! What's going on?" And then you look out to the parking lot and you see all these cars with American flags. . . . And yeah, it was terrifying for me. I was like, "Whoa, what's going on?" . . . That's when everybody started, like . . . chanting racial slurs.

You say they were chanting, like, in the hallways?
Yeah, it was pretty much every hallway, the library, I don't know. When I saw the flag, it was in the hallway over here. I remember Ms. S——, I was walking, and I even see a teacher with the American flag shirt, and I was like, "Whoa, the teachers are like that, too?" It was pretty terrifying to be a freshman, 'cause you're not used to the high school environment, you know? You're just getting used to it. And then you see this happening and you're like, "Whoa!"

Rumors spread that one group of white students was planning to burn the Mexican flag in the parking lot and that a group of Mexican American students would retaliate if that happened. The action shifted to the parking lot outside the building, where, in Gabriela's words:

There was some American people with their flags on . . . saying, "Oh, go back to your country." . . . Then the American people thought they were so tall and bigger, they were pushing everyone and this kid was wearing like a soldier theme. It said border patrol.

Additional people, including students and staff, reiterated versions of these stories in interviews and writing. Jennifer, a native Spanish-speaking student in Luis and Gabriela's class who was learning English as her second language, wrote the following in response to her teacher's prompt to recount her experiences on Cinco de Mayo at the school:

My experience with Cinco de Mayo in the past years are a very strong negative because many Mexicans get excited to celebrate/party with their familys. Get all together and remember Mexican tradition.

Throughout school days in cinco de mayo made me feel worthless and no power because many americans here in the united states make unappropriate comments. Every Mexican student waking up in the morning happy to wear their Mexican flag colors and to get threaten by it saying "to go back to our country" makes me feel like were nothing.

There's a lot going on in these accounts: Nationalism. Xenophobia. Racism. Contested space. Competition over who belongs and who can claim rightful space in the school. As Luis later told me, Why did the white students decide to express their patriotism on this particular day? For the Latino students, it was a message of exclusion: *You don't belong here. Go back to where you came from.* According to Luis, a U.S. citizen, it was "terrifying." It must have been even more threatening for those students who were undocumented and whose families were at risk of deportation during one of the most punitive eras in U.S. immigration policy.

Imagine you were a teacher at the school, or an after-school provider, or a school counselor: How would you approach this problem of racism and intergroup conflict at the school? In particular, if a student like Jennifer, who in the excerpt above described feeling "worthless and no power," came to your door, what developmental theory could you call upon for guidance? How should teachers, after-school youth workers, counselors, or administrators support and guide Latino students experiencing this kind of harassment?

Answers to these questions are not only relevant to situations, like Roosevelt, where racism and intergroup conflict are out in the open. They are important more broadly for educators who seek to be developmental allies for young people experiencing varied kinds of "dispossession."[3] Some might be in a school where they confront everyday microaggressions that disparage their intelligence or work ethic.[4] Others might be undocumented youth experiencing exclusion from legal employment or youth growing up in neighborhoods with high rates of violence and attending dysfunctional schools.[5]

Situations such as these call for an educational approach that encourages *critique* and *collective agency*. Critique refers to the practice of questioning and denaturalizing the sociopolitical context of one's life. Collective agency refers to people working together to dismantle barriers to their education or to forge new educational pathways that did not exist before. Too often students hear exhortations to stay in school or reduce the achievement gap without any acknowledgment of structural racism or inequality. Young people experiencing oppression need more than just good mentors or academic skills; they need opportunities to talk about challenges in their everyday lives, examine root causes of inequality, and take action, broadly defined, about issues that affect them.[6] Opportunities for critique and agency contribute to sociopolitical development, which refers to "a process of growth in a person's knowledge, analytical skills, emotional faculties, and capacity for action in political and social systems (p. 185)."[7]

Luis and Gabriela's effort to change the climate at their high school exemplifies how this mix of critique and agency can contribute to youth sociopolitical development. In this chapter I draw upon data gathered over two years by a small team of researchers, most of which were collected through ethnographic fieldwork by then-doctoral student Elizabeth Mendoza. (This chapter builds on, and departs from, a conference paper co-authored with Elizabeth Mendoza and Carrie Allen).[8] Data included interviews with students over the course of two academic years, student-led tours of the school, and field notes describing classroom activities during the second year of the project.

I draw on these data to characterize the social order of Roosevelt High and show how students questioned and challenged that social order as part of their ESL classroom project. The term *social order* here refers to a constellation of taken-for-granted norms, practices, and hierarchies in a particular social system, such as a school. Excavating the social order requires attention to who has power and which types of students are positioned as the leaders and achievers. I privilege student perceptions of that social order, rather than adult personnel.

By considering their story we can see how Luis and Gabriela developed as sociopolitical actors over the course of a yearlong project they undertook with the guidance of their ESL teacher. I draw on qualitative evidence to describe changes in the way they made sense of the social order of their school and corresponding changes in their participation and voice. This way of theorizing development gives pride of place to how people *transform their participation in social groups over time*: the kinds of roles they take on, the ways they apply knowledge and skills to new situations, and their contributions to changes in cultural practices. This viewpoint, called a "sociocultural" approach, was first articulated by Lev Vygotsky in the Soviet Union in the 1930s and has recently been expanded by Barbara Rogoff, who describes it this way:

It examines individuals' roles in the context of their participation and the ways they transform their participation, analyzing how they coordinate with others in shared endeavors, with attention to the dynamic nature of the activity itself and its meaning in the community. The investigation of people's involvement in activities becomes the basis of understanding of learning/development rather than simply the surface that we try to get past. (p. 279)[9]

According to this view, when we talk about development we must also be explicit about the particular end, or *telos*, toward which people are developing. Social scientists try to measure change over time: but change in what direction? After all, what is good or normative in some cultural communities is problematic in others. In some contexts being "a good citizen" means obedience to laws and devotion to authority; for others it means judging the current government against a set of moral criteria.[10] Beliefs about good citizenship are highly contested and linked to different ideologies around what kind of society we want to be.

From my perspective the kinds of activities in which Luis and Gabriela participated were good—but on what grounds? I draw on key insights from critical theory to articulate the value of sociopolitical development and how it represents an advance over existing paradigms of youth work.

The Limits of Prevailing Approaches to Working with Youth

Zero tolerance policies, which blame young people for their struggles and use criminal penalties to both deter and punish youth, are neither effective nor just.[11] Although increasingly under scrutiny, such policies are still common in schools with high percentages of African American and Latino/a students.[12] You can see the zero tolerance approach put into practice at Roosevelt High after the scuffles that took place on Cinco de Mayo. The following year the school brought in more police cars and heightened security to prevent violence. This strategy suppressed overt demonstrations of hostility among students that day, but did little to address the deeply rooted tensions, mistrust, and misunderstandings among social groups at the school. It was a Band-Aid that did not heal the deeper problem.

A more compelling, but still limited, response is offered by *social and emotional learning* (*SEL*).[13] SEL programs work from the premise that people's social and emotional development is a central part of what it means to function in the world; moreover, social and emotional competencies shape students' capacity to focus on academic learning. For example, are you aware when you are becoming angry, stressed out, or anxious and can you manage those emotions rather than let them manage you? Do you persist even after encountering challenge or failure? Several recent meta-analyses document the positive impact of SEL for young people, such as reduced emotional distress, positive social behaviors, positive attitudes toward school, and improved test performance.[14] Interest in SEL is part of a broader trend toward recognizing the importance of "noncognitive outcomes" in school and life, such as the concept of "grit" studied by Angela Duckworth, popularized in Paul Tough's book *How Children Succeed*, and embraced by inner-city charter schools such as the Knowledge Is Power Program (KIPP).[15] Grit refers to "the tendency to sustain interest in and effort toward very long-term goals" and, like other types of social and emotional attributes, grit is correlated with educational attainment and performance.[16]

Psychological qualities such as grit, the ability to manage conflict, and emotional regulation are valuable, even necessary, in an increasingly high-wire economy with no safety net, but they are not sufficient for young people or the democracy we aspire to live in. A single-minded emphasis on grit or emotion regulation leaves social conditions unexamined and reinforces the myth of self-reliance. Although a rare few will develop the kinds of resilient stances required to persist in a hostile school or overcome years of nonrigorous classes, self-determination by definition does not get at the roots of the structural contradictions that many young people face. The cultivation of grit helps youth defy the odds, but it does not challenge or change them, particularly in an era when social mobility is stagnant and income inequality is growing.[17] Education scholar Mike Rose said it well:

> Given a political climate that is antagonistic toward the welfare state and has further shredded our already compromised safety net, psychological and educational interventions may be the only viable political response to poverty available. But can you imagine the outcry if, let's say, an old toxic dump was discovered near Scarsdale or Beverly Hills and the National Institutes of Health undertook a program to teach kids strategies to lessen the effects of the toxins but didn't do anything to address the toxic dump itself?[18]

Rose makes an important point: The existence of social and emotional interventions becomes an excuse to ignore the social conditions that give rise to the need for those interventions. Youth growing up in affluence get strong schools, safe routes to school, and stable ladders to sustainable employment; those growing up in poverty get interventions to promote their coping skills.

A third paradigm to consider is *positive youth development (PYD)*. Like SEL, this work is sound empirically and represents a major step forward for research and practice. Perhaps the biggest achievement of this literature is to reframe young people as assets rather than deficits. In reaction to earlier decades of interventions that assembled kids based on their shared status as being "at risk" for a particular behavior, youth development advocates shifted to a prevention model that provided universal programming based on building strengths. Youth development scholars have generated valuable policy-relevant findings for youth growing up in poverty: about the power of strong relationships with nonfamily adults, sense of belonging and community connections, and opportunities to develop efficacy and skill in valued domains.[19]

The typical PYD program, if guided by "best practices" in the field, would create a safe space for people like Luis, Gabriela, and Jennifer. It would look a lot like the youth development organization where I worked in the 1990s. If high quality, these are settings where young people encounter caring adults who go by their first names and build relationships that attend to the many parts of a young person's life, including school, family, peers, and future aspirations. They offer rich opportunities for youth to build skills and interests, whether in poetry, digital media, sports, or community leadership.

What is less well articulated in youth development practice or theory, however, is how these caring adults should engage in conversations with youth—who are marginalized because of their race, class, or sexual identities—about the political context of their lives, particularly in ways that don't further pathologize their neighborhoods or peer groups. Put another way, early work on youth programs tended to frame them as safe spaces or sanctuaries from difficult environments. What we need now are strong examples and professional training around how to engage youths' knowledge about their everyday lives and approach them as partners in crafting solutions to problems such as those found at Roosevelt High. To return to Jennifer's example, there are few manuals describing how one might talk with Jennifer about the racism at her school and discuss ways to respond to it collectively. SEL and PYD cultivate important psychological and interpersonal strengths, but, with some notable exceptions, they have been relatively silent about the implications of racism and structural oppression for applied work with youth.

Fortunately we don't need to start from scratch. An emerging network of scholars and educators are developing education frameworks that expand PYD to include a sociopolitical dimension for both classrooms and community programs.[20] Shawn Ginwright and Julio Cammarota call this Social Justice Youth Development.[21] They draw on traditions of social thought that attend to how people come to think critically of their everyday social conditions, such that they do not accept racism, inequality, or substandard schooling as just "the way things are." Developing a critical perspective, as the following section will describe, is tightly bound with developing a sense of agency to change those conditions.

A Brief Introduction to Critical Theory

Critical perspectives in sociology and psychology can generally be traced back to Karl Marx, whose social and materialistic account of human history upended dominant accounts of the human mind in the nineteenth century. In brief, Marx argued that human psychology was a product of one's place in existing class hierarchies; this view, called *historicism*, rejected the notion that there is a universal or timeless "human nature" that exists independent of one's social and material circumstances. (Western experimental psychology, which took the natural sciences as its model throughout the twentieth century, proved increasingly removed from this historicist account of human development.)[22] In this Marxist account, members of the ruling classes develop an ideological superstructure that justifies the existence of inequality through the development of belief systems. Subsequent interpreters of Marx, who have had a major influence on critical perspectives in the human sciences, have developed this idea with greater nuance and contemporary relevance.

Antonio Gramsci, an early twentieth-century Italian writer, philosopher, and communist leader, expanded traditional analyses of class domination.[23] Gramsci's work, written while imprisoned in fascist Italy, aimed to show how the control or domination of a subordinated group is produced not merely through brute force, but also through a process by which members of subordinated groups adopt the values and interests of the ruling class as their own.[24] In this account, existing patterns of inequality become taken for granted by members of a social system such that, over time, what might seem wrong or problematic becomes tolerable or fated. It becomes the "common sense" of the times.

Critical psychologists have picked up on this tradition, and social reproduction theory more broadly, to understand how stratification by race and class plays out in people's inner lives. Isaac Prilleltensky, for example, writes persuasively about the ways in which oppression can occur both at the political level and at the psychological level.[25] The political level, which is more visible, refers to those policies, laws, and institutions that advance the interests of some at the expense of others who are relatively powerless. Psychological oppression, on the other hand, exists when people participate in their own marginalization or stigmatization by internalizing the norms and standards of those with the most power, ranging from ideals of beauty to views of the good life.[26] As Michel Foucault argued in his genealogies of various forms of institutional domination, power need not be exercised through physical coercion, but instead through more subtle ways that, as Prilleltensky writes, "people come to regulate themselves" (p. 120). One of the more pernicious kinds of this political self-regulation occurs when young people in the United States place sole blame on themselves or their peers for their struggles. In such a context, from a critical perspective, a key part of human development is to develop awareness of systems of power and inequality.[27]

The most influential scholar to theorize this learning process is a Brazilian writer and teacher named Paolo Freire, who lived from 1921 to 1997. Although Freire is rarely discussed in developmental psychology journals, he thought *developmentally*, insofar as he theorized a process of developmental change that made liberation from oppression its outcome. Freire was critical of the word "activism," because for him it often implied unthinking behavior, action without reflection.[28] On the other hand, what Freire called "verbalism," critical reflection without action, was also problematic. In their place, Freire argued for *praxis*, or a unification of reflection, theory, and action. Central to praxis was the formation of *critical consciousness* (in Portuguese, *conscientização*).

What is critical consciousness (CC) and how is it relevant to supporting the development of young people such as Luis and Gabriela? First, CC involves the recognition that current features of the social order—and the intellectual frameworks that reinforce it—are not natural or inevitable, but instead socially produced. Rather than view discrimination or inequality as part of the natural course of human social organization, it begins to see such phenomena as human-made and therefore alterable.[29] A second element to critical consciousness, which follows closely from the effort to denaturalize social circumstances, is the recognition that individual actions are embedded in a matrix of institutional structures, cultural norms, and social forces. This can be important when young people come to recognize that their own experiences are not isolated or unusual. Recognizing that personal experiences are shared by others diminishes feelings of stigma or isolation. Social psychologist Michelle Fine, for example, describes an encounter between youth from Tucson and New York City. After listening to a New York student describe his special education class, a Tucson youth observed, "Your special education is in the basement? Wow, all the way across the country, and ours is, too" (p. 226). This kind of recognition of the interconnectedness of experiences can be powerful for young people who previously interpreted experiences of suffering or hardship as theirs alone.

Both these insights—to denaturalize social realities and to counter isolation—are valuable for youth struggling against institutional and cultural barriers, such as tracking, linguistic discrimination, or xenophobia. Without the chance to talk with others and to, in Fine's words, "analyze, mourn, and make sense out of these contradictions," young people might otherwise remain isolated and powerless. Such conversations are important for all people, but especially relevant to low-income youth of color who have experienced a disjuncture between the American ideals of equality and achievement and their lived experiences of poverty, racism, or stratified schooling.[30] They lead to a greater recognition of the complex ecological systems that shape one's life and a stronger sense that these systems can be changed; that they are not natural and immutable.

Recent quantitative research has begun to show links between critical consciousness and an array of positive developmental outcomes, including political engagement, employment, and psychological well-being.[31] Critical conversations about racism and inequality can also contribute to stronger teacher-student bonds.[32] Educational scholars such as Jeffrey Duncan-Andrade and Eric DeMeulenaere have written about the corrosive effects on students' trust in teachers when the latter fail to acknowledge or witness the stresses or barriers in their everyday lives.[33] Experiences of racial microaggressions need to be brought out into the open where people can talk about what they mean and how to dismantle them.

This kind of educational work is challenging, even risky, if not carried out in a way that is respectful of young people's dignity and agency. The point is not to persuade someone she is oppressed or deliver a lecture about how she should see the world. One of Freire's biggest targets of criticism was what he called the "banking model of education," which presumed that the teacher possessed the right information and just needed to deposit it into the learner's head. Critical education, instead, is dialogic and egalitarian. You ask questions, you share experiences, you encourage deliberation about different perspectives. And, perhaps most important, these critical conversations must recognize and support people's sense of hope and agency. They are not intended merely to substitute self-blame for system-blame, without action. Freire was as skeptical of idle talk as he was of mindless activism. Praxis signals a mix of smart analysis and efforts to change things.

Luis, Gabriela, their classmates, and the teacher demonstrated this potent mix of critique and collective agency in a project they developed over the course of the year to address the problems of racism and xenophobia that surfaced on Cinco de Mayo.

Challenging the Social Order of Roosevelt High through Critical Civic Inquiry

Luis, an eleventh grader at Roosevelt High, identified as Mexican American. His father and mother had met in Mexico, but his father left for the

United States to save money. After saving money, he returned to Mexico, married Luis's mother, and they returned together to the States, ultimately settling in Colorado where Luis's uncle reported that there was plentiful work. Luis was born in the United States and was therefore an American citizen. Luis embraced a multicultural view of the world: he said proudly that his two closest friends were Indian (from South Asia) and expressed his interest in being exposed to different worldviews. He also treasured his participation in his family's cultural practices, such as celebrating Las Posadas or speaking Spanish with his parents. Although Luis grew up in Colorado, he was placed in an ESL class in his high school because of his performance on a state mandated language test (CELA), much to the consternation of his ESL teacher who believed he was capable of more challenging academic classes.

Gabriela was also a junior at the school. She identified in her interview as "straight up Mexican." Gabriela had left Juarez, Mexico, with her family after witnessing a family member's murder. She talked in an interview about wanting to be a writer after high school—"writing about real stories"—and shared an example of a story she had written about her friend's life. Aside from writing, Gabriela's life outside school was occupied with helping out her family: at night she helped her mother clean offices; she also looked after her nephew regularly. Despite her fluency speaking English, like Luis she was in the ESL course because of her performance on the CELA test.

I know of Luis and Gabriela because their ESL teacher—Mr. Monteith—enrolled in a graduate seminar that I co-taught with Shelley Zion, which provided an intellectual space for teachers to support each other in facilitating a project called Critical Civic Inquiry (CCI). CCI is a school-based intervention that provides opportunities for students to develop critical awareness about education systems and take collective action to address a problem. CCI adopts the inquiry cycle in participatory action research (PAR), which includes identifying a compelling problem motivated by tensions between students' everyday experiences and dreams for the future, studying that problem through original research, and then advancing their ideas through meetings with policy makers or presentations to public audiences. The three core practices of CCI are summarized in Table 1.1.

TABLE 1.1. Critical Civic Inquiry in Schools

Key practices	Definitions
Sharing power with students	Examples include using periodic surveys to get feedback from students, creating opportunities for students to share their own knowledge and educational histories, and practicing group decision making
Critical conversations about educational equity	Students talk about their school experiences and how issues of power and privilege play out in their lives
Participatory action research	Students enact the action research cycle and communicate their experiences and policy solutions to external audiences

A separate quantitative study of student experiences in CCI reported promising evidence of its impact on students' academic engagement and civic efficacy.[34] Carlos Hipolito-Delgado, a co-Principal Investigator, surveyed CCI participants (including the students from Roosevelt) at three time points and compared their responses to a control group of students who were similar demographically. Whereas the CCI students reported increases over those three time points, the control group reported declines in academic engagement and civic efficacy.[35] This chapter helps to fill out those promising results by showing what the experience looked and felt like for two students at Roosevelt. I chose to write about Luis and Gabriela because they showed up so frequently in the field notes and they participated in interviews at the end of the year.

Mr. Monteith was a veteran white teacher, bilingual in Spanish and English, who served as chair of his school's ESL department. He was a devoted ally to his students—most of whom were Latino—as illustrated by his annual role as faculty advisor for students to participate in a statewide Raza Leadership conference. As a participant observer in the class, Elizabeth Mendoza made weekly visits to get to know students and document discussions in field notes. The class was composed of seventeen students, roughly split between juniors and seniors and females and males. Most identified as "Latino/a" on an open-ended written survey, but one said "American," one said "Asian American," one said "white," and three declined to identify their race or ethnicity.

The Naturalized Social Order at Roosevelt

Racism was for all intents and purposes a taboo subject at Roosevelt. Well, to be more accurate, race talk was ubiquitous when it came to sorting and reporting the performance of various groups on state tests; and it shaped many of the patterns and rhythms of the school, including where you sat in the building during free periods, whom you sought out as friends, whether you were targeted for the new STEM "school within a school," and which, if any, afterschool clubs you joined. But people were relatively *color mute* when it came to talking about these issues in public. *Color muteness*, coined by anthropologist Mica Pollock, refers to a tendency in American schools for people to avoid talking about race or using racial labels despite the relevance of racial categories in the way people are treated.[36] Color muteness is problematic because it tends to naturalize—to enshroud as common sense—tracking and other forms of racial inequalities.

Finding evidence of color muteness can be difficult because one is looking for examples of absence. But several sources do point in this direction. The teacher, Mr. Monteith, expressed concern in multiple conversations that the overwhelmingly white school faculty and staff did not reflect the school population and were not equipped to understand or address the daily realities of Latino/a students. He worried that the development of a new STEM program was motivated to recruit white middle class families and would not meet the needs of Latino/a students.

Evidence of color muteness also emerged in Gabriela's accounts of conversations she had with adults in the school. Inspired by discussions in Mr. Monteith's class, she sought out interviews with security guards and deans of the school about whether discrimination existed at Roosevelt. She reported that a police officer told her, "There was a lot of discrimination in this school that nobody knows about." Similarly, she said that the deans told her that there was "a lot of discrimination, but they don't like to talk about it. . . . They don't really want to put it out there." Gabriela's account suggests a pattern at the school in which adults acknowledged discrimination at the school, but tended not to address it as part of public discourse. The school's solution to the prior year's Cinco de Mayo conflicts is further evidence of this tendency to avoid forthright public discussion: the extra police cars led to a quiet

May 5, but not to public conversation about any of the issues lying below the surface.

Some students too voiced the view that everybody got along and race didn't matter at the school. As part of our research methodology to understand the school from students' perspectives, on two separate occasions we asked students to give us a guided tour. On both tours we noticed that students did not voluntarily share examples of racial tension or discrimination. It was not until we explicitly asked about how different racial groups got along that we heard about examples of harassment. Interviews, as well, suggested a tendency among students to articulate a color-blind discourse when asked about race relations at the school. We heard comments such as, "It doesn't matter what race you are," and "I don't know, I don't really feel different than anybody else." Another student said, "You know, it's just, it's just skin color, you know people can be just like you."[37]

Early in the year Mr. Monteith's classroom was also a place where students resisted his invitations to examine the topic of racial inequality. For example, in September Mr. Monteith brought in charts showing differences in achievement and attainment by different racial and ethnic groups. Elizabeth, curious about the subdued response in the room, asked the students how they felt about the graphs and how they would explain them. Later she wrote in her field notes:

> There was a pause and then Luis, adamantly (in a strong voice and greater hand movement), said, "I don't think race has anything to do with it." Gabriela . . . said she agreed with Luis. She said that "it is not about race." (9/28 field notes)

After this class, Ana, one student hung around chatting with Elizabeth and Mr. Monteith about how the class had been. Ana said:

> Other students don't know why we are talking about race and they sometimes they think that it is racist what we talk about in the class. . . . "Why are you talking about this anyway, Mr.?" (9/28 field notes)

Mr. Monteith felt that segregation and discrimination were problems at the school, and he wanted students to talk about them. At one point, in a class brainstorm about problems at the school and why many students were not feeling motivated, he said, "You tend to blame yourself, but maybe there are other reasons you are not engaged in school." In this example, Mr. Monteith was trying to challenge a meritocratic ideology about student success and failure, which assumes that people are competing on a level playing field.

Another case of the meritocratic ideology can be seen in interviews with Luis and Gabriela about student voice at the school. We wanted to know which types of students were heard at the school in terms of having their ideas listened to or their interests met. Both Luis and Gabriela, when asked to talk about who got heard at the school, hinted at inequalities but then justified those inequalities through a meritocratic lens. Luis said, for example:

> I think those students who are more involved in the school are mostly heard more than others, like, if they're part of clubs, sports, honor society, they'll be heard more than others.
> *And who isn't heard as much, then?*
> Uh, the people that, like . . . they're not involved, they just go to school, take care of their business and go home.

Gabriela responded similarly. When asked which students were heard at the school, she said it was the students who are part of various extracurricular activities. Elizabeth followed up by asking why she thought some students "get involved in school and some students don't."

> Because they want to, like, have a good resume for the college. [Laughs]
> I would do that. [Laughs]
> *What do you mean, you "would do that?"*
> If I was to, like, actually get to do something big for college or somethin', I would actually, like, get into a [*student leadership*] thing or participate in stuff.

Both Luis and Gabriela said that those who were heard were "involved" in the school through athletics or formal student leadership. Luis contrasted the involved people with those who were "not involved," who "just go to school, take care of their business, and go home." Gabriela indicated that she would have participated if she thought she could "get into something big for college." They appeared to be legitimizing this social order: those who were "heard" had earned that right: they participated, they were active, they got involved.

But as the interviews continued, when Elizabeth asked them to talk about why they were not involved, the story became more complicated. It turned out that Luis used to play baseball but stopped because of the exorbitant fees ($400 per season). He instead joined a team from another high school that was cheaper and left him more time to work after school. This left him in the paradoxical situation of being quite active and engaged outside school but still "uninvolved" in the eyes of the school. Gabriela's reasons for not joining the student leadership program were similar. When Elizabeth asked her why, she said:

I don't know. Like, I work . . . with my mom.
How many hours do you work usually during the week?
Oh, it takes us, like, we work from 5 to, like, 2 in the morning. It's at night.
Oh, that's a lot. What are you doing with your mom?
Cleaning offices. [Laughs]
You do it every night?
Yeah.
Wow.
And I would have to baby-sit my nephew sometimes.

Luis and Gabriela, as it turns out, were highly involved in extra-curricular activities. Although I can imagine Gabriela and her mother would have preferred for her not to work that many hours, it is important to acknowledge the kinds of strengths work likely fostered.[38] One can imagine the time management skills that these activities promote, not to mention the experience of maturity that comes from contributing to her family's sustenance. Luis too was juggling multiple commitments that demonstrated his self-sufficiency and self-discipline.

But they went to a school where their out of school activities were not recognized and therefore they could not parlay them into access to high-status opportunities or new kinds of visibility at the school.

According to Luis and Gabriela's account, other students—typically white and middle class—were recognized as the "involved" students because of their participation in sports or afterschool clubs. This image was made more visible and explicit by the pictures of clubs and sports teams that adorned the hallways of the school and its "wall of fame." This is a powerful example of how certain behaviors that are shaped by one's class privilege end up being endowed with a certain moral quality; inequality in who gets heard becomes naturalized.

Critique and Collective Agency

The Critical Civic Inquiry project in which Mr. Monteith's class participated was intended to be a vehicle for students to denaturalize and inquire about injustices at their school. Mr. Monteith guided his students in a participatory action research sequence that started with conversations about race and inequality and culminated in efforts to change their school.

CRITICAL CONVERSATIONS ABOUT INEQUALITY

Students participated in multiple activities in the fall that raised topics of inequality and institutional racism, including ten- to fifteen-minute presentations to define "oppression," "privilege," "power," and "domination"; open-ended discussions about the recent passage of an Alabama anti-immigration law and its impact on Mexican neighborhoods; and watching a video about Arizona's decision to outlaw "ethnic studies" in Tucson high schools.

Classroom conversations about power and privilege were linked to assignments to study policies and practices at their own school. Students completed a "school report card" in which teams of students collected data about different aspects of the school such as test performance, the school lunches, and support for low-income families. They developed their persuasive writing skills through assignments that asked them to redesign their school for the twenty-first century: "What changes would you make? What would you add, and what would you keep? What is missing that would make our school a better place?"

This combination of activities, assignments, and discussions culminated in a decision-making process with the class, which took place over several weeks, to winnow its list of problems and select one as their CCI project. Eventually the class chose to take up the topic of Cinco de Mayo. When asked why this was the topic, Luis said: "Everyone already . . . had a negative outcome out of that day, like, the whole class did, so we were like, 'Yeah, we should do this. It's going on in our school.'" As described by Mr. Monteith, the goal of the project was to get teachers and administrators to think about Cinco de Mayo as a celebration of cultural diversity, not a threat that should be monitored with extra police. They aimed to educate students about the holiday and create forums for students of different backgrounds to share their cultures.

FROM PRIVATE TO PUBLIC

After agreeing on Cinco de Mayo as their topic for research and action, the students' first assignment was to write down their own experiences with Cinco de Mayo, either positive or negative. This idea of inviting personal narratives, also called *auto-ethnographies*, is a signature practice in Participatory Action Research because it elevates the stories and experiences of people as forms of knowledge production. Students wrote in vivid and emotion-laden language about their recollections. Gabriela wrote one of the more detailed accounts:

A negative experience I had with Cinco de Mayo was 2 years ago in my freshman year. There was a lot of conflicts. There was people fighting and Mexican/Americans[39] trying to burn each others flags. In the halls ways there was a lot of people pushing each other which caused Student Relations[40] full of Mexicans/Americans. Well mostly Mexicans. They sent me to the office just make sure I wasn't wearing any Mexican colors (which I wasn't) also to see if I was causing problems with others (Americans). That made me mad which made me want to do stupid stuff. For example this American kid pushed me and I pushed him back and talk crap to him because if I was going to get sent to the office for no reason why not give them a reason to send me to the office. At first I was mad because Americans were been all annoying. But then I ignore them but they kept pushing and pushing and that's when I snapped. Then they burned a Mexican flag and spit on it and stepped on it which there's a difference between annoying and disrespect but at that time they were *both*.

Even Luis, who had at other times voiced his sense that kids generally got along at the school, wrote a very detailed story about the fear he felt on Cinco de Mayo:

> It was my freshman year I was brand new to the high school environment & Cinco de Mayo came up. I wore a Mexican flag behind my t shirt to honor my parents country. At the time I thought [Roosevelt] high school will fill with Mexican flags but I was wrong as soon as I walked through the hallway I find myself surrounded by American flags all over. Furthermore students screaming racial things like "GO BACK TO MEXICO"! & "Fucking Beaners!" I was terrified at the time so I acted like nothing was going on. That was a negative experience that I had during Cinco de Mayo.

There are many ways one might interpret these rich and layered narratives. Here I focus on their significance as academic artifacts that were shared publicly in the class. Students read and, consistent with qualitative data analysis methods, "coded" each others' narratives so that they could identify themes that cut across the group. All of them had experienced Cinco de Mayo, so writing down their experiences was not new knowledge or new information. What was novel about it was that it enabled the students to see how this experience was one that many of them shared. This notion of taking private or personal experiences and seeing how they are part of a collective experience is central to sociopolitical development.

Moreover, Mr. Monteith treated these narratives as building blocks for a survey that the class was developing for the whole school. The essays produced knowledge that would then be examined in relation to the experiences of a broader and more diverse mass of students from the school. The surveys focused on a few key elements, such as: Did people think it was wrong to celebrate Cinco de Mayo? Did people think Cinco de Mayo was different from St. Patrick's Day? Did people know what Cinco de Mayo commemorated?

TABLE 1.2. Survey Results*

	Somewhat or strongly agree		Somewhat or strongly disagree	
	Hispanic students (n = 138)	White students (n = 98)	Hispanic students (n = 138)	White students (n = 98)
Should students celebrate Cinco de Mayo in school?	54%	36%	18%	41%
Do you think people who wear American flags on Cinco de Mayo are provoking racism?	80%	38%	12%	43%

* Responses of "Don't know" are not included in this table.

GATHERING EVIDENCE

The students administered and collected 281 surveys. With Mr. Monteith's coaxing and guidance, they tallied the data, studied it, and used Excel spreadsheets to compare responses by different independent variables. They organized the charts into different findings to share at a student forum held at the local university, where CCI student teams from around the area shared the results of their action research projects. Much of the Roosevelt students' analysis focused on comparisons between "Hispanics" and "whites" (their terms). For example, they found widespread recognition of a problem on Cinco de Mayo: A majority of whites and Hispanics reported "witnessing violence" on Cinco de Mayo at the school in the past. It also showed disagreement about whether or not students should be allowed to celebrate Cinco de Mayo at the school and whether wearing American flags promoted racism. Table 1.2 summarizes some of the results.

The data revealed differences depending on one's self-reported identity: Hispanic students for the most part thought students should be able to celebrate the holiday; they interpreted the wearing of American flags on May 5th as provoking racism. The responses of white students differed: although there was a multiculturally oriented faction of white students, there was a marginally larger group who thought that students should not celebrate Cinco de Mayo at the school and who did not think that wearing the American flag on that day was provocative. According to Gabriela, she and her colleagues were surprised by the results:

At first we didn't think it was a big problem. But then when we actually looked at all the surveys and stuff, it was, like, a big problem. More than half the students have witnessed fighting or been in fights.

When I saw the surveys, I was really surprised at some of the comments.

We saw there was, like, a lot of discrimination in school, 'cause usually people don't actually show it, but if you actually ask 'em, they'll be like, "Ugh!"

Analysis of the survey results fueled conversation and reactions among the students. Ivan, one of the quieter students in the class, made a joke that perfectly evoked the contradictions that the students were finding:

JESUS: "I don't like St. Patrick's day because if you don't wear green you get pinched."

IVAN: "Yeah, and on Cinco day Mayo if you wear green you get put in the back of the police car." (field notes)

Gabriela and Luis were two of the most engaged and outspoken members of the class when it came to investigating this issue. Both frequently weighed in on decisions about the direction of the project. When asked about her role, Gabriela said, "I was everywhere. . . . I did some surveys, I asked the teachers, I asked the principal, I talked to the cop, I talked to the deans." Elizabeth asked if talking to those people was "for class" and Gabriela said, "I just wanted to know. Not really for class, I just wanted to talk to [them]." These examples of role taking by Gabriela and Luis are signs of sociopolitical development, because they reflect new kinds of participation in the social world of the school. Gabriel, in particular expanded her social networks and in her interactions with powerful adults at the school projected confidence and agency.

SPEAKING UP FOR CHANGE

The students in Mr. Monteith's class had varied goals for what they wanted to see changed at the school. They invited a writer for the school paper to write an article providing a history of the holiday. But they wanted more than that—as one student said, "No one reads the school paper." So Luis, Gabriela, Eli, and a few others requested a meeting with the principal. They wanted her to see the findings and discuss strategies for change for the subsequent year.

Students' accounts of the meeting overlap but pick up on different themes and subtexts. First, according to Gabriela and Luis, they encountered trepidation from the principal. Gabriela recounted that the principal's first reaction upon seeing them at the door was, "Ugh, students." Luis also perceived a general tone of resistance:

> We told her what was going on and she was like, "I don't want to see the survey."
> *She didn't want to see it?*
> Like, she saw it, but she was like, "I shouldn't be seeing this," 'cause it made her look bad, you know, I guess.

After this rocky start they started to get into more details and the principal showed her openness to their ideas. Both Luis's and Gabriela's accounts communicate a sense of affirmation from the principal but also frustration with her response. Here is Luis:

> *So did she listen to you guys?*
> Yeah, she listened, but then again, she was like, she didn't want to take action. We told her, "You should do this and this," but she didn't agree. She was like, "No." Then I told her, "I strongly think that you should educate people," and she said, "Yeah, I think that's what needs to be done."

Gabriela's account followed a similar arc:

> She didn't even want to look at the graphs or anything, 'cause she was, like, surprised at how many fights there was and how many things there was, especially 'cause our school is in the lowest from her district, like—
> *Lowest what?*
> Performing. It's on the lowest. [Laughs] So she's more disappointed and stuff like that, so she wants, like, everyone to learn about Cinco de Mayo. And then I was tellin' her, like, "Not just Cinco de Mayo, I think it should be more cultures, 'cause if they don't even know what Cinco de Mayo is, they probably don't even know what other cultures did."

But Gabriela also communicated a sense of being heard and supported by the principal:

> She (*the principal*) was actually like, "No, you know what? This is a problem. We are going to make a video. How about this? How about this?" She was, like, giving us options of what to do.

So the meeting ended but it was unclear what the next steps would be. Another student in attendance left it feeling frustrated, as she later told Elizabeth: "I don't think anyone, the principal or anyone, did anything about it." Mr. Monteith, in a later email, corroborated these accounts, saying that the principal "was friendly and welcoming," but

> never actually offered any kind of solution to the problem. . . . She was convinced that we wouldn't have much of a problem with students since Cinco de Mayo fell on a Saturday that year and on a Sunday this year. She did not want to really address the issue.

Sociopolitical Development at Roosevelt High

The students in Mr. Monteith's class did not succeed in accomplishing dramatic changes at their school. They were unable to persuade the principal to organize a more proactive approach to race relations there, nor did they develop other change strategies for the school, other than the article about Cinco de Mayo that was published in the school paper. This challenge—of mounting student-driven classroom projects that lead to sustained and meaningful change inside schools—was experienced by other CCI classes as well.

But for the students who participated, particularly Luis and Gabriela, whose participation I have foregrounded here, it was not just a class exercise. It gave them a chance to develop as sociopolitical agents. Luis and Gabriela practiced a powerful combination of critique and collective agency. They took part in dialogues that raised questions about the social order of Roosevelt High. They developed autobiographical narratives that highlighted commonalities in their past experiences of harassment and discrimination and motivated further inquiry. They talked—a lot—about race and racism and joked about contradictions in their experiences, such as Ivan's wry observation that wearing green was so much more dangerous on May 5 than March 17.

These practices of critique were accompanied by the opportunity to work together to change the climate at the school. This was a school project that shifted the typical unit of measurement from the individual student to the class as a whole. They gained practice working with peers, investigating the roots of the problem, formulating strategy about how to accomplish meaningful change, and meeting with a powerful decision maker. Their accounts of the meeting with the principal reveal a sophisticated give and take in which they engaged in persuasive argument. They framed their argument in a nonantagonistic way and persisted despite initial defensiveness. Moreover, in a school where Luis and Gabriela had been positioned as uninvolved and low track, taking up space in the principal's office and demanding that she recognize them as public actors represented a challenge to business as usual.

Luis's and Gabriela's reflections about their experiences lend credibility to the claim that this opportunity to engage in critique and collective agency was unusual in their schooling experiences. When asked to talk about the class in an open-ended interview, they both emphasized its novelty—that it was "different." One of the key differences was its scope: It was bigger, more ambitious, and harder work. Gabriela described how her initial impressions changed over time; she particularly liked that it had an audience that went beyond the typical class assignment:

> At first it was kind of boring. . . . We started doing the project thing, and at first we were like, "Ugh, it's a project, we don't wanna do it. Ugh." And then we started getting into it, and we're like, "Oh, we're actually doin' it," you know? "We're actually doin' a big project, not just like a little class project." And it got better each day. [Laughs]
> *And when you said you were doing something that's bigger than the class project, can you tell me more about that?*
> Well, usually we present only to the class, but this time we presented to more other people, not just ourselves or others at our school. We actually did it to other schools.

Luis too emphasized a transition from initial boredom to interest, saying:

> At first I didn't like it, honestly, thought it was boring, but then when we started doing CCI, I was like, "That's pretty cool." I just started coming to class. 'Cause I used to ditch a lot.

Later in the interview Luis returned to this point, saying that he goes to "second hour (*CCI class*) almost every day, just so that I wake up." Interpreted literally, I think Luis meant that the CCI class rejuvenated him for the day ahead; but to play with the metaphor a bit, perhaps he also meant it as a process of waking up to new awareness or insight.

Luis returned to this imagery of waking up—seeing things differently, gaining awareness—throughout the interview. He was initially reluctant to acknowledge inequality of opportunity; as mentioned in the example from the field notes, he voiced skepticism when Mr. Monteith brought up a term like "institutional oppression." Elizabeth asked him to give an example of what he meant by saying he had gained more "awareness of his surroundings."

> For example, [pause for 4–5 seconds] like, the minorities, how they don't have as many opportunities as the whites, like, after I saw that, I was like, "That's not true. That's not true. I'm sure that's not true."

A minute later he echoed this point when asked about the class:

> Like I said, it makes you find yourself, helps you make, like—it gives you a different view on life. At first I was like, "Oh, nothing's wrong with this world. Like, everything's perfect." And then, once you get informed of this stuff, you're like, "Whoa, you better be aware of this stuff and be careful."

Luis identified a specific event outside class, during the fall semester, which prompted his change in thinking. While leaving the school parking lot in his car, he was pulled over by a police officer and told to produce his social security card: "It was crazy, 'cause it was during the CCI class, and I was like, 'Whoa, this is actually happening!'" Luis felt that he was being profiled by the police officer because of his skin color and appearance; he said to himself, "This (the stuff we've been talking about in class) is actually happening!" Luis recounted a shift in perspective from denial ("that's not true, that's not true") to recognition ("you better be aware of this stuff and be careful"). Rather than dismiss his experience with the police officer as an exception or due to his driving skills, Luis started to draw a connection between the event and what he was learning in class about racism.

Gabriela also talked about learning important insights during the class. She focused on the concept of "culture." When Elizabeth asked Gabriela to elaborate on her statement that the class was "productive," Gabriela said:

> You could actually learn about stuff instead of just going to class and just sitting there. You could actually learn somethin' about your own culture or . . . not just yourself, but about somethin' else.

When Gabriela was asked to describe her learning, she talked about learning "not to give up on projects" and that "you actually learn who you are and also what other people are."

It's difficult to know how enduring or robust these lessons were. I caution against thinking of sociopolitical development in terms of a linear process, from absence to presence or ignorance to awareness. It is more incremental and situational. Also, I tend to treat interview data with some skepticism because of the strangeness of the interview as a social interaction and the possibility of people wanting to share "good news" with the researcher. Therefore I look for examples or stories that give life to people's statements. Luis and Gabriela, for example, each told stories that show them applying their learning to new contexts. Educational psychologists describe this as a question of "transfer"—does a new insight or skill or interest travel to new settings or does it remain confined to the original setting where it was learned?[41]

Luis's story about his interaction with the police officer suggests a highly consequential form of transfer. When asked for an example of what he meant when he said the class was "a good way to learn and to know your surroundings," Luis responded by recounting when he was pulled over by a police officer and asked for his social security number. Luis explained that when he went to court, he "told them" that if he had been white, they wouldn't have asked for that information, but the judge told him that the police officer could still ask. Luis then persisted in challenging the court officials with a new question: "Yeah, I know, but why was he asking me?" Luis's story, believable to me in its detail, is evidence that he was applying lessons from the class to a different context. Specifically, he transferred the practice of critical questioning—and a general sense of empowerment—to a new, presumably more intimidating setting.

Gabriela too gave several examples that suggested transfer outside class. Like Luis, she transferred a practice of critical inquiry and questioning directed toward people with institutional power. As mentioned earlier, she interviewed school security, teachers, the deans, and the principal about whether there was discrimination at the school. In addition, she brought these inquiry practices inside her home, making use her family's internet connection: "When I would get bored, I would, like, research how many actual schools have a lot of racism and stuff like that. There was a lot of schools with racism." Gabriela recounted a time she was doing this research and her mom entered the room.

> My mom . . . was like, "What are you doing?" And I'm like, "Oh, searching." [Laughs] She's like, "What are you searching now?" "Oh, about cultures and stuff." She was like, "What kind of cultures?" I'm like, "Oh, Mexican American." And she goes. "Oh, OK. Why are you kids learning this?" And I'm like, "Oh, 'cause it's an ESL class about, like, Mexicans and learning more about Americans and stuff." And she was like, "Oh. What's it about?" And I'm like, "Oh, my God." [Laughs] And I explained to her the whole thing that we're doing, the survey, and she goes, "Oh, that's interesting." I'm like, "Yup." I showed her, like, how many people were discriminated, and she goes, "Daaammnnn." And she goes, "I did not know that." She was, like surprised by it, too. I was like, "Yup, that's what happens."

Gabriela's story shows her curiosity about the issue of discrimination and how she brought it into discussions with her mother—another form of transfer.

Luis and Gabriela's experiences with the project help to illustrate the exciting quantitative evidence from surveys of CCI students, which showed significant increases in academic engagement and self-reported civic efficacy in contrast to a comparison group.[42] With regard to academic engagement, we see in Luis and Gabriela's stories how they felt the relevance of the projects to their lives. The opportunity to do something "real," something that had a public audience and significance for their sense of belonging in the school, motivated their engagement. With regard to the growth in civic efficacy, it is plausible that the opportunity to think strategically about how to bring about change, persist despite adult indifference or skepticism, and ultimately be recognized for having expertise and value, would lead to such changes. Consistent with a sociocultural account of development, this process was not just an internal psychological shift but one that played out in an institutional context where previously marginalized youth stepped forward and claimed public roles. Far from diminishing their sense of agency, the conversations about racism and discrimination, which early on provoked skepticism or resistance, catalyzed a greater sense of confidence and repertoires for action when dealing with institutional authorities.

* * *

This chapter offered a case study of sociopolitical development for two young people, Gabriela and Luis, who experienced marginalization linked to their class, ethnic, and linguistic backgrounds; this marginalization became most conspicuous in displays of anti-immigrant sentiment on Cinco de Mayo. I have tried to show what practices of critique and collective agency looked like as they unfolded in the course project and how Gabriela and Luis made meaning of their experiences. Experiences like these should be more common for all young people, but particularly for those struggling with a social order that tracks and excludes them in ways that go unrecognized.

Sociopolitical development, in this account, extends, but does not replace widely accepted practices of Social Emotional Learning (SEL) and positive youth development (PYD). After all, Gabriela's and Luis's experiences in Mr. Monteith's class included many of the competencies prized in the SEL and PYD literatures. One can see, for example, students sharing their emotions in their narratives about what happened at the school on Cinco de Mayo and managing relationships in their negotiations about what topic to focus on for their CCI project. One can also see prized features of the PYD literature at work: providing opportunities for leadership and mattering, supportive relationships with a devoted teacher, and the development of key academic literacies in their writing and survey analysis.

Where the project went beyond typical SEL or PYD activities was in its focus on problems with the social order at Roosevelt High and willingness to engage students in conversations about race, power, and privilege. Instead of positioning students as the target of remediation, the project targeted the complex ecology of the school. Just as significant, it positioned students as key actors in interrogating and changing a complex ecology. The source of their dispossession became the object of their work together. In such a context, activism contributed to human development.

Schools and youth programs need to offer opportunities for students from historically marginalized groups to participate in sociopolitical practices like these. Students will be most likely to engage in school when they see academic work as being relevant to their everyday lives and are invited to participate with adults in making their schools better. Youth will benefit when they are treated with dignity as partners in school or community transformation.

2

Millennial Youth and the Fight for Opportunity

The Soweto Uprising of June 16, 1976, widely credited with jumpstarting the struggle to end apartheid, was planned and coordinated by high school students.[1] Somewhere between ten and twenty thousand learners walked out of their schools in a coordinated effort to protest South Africa's education system under apartheid. Steven Biko, founder and organizer of the Black Consciousness Movement, and at the time only thirty, said, "It took us all by surprise."[2] Elliot Ndlovu, the father of fifteen-year-old Hastings Ndlovu, one of the first two students to be killed by police that day, recounted, "On June 16 1976 I woke up as usual. I did not know anything, these kids were too secretive." Hastings, walking near the front of a procession, was shot and killed before the march could get to Soweto's Orlando Stadium, where students from a number of schools were to gather.

Another victim, Hector Pieterson, a primary school student, was not supposed to be part of the demonstration at all, but joined in when he saw relatives among the marchers from his classroom window.[3] Teachers tried to stop the younger students but they couldn't. Hector's sister recalled, "Hector joined me because he saw the uniforms of the schools involved in the march. 'My uncle is there, my sister is there, why can I not join?'" The photograph of Hector's prone body, being carried by a distraught teenage boy, became an infamous symbol of the evil of the apartheid regime.

The immediate catalyst for the walkouts was the national government's decision to require that Afrikaans be the medium of instruction in "African" schools (meaning schools attended by Xhosa, Zulu, and other indigenous black youth). The policy was opposed by black school boards and teachers, in part for practical reasons (many were not fluent in Afrikaans), but more importantly to resist its destructive consequences for the cultures and languages of black South Africans. Many teachers were inspired by Biko's Black Consciousness Movement and carried its message into their work with black students. Afrikaans was the language of the oppressor. During the early months of 1976 the policy pushed forward in fits and starts, with some principals actively opposing it and others submitting to the national authority. Students began meeting during afternoon periods to discuss their frustrations and help each other with their studies. These sessions led to a decision in May to shift tactics toward visible public protest. *The World* (a Soweto paper) reported events on May 17 at Phefeni Junior Secondary School:

> Students threatened to beat up their headmaster and threw (Afrikaans) textbooks out of classroom windows in a demonstration against being taught some subjects in Afrikaans. The 600 students from Phefeni Junior Secondary School, Orlando West, then went on strike and refused to attend any classes.

By June 1 seven secondary schools had joined the strikes. Parents and school board members convened and, although they were also opposed to the Afrikaans instruction, called for students to return to school while they sought to address the matter. Students, however, continued to strike. By this time college students, who were part of the South African Students Movement (SASM), took an interest in what was going on and organized a conference where they officially endorsed the actions by the younger students.

Hector Pieterson and Hastings Ndlovu were the first of scores of youth to be killed on June 16. The police force responded to the marchers with stunning brutality and force. Young people responded by setting fire to police cars and vandalizing government offices and liquor stores.[4] Police action resulted in another ninety-three deaths over the next two days alone.[5]

The story of the Soweto Uprising resists nostalgia or romanticism. Too many deaths for that. The students of Soweto did not show the caution of their elders, who were also angry about the new policy. Their defiance of a brutal police state led to death and suffering. But it also inspired others to continue the fight and show the world that apartheid would not be passively tolerated. The events of June 16 fueled further uprisings and student strikes throughout South Africa and led to an international outcry against the apartheid regime. Thousands of students fled South Africa to join militant groups outside the borders.[6] According to South Africa's Apartheid Museum:

> The protests by Soweto school children on that day marked the end of submissiveness on the part of the black population of South Africa and the beginning of a new militancy in the struggle against apartheid.

Rian Malan, an Afrikaner intellectual, writes, "The tide of history had turned."

* * *

It is risky to begin a chapter about young people's contributions to grassroots democracy with stories from almost forty years ago. It is even more risky to profile a movement outside the United States. Doing so may reinforce the presumed exceptionalism of youth political activism: it's a thing of the past, it happens elsewhere.

But I start this chapter with the Soweto Uprising because it offers proof of young people as historical actors—people who organized against oppressive conditions, built power in numbers, and took great risks to galvanize the struggle against apartheid. This was high-stakes civic engagement. The facts of the Soweto Uprising challenge paternalistic and apolitical views of civic engagement that would situate it solely as a developmental exercise.

Too often the literature about youth civic engagement only focuses on what it means for the future civic participation of the actors. Youth's experiences with volunteering, speaking at a city council hearing, or creating a peace mural are discussed in terms of their significance for their likelihood to vote or their growth in civic efficacy. We need to remember, however, that there have been times and places where youth action has changed history. Recognition of youth's roles as historical actors—typically in collaboration with adult organizers and movements—helps to dismantle the condescending future-orientation of much of the civic engagement discourse. Yes, youth are the "leaders of the future," but they also interpret, critique, and, sometimes, take action to change oppressive conditions.

So where are today's cases where once-marginalized youth assert their public voice and make an impact on policies affecting youth? If, to quote a South African youth organization called Equal Education, "Every generation has its struggle," where are today's struggles? Are there movements among today's "millennial generation" that will be discussed by historians in twenty-five years? Where are low-income youth of color stepping forward, speaking up, organizing each other, and calling attention to inequities? Before answering those questions I first clarify the landscape of civic engagement for young people in the United States.

Trends in Civic Engagement among Millennial Youth

The millennial generation refers to young people in the United States born between 1980 and 2000.[7] One could be forgiven for being confused about the civic health of millennials: There is reason for both alarm and optimism. Evidence for alarm starts with concerns about American democracy in general. Congress is more unpopular than ever and appears to be broken in fundamental ways. Gerrymandering makes congressional representatives less accountable to a broad and diverse public. Private wealth, through campaign donations and lobbying, shapes legislation. The ratio of citizen to congressional representative has gone from roughly 30,000 to one at the country's founding to more than 700,000 to one in 2010.[8] Policy makers' tendency to reduce social problems to technical challenges—reinforced by tortuously complex laws and regulations—creates the need for specialists who crowd out ordinary people from public problem solving or deliberation.[9] These manifold problems with the electoral system and widespread disenchantment contribute to a discourse about a decline in the American political system.

A subcomponent of this discourse of decline is the allegation that youth are especially apathetic or uninvolved politically. "Youth" sometimes refers to those under eighteen but in discussions of voting rates, the term tends to be used to refer to those in the 18–24 or 18–29 age range. As with the decline discourse, there is some evidence that bears out concerns about youth civic engagement. According to one study, youth perform lower than prior generations on 9 of 10 indicators of civic engagement, such as working on a community project, voting, belonging to a union, and being contacted by a political party.[10] The one exception, volunteering, likely reflects the significant growth of community service programs in the 1990s and 2000s. Although rates of youth voting (18–29 years old) increased in 2008 and 2012, they remained below the rates of older adults by about 20 percentage points.[11] More than half of young people between 18 and 29 *did not vote* in 2012. Additionally, only 10 percent of youth between the ages of 18 and 24 met strict criteria for "informed voting," which included accurately answering questions about political knowledge and campaign issues.[12]

Parsing this generational distinction still further reveals evidence of a civic engagement gap related to race, class, and educational attainment. Meira Levinson, an educational philosopher, summarized data showing that "African American, Hispanic, non–native-born, and poor students perform significantly worse on standardized tests and surveys of civic knowledge and skills than White, Asian, native-born, and middle-class students do."[13] Comparisons also show higher rates of volunteering among white people than African Americans and Latinos.[14] The most robust predictor of civic engagement and voting is educational attainment. In 2008, for example, more than 70 percent of those with a bachelor's degree voted, whereas just 40 percent of those with only a high school diploma voted, a trend that has been stable for several election cycles.[15]

Writers who call attention to a civic engagement gap also point to attitudinal measures related to trust, efficacy, and belonging.[16] The general finding is that youth from low-income families and youth of color tend to feel less trusting toward government and articulate lower rates of civic or political efficacy.[17] Albert Bandura, a social psychologist, wrote in 1997 that African American youth "have a lower sense of political efficacy and higher political cynicism than do white youths" (p. 491).

But as one begins to investigate the "gap" discourse it breaks down, or at least become more complicated, as do generational laments about youths' apathy and civic decline. In fact, the literature is almost contradictory on this point. Consider the civic status of African Americans. In defiance of allegations of alienation and disconnection among black youth, there is a great deal of evidence that young African Americans are *more active* than any other ethnic or racial group, including whites.

For example, a 2007 fact sheet from CIRCLE, a nonpartisan research institute, reported that

> African-American youth are the most politically engaged racial/ethnic group. Compared to other groups, African-Americans are the most likely to vote regularly, belong to groups involved with politics, donate money to candidates and parties, display buttons or signs, and contact the media.[18]

CIRCLE also cited data that African Americans were far more likely than any other group to address community needs by gathering with others and participating in community meetings.[19] In the 2008, 2010, and 2012 elections, African American youth between 18 and 24 voted at greater numbers than any other racial group.[20]

This high level of participation can partly be attributed to Obama's candidacy, but it also shows up in other areas of civic engagement. Mass protests against Stand Your Ground laws, motivated by Trayvon Martin's homicide, as well as earlier protests in Jenna, Mississippi, attest to the political engagement of black youth.[21] A report published by the MacArthur Foundation's Youth Participatory Politics network reported that "engagement is highest among black youth," measured in terms of voting, online participation, or membership in political organizations. Even the numbers around volunteering, which have shown lower rates among African American youth, have been convincingly critiqued for a class and cultural bias. Some conventional surveys are biased to count service that is formally recognized by schools or community service programs but tend to undercount other forms of volunteering, such as caring for neighborhood children or helping out in one's church.[22]

Evidence about Latino youth also defies the familiar narrative of disconnection. Although they have shown lower rates of voting than African Americans and whites, Latino youth, including those with and without legal citizenship, have joined the movement for immigration rights in great numbers to press for changes to state and federal laws.[23] In a 2006 survey, 23 percent of Latino/a young people reported that they had participated in a march in the past twelve months.[24] William Perez, an educational psychologist, in research with a sample of undocumented Latino college students, found that 73 percent participated in some form of civic engagement in high school, ranging from tutoring others, volunteering, to political activism.[25] Undocumented Latino youth are by definition a highly marginalized political category, by virtue of not being citizens, and, for many, living in poverty. Yet they have contributed to an impressive number of progressive policy victories since early 2000.

Millennial youth can also be credited with accomplishing radical change in rights and dignity for gay, lesbian, and transgendered people. It wasn't just *Will and Grace* that changed public opinion. Consider the growth of high school Gay Straight Alliances (GSA) in the United States. The first official "network" of GSAs was founded in California in 1998 "to empower youth activists to start Gay-Straight Alliance clubs to fight homophobia and transphobia in schools" and it expanded from forty clubs during the 1998–99 year to over nine hundred clubs in California in 2013.[26] These clubs can be thought of as intergenerational youth–adult partnerships because of the important role that teachers or advisors play in providing stability, continuity, and safety on the school campus. This network fueled school-based change but also engagement with politics, such as its leadership role in the successful passage of a California law in 2000 that prohibits discrimination on the basis of sexual orientation and gender identity. The network became a national one in 2005. There are now roughly three thousand Gay Straight Alliances in the United States.[27]

Still more examples of youth engagement can be seen in the rise of community-based youth organizing in the 1990s fueled by dissatisfaction in communities of color with issues such as safety, education, and policing.[28] Youth organizing offers a strategy for marginalized or disadvantaged young people to build collective power and make public institutions more accountable to their interests.[29] Such an effort signals a distinctive brand of civic engagement—one that is generative—because it works to contribute to a public good, but it is also self-interested, because it seeks to improve life chances or quality of life in one's own community. A 2010 review by the Funders Collaborative on Youth Organizing found that there were 160 "youth organizing groups" around the United States primarily focused on education reform, followed by racial justice, environmental justice, the economy, juvenile justice, immigration rights, health, and gender issues.[30]

So what are we to make of these competing stories? On the one hand there is evidence of youth disengagement in terms of comparative voting rates; certain indicators suggest that low-income African American and Latino youth demonstrate less trust in government and lower performance on tests of civic knowledge. On the other hand more young people between the ages of 18 and 29 voted than ever before in the 2008 presidential election and millennials are widely credited with winning the election for Obama in 2008 and 2012.[31] Progressive youth-based campaigns have made a real impact, including DREAM Activism, GSAs, and youth organizing in communities of color.

These competing narratives stem in part from different kinds of evidence. Whereas some rely on responses to surveys in nationally representative samples, others rely on case studies of self-selected groups of people. Confusion also stems from the lens through which one defines civic engagement or citizenship. Is a good citizen one who volunteers, one who shows up at city council meetings, or one who walks out of school to protest immigration policies?[32] Does one's research paradigm prize social maintenance or social change?[33] Researchers might mistakenly define feelings of disconnection from or mistrust of government as alienation, when in fact it motivates civic action.[34] Statements that get tagged as apathy or lack of efficacy perhaps sound that way to middle-class ears that see high levels of trust in government as normal and experience American society as fundamentally fair. But if one adopts a different metric, which is to look at the participation of groups in system change-oriented activities, motivated by feelings that government has either actively discriminated against them or not adequately protected them, then the "civic engagement gap" looks quite different. In fact, the gap should be seen as one where historically marginalized youth are leading the way for their generation.

Expanding Opportunity through Sustained Activism

Two youth-driven movements that deserve special attention for their success in expanding access to education and opportunity are campaigns for immigrant rights and ending the school to jail track. To identify these cases I drew on a framework articulated by Ethan Zuckerman, the Director of Civic Media at MIT. Zuckerman argues that we should

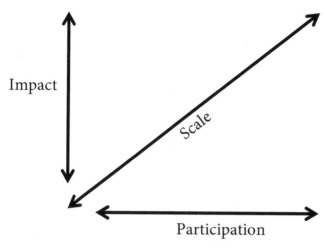

Figure 2.1. Civic Agency Dimensions from Zuckerman (2013a)

be much less concerned about alleged declines in civic knowledge and instead focus on questions of agency: Do people have the ability to influence their government or society around issues they care about? He offers a three-dimensional framework for mapping civic change initiatives and groups (Figure 2.1).[35]

Zuckerman begins with a distinction between thin and thick *participation*. Thin forms of civic or political participation ask for minimal levels of involvement. Consider the ubiquitous Facebook request to "like" an organization or, perhaps slightly more difficult, donate money to a cause. Thick participation, in contrast, asks for high levels of involvement and dedication from participants. The second dimension is *impact*. Thick participation, although important, does not always predict impact. Some *thin* types of participation, such as voting, can lead to meaningful impact. The third dimension in this framework is scale. One can find instances of thick forms of participation that are impactful, but there are more examples of powerful and thick *local* impact than of national or global impact.

I selected cases of political agency that boast "thick" participation by young people from marginalized backgrounds, "impact" on laws, policies, and cultural norms, at a "scale" that transcends single neighborhoods or school districts. In looking for cases, I did not require that they be exclusively youth-led or independent of more established organizations because the most impactful movements of young people are often intergenerational.

DREAM Activism, for example, is part of a movement for immigrant rights. In ten short years the political identity of a DREAM Activist materialized and fueled a collective movement that has made a major impact on state and federal policy. A second example can be seen in youth participation in the national movement to end the school to jail track, which since the early 2000s has achieved major policy victories. Padres & Jóvenes Unidos, a community organizing group in Colorado, has accomplished a series of school district and state level wins to limit the role of police in minor misbehavior, reduce racial disparities in punishments, and develop new restorative justice policies. Both these cases show the ways that young people have organized each other to engage in critique and collective action to make democratic institutions more responsive to their aspirations. To tell their stories I rely primarily on published and online sources.

A Youth Movement for Recognition and Rights: The Dream Activists

THE PROBLEM

DREAM Activism was inspired by a painful contradiction that confronted young people who came to the United States as children without legal citizenship. Because of the 1982 Plyler v. Doe Supreme Court decision, which designated that undocumented children are "persons" under the Fourteenth Amendment and they could not be denied access to public education, schools served as sanctuaries.[36] But as they began to seek more autonomy in adolescence, whether by getting a driver's license, exploring possibilities for formal employment, or looking into college, they discovered that their legal status barred them from these options.[37] Sociologist Roberto Gonzales called this developmental process "learning to be illegal." Even those who found ways to pay for college faced limited or precarious employment prospects after graduation because of their undocumented status.[38]

To be undocumented required concealment and secrecy, but this very invisibility contributed to feelings of isolation and made it difficult to find support. For example, because schools were barred from asking about citizenship, counselors and teachers tended to avoid the subject altogether.[39] Many undocumented youth "looked" and "sounded" as American as their citizen peers, so often they would get curious questions if they said they couldn't drive or get a regular job. They had to stay quiet about their fears that a friend or relative could get deported at any moment.[40] A young activist recounted this kind of invisibility—as well as a pathway out of it—in an article she coauthored about the experiences of undocumented high school students:

> During my 11th grade year I remember a day when congressman Mark Udall came to speak to this group of "at-risk-youth," of which I was part due to the fact that I learned English as a second language and because I am Latina. He came to speak about the importance of education. By this time I had already realized that I was not going to be able to go to the university of my choice, even if I were to have the grades for it, because I do not have a particular nine-digit number. I also knew that financially it was going to be almost impossible to go to college as a full time student due to the fact that I would have to pay out-of-state tuition as an international student. Considering the fact that I was not going to be able to access financial aid and hardly any scholarships college seemed like a far off dream. I remember sitting at my desk bawling throughout Udall's presentation. I was crying out of frustration, the uncertainty of not knowing how I was going to do it and knowing that what I wanted most in life was to get a good education. Then I remember that some teachers and the senator saw me crying and were surprised. Eventually a different teacher told him why I was crying. At that moment another teacher asked the rest of the students to lift their hand if they were undocumented and I saw nearly all the hands go up.[41]

The writer's initial state was defined by isolation, stigma, and despair—"sitting at my desk bawling." The teacher's request for a show of hands posed risks for the students, of being seen not just by their peers and teachers but by a representative of the federal government. But as risky as it was, the act of hand raising also made it possible to be seen and to see others.

The transition described in the passage—from isolation to solidarity, from concealment to being "out"—became one of the transformative features of DREAM Activism. It offered both a way out of a burdensome secret and a way to find solidarity with fellow youth who were struggling with the same hopeless situation.[42] More than just solidarity, it offered a political solution to the problem of broken immigration laws and a chance to fulfill aspirations for education and professional careers. This shift did not happen spontaneously, but was instead nurtured and supported by immigrant rights organizations.

THE DREAM ACTIVISM MOVEMENT

DREAM activism, which coalesced around the demand that young people raised in America but born abroad should have the opportunity to realize their dreams as legal citizens of the United States, developed in the context of a broader push for comprehensive immigration reform. This can be thought of as an ecosystem of activism that was highly interdependent but also experienced periodic disagreement and fracture, particularly between national, professionalized nonprofit organizations and local, youth-led chapters and networks. DREAM Activism, which is my focus in this chapter, is a term that some activists and researchers use to refer to the portion of the movement led by youth, in part because of its centerpiece DREAM Act (Development, Relief, and Education for Alien Minors).[43] Although populated mostly by youth of Mexican or Central American descent, DREAM Activists included youth from many countries including leaders with origins in Iran, Vietnam, Nigeria, and Poland.

In the policy domain, DREAM Activism worked on several fronts. State campaigns focused on gaining in-state tuition for undocumented youth who had attended American public schools as kids and wanted access to the same rates as their peers. National campaigns sought throughout the 2000s to pass the DREAM Act, first introduced in 2001, and also to reduce deportations.

Through most of the 2000s the ecosystem of immigration policy activism was led by national groups and showed strict and unified messaging, as indicated, for example, by the ubiquitous presence of American flags at the massive immigration rallies of 2006 and 2007. In many cases there was a harmonious set of intersecting interests and strategy linking young and old. The successful 2001 effort to pass AB 540, California's in-state tuition bill, relied on an alliance between undocumented youth and Chicano/a and Latino/a policy makers. These veteran leaders, who saw the rights of undocumented youth as an extension of earlier struggles of Latinos, facilitated access by youth to the highest decision makers in California. In turn, young activists, who had the most at stake, contributed compelling personal testimony that was essential to the passage of the bill. As anthropologist Hinda Seif writes:

> Youth like David assert a political voice with the support of Latino legislative professionals, who in turn rely on these courageous teens to humanize the plight of undocumented immigrants and challenge popular stereotypes of the "illegal alien." The presence of David and his peers at press conferences and legislative hearings and visits compels elected officials and voters to look these California students in the eye as they make important decisions about their educational access and futures.

This interdependence was also evident in the training that professional groups provided to undocumented youth in terms of messaging and narrative frames. Established groups provided strict guidelines and training about how people should tell their story, which returned to a few key messages about undocumented youth: they are high achievers and hard workers, seeking the American Dream, and in the United States through no fault of their own. Sociologist Walter Nicholls argues that in the early stages of the movement this kind of training and guidance was necessary for young people who otherwise were not skilled in the codes of power.

Over time, however, youth began to assert greater ownership and leadership of the direction of immigrant rights campaigns. One of the defining features of the emerging youth voice in the movement was a focus on building identity narratives that challenged the silence and stigma of being undocumented.[44] In a fortuitous confluence of political organizing and technological innovation, youth participation was increasing just as social media was in the ascendance, typified by YouTube (founded in 2005), Facebook (opened to the public in 2006), and Twitter (2006). As media scholar Arely Zimmerman explains in a study of DREAM Activism and social media, undocumented youth began to use new media tools to forge collective identities as "undocumented and unafraid." Young people used new media to share stories with each other about their own experiences and "reframe [their] identity as a source of pride rather than shame." Zimmerman recounts one such story, shared on YouTube by a young man named Gabriel:

> Gabriel tells his viewers about coming out as undocumented, "it doesn't roll off your tongue, but every time you say it, it gets easier." He confesses he was once ashamed to say "it. " Every time he said "it," he would shake with nerves. . . . Gabriel ends by inviting others to join the movement: "My name is Gabriel, and I am undocumented, and I invite you to come out."[45]

This metaphor of "coming out"—an allusion to the struggles of LGBTQ youth to make their identities public—was common among many of Zimmerman's respondents. Another young person, Agustin, told her that after telling his story in public he "didn't feel ashamed anymore. I feel like I came out and I felt safe to come out. . . . . I think it's time where we should not be afraid of saying who we are" (p. 46). This feeling of safety was directly linked to activism. As Agustin said, "[L]et's stop being afraid and let's start taking action because if there is no action there is never going to be a change." Agustin's language echoed the organizing slogan that gained popularity in 2010: "undocumented and unafraid."[46] In tandem with building a sense of collective identity, the process of going public with an undocumented identity paradoxically reduced the risk of deportation because of the large networks of supporters who could be called upon to protest and lobby officials. Those who remained "in the shadows" did not have access to the same networks.

In 2010, as the promise of comprehensive immigration reform (CIR) looked more and more distant to the young and undocumented, a cleavage occurred between the professional, established national groups and loose networks of emergent, youth-driven chapters often based in colleges but also including community organizations and high school clubs. Some of the more radical youth activists grew frustrated with the failures of CIR and what they perceived as their marginalization in the broader immigrant rights movement. These groups shifted toward direct actions and civil disobedience, exemplified by the occupation of Senator John McCain's Arizona office by four undocumented youth and one ally.[47] One of these new organizations, the National Youth Immigrant Alliance, articulated the new stance on its Facebook page:

We have reached a point where lobbying alone is not adequate to accomplish our mission. We strongly believe that our movement needs to escalate and we will use mindful and intentional strategic acts of civil disobedience to be effective.[48]

New youth activists also challenged narrative frames from the early 2000s that, by strategically seeking to appeal to the American center, privileged rights only for "good immigrants." The earlier strategy created a problem, because it unintentionally implied that there were also "bad immigrants" undeserving of citizenship or human dignity.[49]

Published research about the post-2010 "undocumented, unafraid, and unapologetic" phase of youth activism tends to portray college students as the protagonists. This finding is consistent with other research showing that colleges and universities offer a robust ecology for student clubs and networks that nurture civic engagement.[50] But the foregrounding of college students in the literature may be in part a consequence of their greater accessibility to university researchers. Nicholls points out that there were many talented and energetic young people who were blocked from either college or employment and who lent their skills to the movement.

More work is needed, in particular, to identify and uncover the roles played by *high school youth* in these struggles. Qualitative studies describe involvement by high school students in school walkouts and DREAM Activism action camps.[51] Where I live, in Colorado, Jóvenes Unidos, the youth component of Padres & Jóvenes Unidos, has been organizing students in the Denver area to understand their rights and press for immigration reform. Several high school student clubs in Colorado's Front Range organize undocumented students and speak up about not just federal policy but how their schools can better support them. A systemic and comprehensive account of the roles of high school students in the DREAMer movement remains to be written.

IMPACT

In the span of ten years young DREAM Activists have built a collective political identity that has shaped American policy and culture. In the policy domain, from 2001 to 2013 the broader coalition of immigrant rights groups achieved a series of victories. For example, fifteen states adopted in-state tuition for undocumented students, in a climate when public investment in higher education was otherwise shrinking and in some states that were generally hostile to immigrant rights. In a stopgap measure designed to ease the pressures on immigrant youth (and enlist support for his reelection campaign), in spring 2012 Obama signed the Deferred Action Bill to protect undocumented youth from deportation and give them a chance to get employment authorization for two years. Although the U.S. Congress had not, as of 2014, passed the DREAM Act or comprehensive immigration reform, steady organizing and lobbying kept it at the front of Obama's domestic agenda. The key role played by Latino voters helping Obama win a second term endowed this complex demographic group with increased political power. Whereas the pre-2012 Senate could not get a vote on CIR, in 2012 it passed a comprehensive immigration bill that included the DREAM Act, with significant bipartisan support. (CIR did not get a hearing in the more conservative House of Representatives.)

These successes in the legislative and policy realms were matched by a series of cultural shifts in attitudes toward immigrants. Polls in 2013 showed that a majority of Americans supported a pathway to citizenship for undocumented immigrants.[52] Gallup reported that Americans were more "pro-immigrant" than in the past. Major news outlets including AP and the *Los Angeles Times* dropped their use of the term "illegal" to refer to people without citizenship papers in the United States. In 2012 *Time Magazine*'s cover, "We are Americans, Just Not Legally: Why We're Done Hiding" signaled mainstream representation of imagery that was a direct appropriation of the cultural productions of younger activists, such as the slogan "undocumented and unafraid."[53]

These cultural attitudes are particularly evident with regard to discourses about undocumented *youth*. The early narratives about undocumented youth—as innocent of wrongdoing, as hard workers, as culturally American—began to show up in the statements of political figures and newspaper editorial boards. President Obama, for example, said, "It is heartbreaking. . . . To have kids, our kids, classmates of our children, who are suddenly under this shadow of fear, through no fault of their own."[54] Rick Perry, Republican governor of Texas, evoked a similar sentiment: "If you say that we should not educate children who have come into our state for no other reason than they have been brought there by no fault of their own, I don't think you have a heart."[55]

And then there is the less quantifiable but more significant impact on the identities and empowerment of undocumented young people. Laws regarding eligibility for college, such as California's AB540 students, created identity categories for undocumented students that countered stigma and were infused with a new political status and legitimacy.[56] I have seen this shift firsthand in the presentations that young immigrant organizers in Colorado have given to my education classes over the past few years. I remember clearly the first presentation, in 2007, when the speaker communicated her pain and frustration at the seemingly insurmountable barriers she faced. The following year another young person concluded his presentation in tears after describing his sibling's deportation. It felt then like a hopeless situation. But the tone of these presentations shifted dramatically in later years. In 2013, for example, a group of seven speakers showed up, a mix of high schoolers and community college students. Their hopes were bolstered by the state legislature's passage of a tuition equity bill. Congressional representatives who had previously given their group the cold shoulder were now seeking opportunities to meet. The speakers were hopeful and energized.

Undocumented youth were invisible as a political category prior to 2001. In 2010 the *New York Times* editorial board wrote: "If the DREAM Act passes, credit must go to those who have fought for it most strenuously: the young people whose futures it will decide."[57] The irony is worth noting: Arguably the most effective civic renewal movement in the United States since civil rights has been led by young people who were not officially recognized as American citizens.

Fighting the School-to-Jail Track

THE PROBLEM

You may have heard the phrases: "from schoolhouse to jailhouse," "school to prison pipeline," "the new Jim Crow." Since the early 2000s activists and scholars have been calling attention to the consequences of zero tolerance policies that began during the Reagan era and became state and federal law in the 1990s.[58] Many states expanded the kinds of infractions that could lead to expulsion from school, such as drugs, harassment, or threatening speech. The passage of zero tolerance rules meant that infractions would be punished with suspension or expulsion. California passed Proposition 21 in 2000, which required more juvenile offenders to be tried in adult courts and increased penalties for "gang-related" activities.[59]

But students, parents, and community members started to notice a problem with this zero tolerance approach. First, students were getting sent to the police for offenses that in past eras would have been handled by a principal. The Advancement Project (AP) documented the most egregious of these: a 10-year-old who was handcuffed and brought to the police station for bringing scissors to school; a 7-year-old brought to the county jail because he hit a classmate, teacher, and principal; a 14-year-old girl arrested and charged with battery for pouring chocolate milk over the head of a classmate.[60] The Annie E. Casey Foundation reports that there was a 72 percent increase in referrals to juvenile detention facilities from 1985 to 1995, despite the fact that less than one-third of the youth in custody had been charged with violent acts.[61]

Second, these referrals to the police were disproportionately levied against students of color, mostly African American and Latino. UCLA's Civil Rights Project reported that students being suspended or expelled for minor infractions were "more likely to be Black or those with disabilities."[62] Racial disparities also show up in who gets sent to juvenile jails after being arrested. Among youth with no prior detentions who were charged with the same offenses, African American were six times and Latino youth three times more likely than white youth to be incarcerated.[63] White youth represented 71 percent of the youth arrested for crimes nationwide but only 37 percent of youth committed to juvenile prisons.[64]

Third, referrals to the police from school were creating a record for students that could track them into future employment. Getting suspended or expelled is correlated with lower education outcomes and higher likelihood for jail in adulthood.[65] Zero tolerance policies, when added on top of an existing "war on drugs" that imprisoned minorities in massive numbers, led to a situation where more and more people of color were ending up in prison. Aside from the destructive impact on families, education, and employment, in many states serving time in prison leads to a permanent loss of voting rights. Michelle Alexander, a civil rights attorney, calls this the "new Jim Crow," because it replaces racial status with prison-time status in the systematic and legalized disenfranchisement for a whole class of people, who are mostly African American and Latino/a. A recent opinion piece in the *New York Times* argued persuasively that the United States is now a "racial democracy" that "unfairly applies the laws governing the removal of liberty primarily to citizens of one race," akin to apartheid in South Africa or the pre–civil rights South.[66]

THE CAMPAIGN TO END THE SCHOOL-TO-JAIL TRACK

Padres & Jóvenes Unidos (PJU) became involved in this fight when they began to see their membership facing increased criminalization in schools.[67] PJU is a multigenerational and multiracial community organizing group based in the southwest side of Denver, Colorado. It was founded in 1991 to support Mexican American parents who wanted to see justice after an elementary school principal punished their children for speaking Spanish by forcing them to eat their lunch on the cafeteria floor. Since then, Padres & Jóvenes Unidos has built an organization of parents and youth that works for "educational excellence, racial justice, immigrant rights and quality healthcare for all."[68] It has expanded from its original core membership in Latino communities and now organizes youth and parents throughout Colorado. This means that on any given week it is organizing multiple campaigns in different policy sectors. For example, PJU has been active in the immigrant rights movement, including playing a leading role in the campaign for tuition equity in Colorado—which was successful when the ASSET Bill was passed in 2013—and training hundreds of young people in how to apply for Deferred Action after Obama's executive order in spring 2012.[69] PJU's youth arm, Jóvenes Unidos, was formed when young people asked for their own space to discuss issues and organize their peers. This intergenerational structure means that young people's efforts are connected to the work of parents and adult organizers.

I first learned about Padres's work related to zero tolerance policies from a report about the school-to-jail track that it coauthored with a national civil rights organization called the Advancement Project (AP).[70] A team of youth and adult PJU members had worked with AP to study the problem in Denver schools and document existing discipline policies. Soon after, PJU persuaded the Denver Public Schools (DPS) to form a task force with community membership to develop a new set of disciplinary policies that prioritized restorative justice and deemphasized referrals to law enforcement.[71] This new disciplinary code was approved in 2008, but, in a pattern that would continue over the next several years, this victory was just the beginning of PJU's more challenging work to ensure that statutory changes led to actual changes for students of color. PJU, no doubt because of its membership of youth and parents, was acutely aware that policies can be written down but too often front-line implementers (teachers, principals, and school security officers, in this case) are resistant to change, poorly trained, or unaware of its details. This kind of monitoring requires a grassroots organization whose youngest members know their rights, can document their experiences in school, can analyze and present data, and know how to hold public officials accountable. It requires youth organizing. Much of Jóvenes Unidos's work has focused on this issue since then.[72]

District-Level Organizing

A core group of youth leaders, made up of high school students and recent high school graduates, learned the details of policies and developed advanced skills in public speaking, group facilitation, training other young people about their rights, and negotiating with district officials. In 2010, for example, Jóvenes Unidos held a "Know Your Rights" assembly in North High School, where students performed "before and after" skits highlighting key changes in the new discipline policy. Youth leaders also participated in ongoing meetings with district officials to monitor the progress of the policy. High schoolers prepared for these encounters by meeting with more experienced organizers the day before to role-play how the meeting might go. These role plays were geared toward preparing youth to think on their feet, know the details of policies, and not be overly reliant on scripted talking points. At the meetings themselves, youth sat around the table with the DPS officials with adults to the side, to visibly reinforce their position as protagonists. Students reviewed the data about disciplinary referrals, raised concerns about inconsistencies in implementation, and put officials on the record about their plans: "What is DPS's plan to eliminate racial disparities?" "What schools have restorative justice?"

These regular meetings were punctuated by a yearly accountability meeting with the superintendent and district staff, where PJU issued a report card to the district and proposed specific actions that the district ought to take. Whereas the regular meetings tended to focus on discussion and negotiation, the accountability meeting was geared toward the public and aimed at highlighting the accomplishments and failures of the district.

I attended the December 2012 accountability meeting held in the Padres & Jóvenes meeting space. Sitting at the front, behind a table, were representatives from the Denver Public Schools, including the superintendent. Next to the panel was a poster showing the report card with results in different categories for the district. In the audience were community members, reporters, and PJU members and staff. Two youth leaders MC'd the event. For each category of the report card, a young person stood up, announced her or his future goals ("I'm Dolores and I'm precollege, premed, and not preprison!"), then explained the grade and asked the superintendent for his comment. PJU assigned one B+ but also Ds and Fs, with the worst marks going toward the continued problem of racial disparities in referrals to law enforcement.

After seeing certain patterns of racial disparities persist, PJU leaders developed a new strategy, which called for revisions to the "intergovernmental agreement" (IGA) between DPS and the Denver Police Department (DPD). The IGA agreement was a formal contract between the Denver police and Denver schools delineating the role of police officers (called "school resource officers") within public schools. PJU wanted to see revisions made to the IGA limiting the role of police in minor disciplinary issues. In their estimation, the school resource officers were not implementing the new policies properly. In February 2013, PJU successfully negotiated a new IGA "that emphasizes the use of restorative approaches to address behaviors, and is designed to minimize the use of law enforcement intervention." This new partnership was hailed as "historic" by the U.S. Department of Education.[73]

State and National Organizing

In 2012, in the midst of their efforts to monitor the new DPS discipline policy, PJU launched a broader statewide campaign to change zero tolerance laws for all Colorado school districts. Now remember, this was a state that had been devastated by school shootings at Columbine High School thirteen years earlier. People were unsure what the popular reception would be for shifting disciplinary policies in the schools. PJU worked steadily to build a broad-based coalition of supporters that expanded on its progressive working-class base in Denver, including district attorneys who were tired of having their police force handle minor behavioral issues,[74] libertarian-leaning Republicans who saw police involvement in schools as an overreach of government authority, and fiscally conscious politicians who saw the high price tag of locking kids up.

In keeping with its intergenerational philosophy, adults and youth worked together to carry out the statewide campaign, with different people playing different roles depending on their experience, interests, skills, and availability. Youth leaders in Jóvenes demanded and won the formation of a youth committee that worked with a legislative task force to develop language for the bill. Youth and adults contributed opinion pieces and statements to major newspapers. Youth and parents participated by speaking to media, testifying to the state legislature, educating peers, and building membership in their communities and schools.

The campaign received an impressive victory in 2012, when its bill, called the SMART bill, for safe schools and smart discipline, passed.[75] This bill gave school principals more discretion over suspensions, drew clearer distinctions between minor violations and those that merit referral to law enforcement, promoted restorative justice discipline practices, and streamlined data collection that could track disparities in punishments across the site. The bill passed by a unanimous vote in the State House and a 27–8 vote in the State Senate.[76]

Similar to the district work, the challenging work began *after* the bill passed, because PJU wanted to be sure students across the state knew their rights and would hold their administration accountable. With that in mind, PJU organized training sessions for high school students throughout Colorado. For example, a team of youth and adult staff traveled two hours south of Denver to the working-class city of

Pueblo, to host a three-day "action camp" for local high school students. Attendees shared stories about their personal experiences with the school-to-jail track, learned the basics of the new law, participated in workshops about the school experiences of lesbian, gay, and bisexual students, and formed social connections that could support future coalitions.

Although this case study has focused on policy work in Colorado, PJU linked its campaign with a national network of groups.[77] In partnership with the Advancement Project, PJU hosted a national "action camp" with groups from Los Angeles, New York, North Carolina, and elsewhere to discuss strategies for ending the school-to-jail track. Visits from the U.S. Attorney for Civil Rights were followed by an invitation to PJU youth leaders to meet with the Secretary of Education, Arne Duncan, in Washington where they pushed for greater commitment to restorative justice and alternatives to the school-to-jail track. In a January 14, 2014 press release, the Department of Education released a new set of policy and practice guidelines aimed explicitly at reducing the school-to-prison pipeline: "A routine school disciplinary infraction should land a student in the principal's office, not in a police precinct," Attorney General Eric Holder said.

IMPACT

It is unusual to see youth organizing groups—even those connected to broader community coalitions—boast the kinds of policy and statutory achievements achieved by Padres & Jóvenes Unidos. Beginning with the revisions to the DPS disciplinary code, and continuing with the new state law about school safety and new roles for police in schools, key elements of the school-to-jail track appear to have been dismantled. PJU's work is ongoing, however. The statutory framework will need to be accompanied by a mix of ongoing public pressure for accountability and monitoring of compliance, local communities of youth and parents who learn to hold school districts accountable, and more engaging learning environments in schools.

Similar to the case of DREAM Activism, the impact of Padres's work is not limited to its statutory achievements, but also in what it means for civic renewal and grassroots democracy. In a social and political context where the participation of regular people—not specialists or lobbyists—in public policy making is rare, and youth participation is even rarer, the End the School-to-Jail Track campaign offers a bright exception. High school students' experience of engaging in high-stakes encounters with policy makers, including praising them when called for and voicing criticism when necessary, contributes to a culture shift, even if incremental, in which young people are taken seriously in the public square.

Practices That Mobilized Youth

Democratic processes in the United States have become vastly unequal. An oft-cited 2004 report from the American Political Science Association (APSA) reports:

> Generations of Americans have worked to equalize citizen voice across lines of income, race, and gender. Today, however, the voices of American citizens are raised and heard unequally. . . . Citizens with lower or moderate incomes speak with a whisper that is lost on the ears of inattentive government officials, while the advantaged roar with a clarity and consistency that policy-makers readily hear and routinely follow.

Movements led by DREAM Activists and Padres & Jóvenes Unidos counter the trend in the United States toward the concentration of political power in the hands of the most affluent and the scarcity of direct democracy by poor and working-class people. To upend the APSA's metaphor, in these two campaigns it was the *least* affluent who roared "with a clarity and consistency" that policy makers could not ignore. This kind of active engagement is essential for American democracy. It draws on the creativity and vision of people who have previously felt silenced and expands their opportunities for future participation.

What do these examples teach us about opportunity structures that mobilize political participation by youth of color?

Leadership by Those Directly Affected

Both campaigns operated on the basic premise that those directly affected by the issue—those most vulnerable or marginalized by the policy—ought to drive decision making, strategy, and public actions. This is a fairly simple point but it cannot be overstated. Imagine, for example, if this principle were taken seriously in a school reform context, and it was a widely accepted practice that students from low-performing schools be at the table to help decide how to turn their schools around. It doesn't happen.

Young people contributed at all levels of a campaign: understanding the problem, formulating strategy, discussing tactics, recruiting members, collecting data, speaking at public events, and communicating with media. Moreover, their stories, their frustrations, and their dreams motivated and guided these campaigns. This does not mean, however, that older, more experienced people were absent. Established professional organizers played a central role early in the immigration reform movement in providing training around strategy and tactics. The intergenerational structure of Padres & Jóvenes Unidos meant that middle and high school students were often sitting around tables with young adults and veteran organizers to prepare for meetings and clarify strategy.

The leadership of young people was most visible in high-stakes encounters with public officials, such as the testimony of undocumented activists in state and federal legislative hearings and negotiations with senior officials from the school district and law enforcement. These performances were intentionally staged in ways that enabled young people to challenge stereotypes and assert their political voice.[78] These public performances can be seen as instances of "counter-staging," which political scientist Celina Su defines as "arrangements of new rules of engagement and interactions, disrupting previous stagings."[79] Given the anomaly of such encounters, they require purposeful choreography until they become routine cultural practices for all involved.

Participatory Cultures

Both campaigns also demonstrated "participatory cultures," a term developed by Henry Jenkins to describe interest-driven online communities.[80] A participatory culture offers low barriers to engagement and membership, social connection among members, and scaffolding for newcomers. Participatory cultures value the contributions of members.

Are newcomers made to feel welcomed, respected, and valued? Can people show up with their friends or a little sister? Are skilled veterans available for scaffolding or advice?

Participatory cultures in the two movements made it possible for young people, many of whom were new to political activism, to participate in a range of ways. Some young people could become part of DREAM Activism through relatively minimal effort, such as clicking "Like" on the Facebook page of the National Immigrant Youth Alliance. Others could engage more fully by making and posting videos or organizing demonstrations. Similarly, PJU had peripheral participants who might limit their participation to phone banking or listening attentively at the Know Your Rights workshops. But there were also those who showed thick participation, by attending meetings regularly, learning about the nuances of policy, and meeting directly with government officials. In both cases youth were drawn to participate because their contributions mattered.

Political but Not Partisan

Both campaigns sought changes at the highest levels of government. They saw value in the electoral system and knew their three branches of government. But at no point did they become arms of or dependent on the Democratic or Republican Party. Part of PJU's strategy was to enlist the support of a range of legislators and ordinary people irrespective of their party affiliation. The unanimous vote for a new school safety bill in the State House is a tribute to their success in finding allies across party lines. Although the immigration rights platform has recently been aligned with the Democratic Party, Dream Activists maintain their independence from political parties, as witnessed in their vocal criticism of President Obama's deportation policies. This stance is consistent with a strategy in community organizing to develop productive relationships with politicians but not be beholden to them.[81]

Extended Timescales

These campaigns differed from many other "youth-led" efforts by their multiyear timespans. They were not quick wins. This extended timescale—beyond the typical unit of time for students such as a sum-mer or a year—required that some people "carry" the campaign during periods of turnover or mobility among youth. This is one more reason why intergenerational groups are structurally set up for successful long-term campaigns. High school students might be active for six months but then want to join a theater production, play sports, or devote more time to helping the family. They may graduate, leave for college, or take a full-time job, but then want to return to pitch in during vacations. In a climate of this kind of dynamic churn, there is a need for steady, long-term staff who can keep the campaign going—carry its vision, maintain partnerships, cultivate relationships, and keep track of wins—and most of all hold the space for youth to jump in when they are present.

Changing Culture, Not Just Policy

Campaigns oriented around social justice issues must engage in culture change simultaneously with passing laws or winning court cases. By cul-ture change I'm referring to the norms, beliefs, and values that support tacit acceptance of a particular policy. Effective change agents accom-plish not just legal shifts, as important as they are, but also shifts in the cultural ecosystem such that the "common sense" about an issue begins to be seen differently by the public.[82]

The two movements sought to change people's beliefs about immi-gration and zero tolerance. This was most effective in their widespread strategic use of storytelling. DREAM Activism, for example, developed narratives about their reasons for coming to America and the dreams for the future; they framed their stories so that they would resonate with mainstream Americans and counter pervasive stereotypes about immigrants.[83] PJU used storytelling as well to call attention to the ways that the culture had become more punitive than in prior generations. For example, in an event called "100 days 100 stories," PJU invited older Colorado residents to submit stories about a time when they had bro-ken a law or school rules and what the consequences had been. These videotaped stories showed how infrequently police used to get involved in misbehavior, and thereby poked holes in what had become the "new normal" around zero tolerance. These stories also normalized the idea that people make mistakes as teenagers. This tactic proved successful in reaching out to not just progressives concerned about racial justice but also to conservatives concerned about the overreach of the state.

In addition to trying to change norms and beliefs, culture change also meant developing the capacity of ordinary people to understand and stand up for their rights in public spaces. For DREAM Activists this meant supporting undocumented young people who wanted to "come out of the closet" even when some adult-led organizations were counseling against it. For PJU it meant holding "know your rights" trainings so that youth would be informed about new policies.

Issue-Based versus Procedural Approaches

Proponents of civic renewal through participatory democracy call for interventions that enable ordinary people to come together and, under well-facilitated conditions, talk, listen, revise beliefs, and develop solutions to problems. *Deliberative democracy*, for example, has gained traction as a way to foster conversations among people from diverse walks of life. As political theorist Peter Levine explains:

> In practice, "deliberation" means convening a diverse group of citizens and asking them to talk, without any expectation or plan that they will reach one conclusion rather than another. The population that is convened, the format, and the informational materials are all supposed to be neutral or balanced. There is an ethic of deference to whatever views may emerge from democratic discussion. Efforts are made to insulate the process from deliberate attempts to manipulate it.[84]

This is a *procedural* approach to civic renewal, because it is more specific about process than outcomes. Its corollary in the youth civic engagement field is the call for *student voice* or *youth voice*, epitomized in the United Nations Convention on the Rights of the Child, which enshrines the rights of young people to give their input on issues that matter to them. Whether deliberative democracy or youth voice, in both cases the virtue is communication, listening, and mutual accountability. It tends to be either neutral or opaque on desired outcomes for a particular issue, and instead focuses on forums where people can represent and exchange ideas. One of its exemplars in the United States is the city of

Hampton, Virginia, which has been lauded for its active youth commission and other structured forums for young people to weigh in on city planning and other public decisions.[85] More recently, in 2014 the city of Boston launched the first youth participatory budgeting process, in which young people from across the city gave input about how the city should spend $1,000,000.[86]

Procedural initiatives to encourage participatory democracy can play an important role in renewing civic life through expanded participation and communication across differences. But, as Levine points out, some aspects of them may not appeal to youth fighting educational dispossession or structural racism. Their procedural quality, which prizes openness to changing one's opinions, may feel too cool or detached for young people who are motivated around urgent demands.[87] Achieving social conditions for communication among groups holding different types of power or social status can be difficult.[88] Also, there are certain issues about which it does not make sense for people to "listen to" or respect other people's arguments, such as perspectives that are dehumanizing or racist. The Black Consciousness movement in South Africa, for example, chose to challenge the basic assumptions of the apartheid state rather than engage in dialogue with its agents.

Both DREAM Activism and the End-the-School-to-Jail Track campaigns prioritized issue-based activism over deliberation. They had clear objectives that were not up for negotiation. Youth who spoke at meetings weren't there to change their demands after hearing from district officials. I conjecture that issue-based campaigns attracted young people because of their clarity about what they stood for and were trying to achieve. Getting police out of schools—particularly if one's cousin or brother got brought into police custody for a nonviolent offense—may be more compelling than the call to be on a student council or speak at a youth forum whose outcomes are less tangible.

Although distinct, these two approaches are compatible and reinforcing. Issue-based activism often represents the culmination of deliberative encounters, such as the discussions held by Soweto students leading up to their decision to walk out of schools. Although a group's public platform may be closed to negotiation, internal decision-making processes often include listening, compromise, and consensus building.[89] The order could also be switched, in which activism mobilizes people for an adversarial form of direct democracy, which prepares them for subsequent interactions of a more deliberative nature. Young people who are veterans of tough negotiations with district officials or the media are more likely to hold their own in deliberative contexts, even in the presence of imbalances of power.

It may be most productive to think of these two distinct forms of political engagement—procedural and issue-based—as having a symbiotic relationship. Deliberative venues in and of themselves are not adequate for engaging the full range of young people in participatory democracy. Social movements such as DREAM Activism and organizations such as PJU enabled young people suffering from damaging policies to step into the public square and find kinship with others going through similar experiences.

But we also face a pressing need to figure out how government-sponsored attempts to encourage participatory democracy can be structured and sustained. Students need more voice in their schools and cities, as is becoming increasingly clear in the epidemic of school closures across the United States, whose unpopularity is compounded by their lack of democratic transparency. The case of Jefferson High School, discussed next, suggests why public institutions need to create enduring structures and processes to broaden participation in decisions that affect young people's lives.

3

"Not Down with the Shut Down"

Student Activism against School Closure

Walking past an empty field, through quiet halls, I took in the murals that spoke about Jefferson's distinguished alumni: the city's first African American female school board member, its first African American mayor, a leader in the Chicano movement, a female African American state legislator . . . the list could go on. I walked past the school's renowned basketball court, whose boys' basketball teams had won more than 20 state championships. The drama department, science classes, library: all empty. I finally found my way to an all-purpose room, populated by a few circular tables, where sat Jefferson High School's student government in exile.

Michelle, Albert, Lucy, Glenda, Betsy, Anthony, and Ivan were assembled with two adults—an African American man named Joseph and a white man named Tom—because of their shared participation in a new entity called the "Student Leadership Council." (Because of confidentiality agreements with the district that were necessary to obtain access to student data, I use pseudonyms to refer to the school, city, and participants). School personnel, community leaders, and youth had formed the Student Leadership Council after a contentious spring had culminated in the closing of Jefferson High School. I approached the group, along with Kristen Pozzoboni, a then-graduate student at the University of Colorado, Boulder, to ask if we could form a research partnership to document their experiences and the experiences of their peers. (This chapter draws upon a publication coauthored with Kristen Pozzoboni.)[1]

Our pitch to the Student Leadership Council dovetailed nicely with the mandate they had taken on, which was to be ambassadors for Jefferson at schools throughout the district and to keep track of how their peers were doing. The students were like a student government in exile—part peer mentors, part protectors of school spirit. They were a peer resource to get help for students who needed it and also provide social cohesion through the occasional dance for displaced Jefferson students.

When we said we wanted to do research with them, Albert spoke up first: "What do you get out of this process?" It was a critical moment, because my answer, I suspected, could either sink or save the research project. I tried to buy myself a few seconds to think through what might be the "right answer." Should I go the benevolent route, saying I was there because I wanted to help them? The phrasing of Albert's question suggested he wanted something else—and that perhaps they didn't want or need my "help," if bound up with a logic of neediness or fragility. But if I went with a more self-interested answer—that I was doing this for my career—it could backfire and I would sound like a jerk. And each of those answers would have missed my real intent. I tried to give the most authentic answer I could supply. Yes, I would benefit from being part of this study: it was part of my job to do research, and if I were to publish articles it would help my career. I added, however, that despite my outsider status to this community, I was motivated to confront wrongs that I saw in this decision—and that it was important to me that young people have a voice in major decisions affecting their education. I saw this project as a chance for them to do research about an important issue and speak up about the results.

There was a pause of a few seconds—during which I wasn't sure if I had passed this first test—then a flurry of additional questions from Albert and his peers followed: *Do you think you understand youth and if so, what makes you think so? What experience do you have in introducing youth-created proposals for policy consideration and what happened? Where did you grow up? What was it like? Tell me about something that changed you or you learned while doing your research?* (Later, Joseph told me that the young people were looking for a "soldier, not a missionary." My response had been close enough to the former to warrant letting me stick around.)

From this first encounter we went on to develop a working partnership that lasted for two years.[2] Kristen and I worked with a group of nine students from October through June and then with four of those students for a second year—to collect data, analyze it, present recommendations to local decision makers, speak at research conferences, and network with other youth activists from across the country. We developed the YPAR project because we believe that young people should have the opportunity to participate in inquiry about institutions and settings that shape their lives.[3] During that time Jefferson students displayed grit—no doubt about that—but also incisive counternarratives about their school and the process by which it had been closed.

Problems surrounding Jefferson's closure stemmed from the absence of participatory democracy. Whereas DREAM Activism and Padres & Jóvenes Unidos offer affirmative examples of young people's role in civic renewal, the Jefferson case shows what can go wrong when young people are not at the table to discuss their experiences and co-develop policy solutions. And it points to the need for neighborhoods and cities to design and sustain open forums for deliberation among students, parents, and school personnel about the future of their schools.

Contested Meanings of the Jefferson High School Closure

Field Notes: Public Forum to Discuss Jefferson's Future

It is 9:05 p.m. and the town hall meeting in Jefferson's auditorium, which began two hours earlier, is supposed to have drawn to a close. But students' hands keep going up to speak. I'm a bit surprised. A few months ago, long before closure was on people's minds, I met with members of a youth organizing group to discuss problems they wanted to fix at Jefferson. They mentioned an absence of elective courses, dumbed-down classes, and arbitrary rules separating Jefferson's three "small schools." I wondered, if a school is failing in these ways, might closing it be an appealing option? Definitely not! Student comments at tonight's meeting convey a strong sense of pride in Jefferson and the neighborhood. . . . A school board member tried to persuade students that the school board had their best interests at heart, saying: "You seem to think we're doing this to you. But we're not. We're doing it *for* you." Her comments fell flat. One student said, "You're putting barriers in front of us instead of removing 'em." Another student called for more elective classes and resources, saying, "Yeah, Jefferson does need changes, but not the way you see it." Others talked about the deep connections they felt to teachers at Jefferson and called for investing in the school rather than shutting it down.

This community meeting was my first foray into the contested politics of the Jefferson closure. One can see stakeholders trying to *frame* the meaning of the closure in different ways; these frames would show up over the next few weeks and in the data we collected throughout the subsequent year.[4]

The school district leadership tried to justify the decision by resorting to a *benevolent paternalism* frame. The school board member, for example, appeared bewildered by students' anger and thought that by framing the decision as a case of the district doing what's best *for* students, she might win over some supporters or at least alleviate the tension in the room. *Trust us, we know what's right,* she seemed to be saying. Her bid for this paternalism frame was repeated several weeks later by the superintendent and school board president, in their public letter that defended the closure decision:

> [T]he Jefferson decision has been characterized as an "attack," an action perpetrated on the school because the students who go there are primarily Latino and African American. Nothing could be further from the truth. We view the decision to move the current Jefferson students to other schools as an admission of complete failure by the district over many years and as a rescue mission for the children that are there.

Here the school district leadership responded to one part of the criticism—that it was racist—but overlooked youths' anger over being left out of the decision. The letter's statement of "complete failure," while laudable for taking ownership of the problem, also served to reinforce its power and authority by doing just that—taking ownership of the problem. Moreover, describing the decision as a "rescue mission for the children" reinforced a paternalistic stance toward the young people—aged 14 to 18—who attended Jefferson.

Students framed what was happening to their school in different terms. Whereas the district framed it as a new opportunity—a rescue mission—students talked about the new "barriers" that it would create and asked why the school with the most African American and Latino students was selected to be closed. What was pitched as a rescue felt more like an attack to them. The community forum was followed by the board's decision the next day to close the school for one year and start over under new leadership with new students. According to newspapers, students reported feeling "blindsided," "stunned," and "crushed" by the board's decision.

The students' alternative interpretation of the closure was accompanied by activism. One day after the decision, students organized a walkout via text messaging. Approximately 200 students left their classes and traveled to the school district headquarters where they stood outside in the cold and chanted "Hell no, we won't go!" In the weeks that followed, students fought to reverse the decision through letter-writing, news conferences, meeting with district officials, and speaking at public forums while wearing T-shirts declaring "not down with the shut down."

This contest about the past and future of Jefferson gripped my attention. I wondered, if the school was so "bad," why did students fight to keep it open? What might policy makers learn about addressing the problems of struggling urban schools by treating students as partners rather than dependent children? Before getting to these questions about the Jefferson case, it is instructive to scan trends in community responses to school closures across the United States.

The Contested Politics of School Closures

Since the advent of No Child Left Behind, school closure has become an increasingly common strategy to "turn around" underperforming urban schools.[5] In May 2009, Arne Duncan, the Obama administration's secretary of education, announced a plan to use new funding resources to "prod local officials to close failing schools and reopen them with new teachers and principals."[6] Closure is one among a menu of options for schools in turnaround status that also includes handing them over to charter schools, turning them into small schools, firing the current teaching staff, or some combination of the above. Schools qualifying for closure under the new turnaround policies are almost always ones serving high percentages of poor and working class students of color. These are the students who, according to a range of peer-reviewed studies, are offered fewer college preparatory classes, have fewer qualified teachers, and experience weaker instruction.[7]

Although there tends to be consensus that the status quo in many turnaround schools is unacceptable, the politics of closure are contested.

Districts, and the national policy makers who support the approach, claim to be offering better options for students by enabling them to attend higher performing schools in the district. They also cite factors not related to academic performance, such as excess building space and financial deficits at the district level.[8] These can be thought of as technical explanations because they claim to be neutral with regard to the racial backgrounds of students or the relative political power of different interest groups.[9]

What these technical rationales overlook, however, are the many ways that schools represent the past history and future aspirations of neighborhoods. Schools are sites of civic struggle that reveal whether communities and families have the political power to shape decisions that affect the lives of their children. Moreover, they overlook the historic disinvestment that often precedes closure: If schools have struggled with shortages of qualified teachers or quality opportunities to learn, then their subsequent low performance is predictable. There is extensive evidence that communities of color in high poverty neighborhoods are most likely to experience school closures and the various kinds of displacement and disruption that follow.[10]

These tangled roots of school closures can be seen in recent closures in Cleveland, Ohio. Community-based researchers pointed out, for example, that the problem of excess building space originated in the 1960s, when the city accelerated school construction in East Cleveland to preserve racially segregated schools.[11] Today it is the city's racially and economically isolated African American youth who bear the burden of closure and must travel outside the neighborhood to go to schools. Pauline Lipman has made a similar argument about school closures in Chicago, which she argues were part of a broader effort to gentrify low-income African American neighborhoods and lay the groundwork for school privatization.[12]

These examples underscore the political nature of school closure. School closures—and community responses to them—have become a focus of youth organizing and community activism around the United States.[13] Although proponents may view closures as technical decisions made in the name of improving achievement, in many cases such decisions reveal political and racial inequities in a city. In Jefferson's case, district officials expressed surprise at the level of community outrage.

Attention to the way students interpreted the closure and what happened to them in their new schools can offer important lessons for broadening participation in future decision making about struggling schools.

A Brief History of Jefferson High School

For over one hundred years Jefferson was a flagship school for the Riverside district and a cornerstone of its historically African American neighborhood. It was known for quality academic programs, champion athletic teams, and strong vocational training. Its halls boast murals of distinguished alumni, including mayors and civil rights leaders.

From 1970 to 1996, integrated by court-ordered busing, Jefferson served an economically and racially diverse student body drawn from multiple neighborhoods across the city. After 1996, with the end of busing, narrower attendance boundaries, and demographic shifts in Riverside, Jefferson's student body became limited to African American and Latino students from the surrounding neighborhood. In 1997, the first year after these changes took place, overall school performance began to decline. In 2000 Jefferson was rated as unsatisfactory based on the results of the state achievement test. The following year Jefferson became one of the early adopters of the small schools movement and was converted from a comprehensive high school into three small schools. According to evaluations of this process, the conversion occurred without adequate support from the district or time to plan and solicit input from teachers, students, and parents. Each school operated autonomously with its own name, principal, and curriculum. Although there were variations in implementation among the three small schools, aggregate test scores failed to increase and by 2005 Jefferson's combined School Accountability Report index was the lowest of Riverside's high schools.

Two of the most prominent problems at the school prior to the closure were dwindling resources and lack of academic rigor. Because of per pupil funding, declines in enrollment at Jefferson contributed to a vicious cycle: Fewer students meant fewer resources such as elective or AP classes, access to technology, and classroom supplies. Jefferson was not the only school in the immediate neighborhood to have undergone changes after busing ended in 1996. The local middle school, for example, was closed in 2004 due to poor performance and converted into a charter school that served 200 fewer students. Its feeder elementary school lost its acclaimed educational programs when they were relocated from the Jefferson neighborhood to other parts of the city. These changes, which amounted to a steady erosion of high quality educational opportunities in the neighborhood, contributed to a climate of mistrust toward the district felt by many neighborhood residents.

In 2005, averaged across the three small schools, fewer than 5 percent of students were proficient in math and fewer than 9 percent of students were proficient in writing. Jefferson enrollment had dropped by 47 percent since the fall of 2002. District officials expressed concern that continued declines in enrollment would mean even fewer resources for the remaining students at Jefferson. A looming district budget deficit, combined with underutilized space in several high schools, exacerbated the issue. After a second public meeting with students and community members, the board decided to close the school for one year and reopen it for a new cohort of 9th graders only. The current 9th, 10th, and 11th grade students were instructed to enroll in other district high schools for the next school year. Current teachers either left the district or applied for positions at other schools.

Tracing Transitions through Participatory Action Research

Soon after the Jefferson closure announcement, a staff person at a local youth organizing group, called Students United, called to ask for my help to find someone who could study the impact of the closure on students. Stories circulated among neighborhood members that two years earlier scores of young people had dropped out of school in the wake of the neighborhood middle school closure, but no one had ever documented this in a systematic way. For Students United, a study of student outcomes could be a key tool in holding the district accountable for its decision. I proposed that we jointly develop a participatory action research study in which youth and adults would work together to study the impact of the closure.

The formation of the team, which took several months and involved negotiations with various organizations, deserves its own chapter, but is not the focus of discussion here.[14] In the subsequent year we formed an interracial and intergenerational group called Tracing Transitions, comprised of ten former Jefferson students (eight in high school and two in college) from three youth organizations, and four adults (including Kristen Pozzoboni and me). The youth received monetary stipends for their work. The group met weekly from late October 2006 through early June 2007 to develop skills and complete project-related tasks such as designing research protocols or analyzing data. The year culminated in presentations to district officials and community members. Subsequent to those presentations, four participants stayed involved for a second year to conduct further data analysis, write a short article, present research findings at national venues, and discuss implications for youth rights with participatory research teams from across the United States. (A full description of the methods used by the Tracing Transitions team can be found in the Methodological Appendix.)

In forming and leading the Tracing Transitions group, we drew on principles of participatory action research (PAR). PAR is a form of public work that links research and civic engagement, in which people with varied training and expertise formulate questions, collect data, analyze it, and take action based on results. The effort to engage youth as researchers is consistent with youth development principles that emphasize opportunities for leadership and mattering.[15] It is also consistent with models of popular education that privilege the knowledge and experiences of ordinary people.[16] Many PAR projects engage marginalized populations of youth whose voices are discounted in decision-making settings and whose experiences are poorly understood in mainstream research.[17] They create venues for young people to articulate *counternarratives*, which contest or disrupt dominant explanations put forth in popular media by elites.[18]

Counternarratives about School Closure

Over the course of the subsequent year the Tracing Transitions team collected 96 open-ended surveys, interviewed 20 students, and led focus groups with 12 students who were eligible for school but had stopped attending since the closure. Evidence from these various data sources spanning the period from the announcement of the decision to roughly one year later suggests that most students disagreed with the decision;

they did not share the district's view that the closure was a "rescue mission." Students articulated their opposition in terms of counternarratives about the decision-making process and features of Jefferson that they valued.

Critiques of the Decision-Making Process

During a data analysis discussion one of the youth researchers stated that students' anger about the closure was more about the process by which it was carried out than the decision itself:

> Some felt that . . . the closure of Jefferson wasn't as bad as the way that they closed it. I mean if you're going to close Jefferson, you can close it but I guess . . . at the last minute . . . I guess the process that they took, or I guess not taking a process, it just kind of made everything like off, just, like, off the wall.
> *What was it about the process they took that made it worse?*
> Like, I don't think that there was . . . any consideration for anyone. It was just like they decided to close it and there was nothing that the community could have did or said.

We did not find any instances in our data where students felt that they had participated adequately in the decision. There were many instances where students articulated the feeling of having been shut out of the process. Consider the following survey responses:

> The Jefferson closure has caught people's attention across the country. What do you think people should hear about it?
> - How they locked us out with no remorse.
> - How they didn't care about how the students feel over this!
> - The district screwed us over and they are probably going to do it again. They don't care about how this is going to affect us. Out of nowhere they decided to close the school.
> - Well I don't think they should hear anything else, or what would be the point of telling more people about it if they already closed the school and nothing and no one is going to change that.

These responses convey students' feelings of powerlessness about the decision. Students referred to the decision as something done to them, against their will, which they had little power to stop. As one student said at a public meeting, "We are your animals to experiment on."

In community meetings, many students and community members argued that the situation would not have played out this way for a school located in a more affluent white neighborhood. Students received public support from the Riverside coalition of ministers, representing predominantly black churches, who said that the decision was racist and who drew connections between the experiences of these students and the struggles that took place during the civil rights movement. Others drew connections between prior school closures, Jefferson's conversion into small schools, and this closure, as evidence of a pattern of disregard for the community. At a press conference organized by Students United, one student said, "It is difficult to look at the eight schools in Southeast Riverside that are struggling without comparing them to the two brand new elementary schools being built a mile away in the shiny new Woodside development."

This topic came up in focus groups with young people who had stopped going to school. We asked them what story they thought was most important to tell about the Jefferson closure.

> They try to make . . . schools for, like . . . rich kids and . . . people that are intelligent. They . . . can . . . change the world . . . go be a president or be a lawyer and stuff. So they really don't care about people down here that have low-income, 'cause they're like, "They're nothing, they're just going to be the people that get welfare and get their income tax real cheap," so that's all they worry about.

These students' reports of discrimination were sometimes tied to recollections that Jefferson was not the first of their schools to close. As one focus group member reported, "They closed all my schools I went to. They closed Jefferson and my middle school."

Despite statements from district leaders that the closure was due to systemic failures in the district, many students felt that the decision to close placed the responsibility squarely on the students. They pointed out that their test performance was cited as one of the principal reasons for closing the school. Also, the decision that the new school would reopen without former Jefferson students implied, even if unintentionally, that their presence would be an obstacle to the reforms there. This theme came up in many surveys, in which students asserted that they were not as bad as people said they were. Fourteen student respondents raised this point when asked for their final thoughts in the surveys and interviews. For example, one survey respondent wrote, "I think they should hear not only bad things but good also. They should know that the students that attended there are smart." Another wrote, "I think that they were wrong about us and that we deserved a chance." In peer interviews, when asked for final thoughts, one responded by saying, "We are not as bad as people think we are." Another said, "People label us as bad, stupid, or useless but people don't know what it feels like to be forced out and no one will ever understand the struggles we face every day." At a community meeting, one student, echoing the language of the School Accountability Reports, referred sarcastically to herself and her peers as "us unsatisfactory students." When I asked members of the Tracing Transitions team what this meant, one person explained it this way:

> I think it's about, "You guys decided to close our school, so that must mean we're bad and we're stupid." So I don't think really anyone from the district said that Jefferson was a bad school, but it's just kinda how students took it. "Oh you're going to close our school so that must mean that we're bad and . . . we weren't doing our jobs and we're stupid and our scores are so low and we can't get kids to come."

This range of narratives from students shows the varied ways that they interpreted the closure decision. They did not see it as benevolent paternalism; instead most felt it was unfair and capricious. Many interpreted it as a comment on their own failings as students and wanted to counter the stigma of the closure. Some students looked across the school district at the range of low-performing schools and concluded that Jefferson was targeted because of what it symbolized as a historic home for African American and Latino/a students. Those who had stopped going to school interpreted the closure as part of a broader pattern of neglect or disinvestment from the neighborhood.

Redefining School Quality

The focus on Jefferson's low scores as justification for the closure echoed a broader national discourse that uses test scores as a proxy for school quality.[19] Jefferson students, however, defined school quality in broader terms than performance on standardized tests. Students told a complex story about the school. In agreement with district decision makers, Jefferson alumnae expressed their frustration at the academic limitations at the school, citing their lack of preparation for college. Members of Students United and Tracing Transitions highlighted the limited resources for learning at the school, such as its lack of AP classes or college preparatory curricula. But criticisms of Jefferson were overshadowed in our data by statements defending Jefferson's reputation and asserting the students' strong attachment to the school. Student narratives about Jefferson amounted to a portrait of a school that provided a rich ecological context for them to develop trusting relationships and feel a sense of connection to the school.

Students' reports contributed to a portrait of Jefferson as a community institution that supported their social and emotional development. Students felt cared for and known. In surveys, they reported that Jefferson was "a friendly place filled with love," a place where "we felt like we belonged," "you could be yourself," and "everyone was understanding and not judging." Students also spoke appreciatively of the caring relationships that transformed their high school into an environment where classmates were "like family" and "teachers were like older siblings." As one member of Students United who had not attended Jefferson, remarked: "These students were actually passionate about their school!" Three themes stood out in students' statements about what they valued about Jefferson.

CONNECTION TO COMMUNITY
Jefferson was described as a foundation for its neighborhood. It graduated scores of neighborhood residents. Many students hoped that

they too would graduate from the high school from which their older siblings, parents, and grandparents had graduated. One focus group participant said:

> I wanted to graduate from there because my brother, he graduated 2006 at Jefferson, so I wanted to . . . It was going to be my brother and then it was going to be my other brother and then it was going to be me. And then it was going to be my little brother.

Many students lived in close proximity to the Jefferson campus and to each other. When not at school students described seeing one another around the neighborhood or at athletic and social events; they knew each others' families and had learned how to navigate existing social or cultural divides in their community. This experience of being known and knowing others translated to feeling understood, protected, or looked after at school. One youth who had dropped out after the closure said, "I don't know, Jefferson was just my home school and I fit there and I knew everybody, I knew I wasn't going to be into no problems." Another focus group participant told a story about how family connections in the Jefferson community had kept him in school. He said, "At Jefferson, I wouldn't leave 'cause like my grandma down there, she'll catch me. So I . . . had more discipline." Students' sense of shared history coupled with a small school environment led many students to describe Jefferson as a place where "everyone knew everyone" and "people were real" (Surveys). As one person said at one of the community meetings, "This is *Jefferson*. This is the 'hood. Holla!" This was a politicized sense of place, in that its symbolic meaning for students was related to the high percentage of African American and Latino residents who lived and went to school there. In the words of one youth researcher, "When you think of Jefferson you think of minorities, mostly Mexican and black." This image was a source of pride and collective identity.

JEFFERSON WAS LIKE FAMILY

Eleven respondents specifically used the metaphor of "family" to describe their experiences at Jefferson. Students spoke of the love they received from and felt for the people and place. "At Jefferson I felt like I was at home. I felt like the staff really did care about us and our education" (Survey). This familial connection was heightened by the fact that many school personnel knew students' family members and did not hesitate to involve them in day-to-day affairs. One youth researcher told us a story about an interaction she had with a Jefferson security guard who had worked at the school for over forty years, who said, "I know your mama and she don't play that way. . . . If you don't quit it [the behavior that initiated the interaction] I will go to your mama's house right now" (Interview). This had its desired effect on the youth researcher who stopped "messing around."

HOLISTIC SUPPORT FROM SCHOOL PERSONNEL

When asked in an open-ended survey prompt to describe Jefferson, the most common response (40 percent) was to express positive views of adults there. No respondents expressed a negative view of Jefferson adults. Teacher-student relationships were characterized as trusting, respectful, and nurturing. Students said they felt connected to the teachers because they could talk openly with faculty and believed the teachers were interested in their lives outside school. For example, students wrote: "I loved my teachers at Jefferson. I trust them for everything" (Survey), and "At Jefferson they actually cared about what you learned" (Survey). Students said they felt as though "teachers wanted them to be in school" (Survey). In addition, students felt respected because teachers expected them to succeed and gave them room to make mistakes.

Five respondents described how trusting and respectful relationships with adults translated into individual academic support to help them to manage challenges at school. Two of these students said, "The teachers at Jefferson would always know when I was struggling and were there to help" and "At Jefferson they helped you more. If you didn't understand something, you got help right away" (Survey). A focus group respondent explained,

> My teacher used to always push me to do my work. So he kept me on track. And like this one teacher, he . . . was trying to boost me up to be more intelligent and help me out and stuff. (Focus group)

Students were motivated by the personal attention they received from adults, perceiving this as evidence that the teachers cared about them and their education.

Consistent with a narrative approach, these stories reveal students' reconstruction of what Jefferson meant to them. Students were probably inclined to highlight the positive features of Jefferson, given the negative attention the school had received through the closure process. Nevertheless, the specificity of examples and the range of data sources showing the students' appreciation for Jefferson give it credibility.

Students' Performance in Their New Schools

In addition to gathering people's perspectives about the closure, the Tracing Transitions group also collected a range of quantitative and qualitative data about students' transitions to new schools the subsequent year. We wanted to find out if graduation or dropout rates had changed for the displaced group, and if their test scores improved. The challenge we faced, however, pertained to causal inference. How would we know if changes in performance were related to the closure? We needed a comparison group that was like the students from Jefferson in key respects, such as race, ethnicity, income levels, and prior achievement. With the expert help of Matthew Gaertner, a quantitative methodologist, we collected academic performance data from three classes of students: displaced Jefferson students ("the Transition Cohort"), students from other district schools during the same year ("Other District"), and students who had attended Jefferson prior to the closure ("Historic Jefferson"). Comparing the performance of the Transition Cohort to these groups enabled us to make inferences about whether there was a "closure effect."[20]

What we found was that closing Jefferson and transferring students to schools with higher test scores aggravated rather than alleviated students' academic challenges. This result is consistent with the literature on school mobility, which reports negative associations between mobility and academic performance, particularly for students from low-income families.[21] The challenges created by displacement trumped, at least for the aggregate, advantages that might have been available at other schools.

Students' struggles showed up in a number of indicators. For example, the Transition Cohort's test score trends changed significantly after the closure announcement. The Transition Cohort scores declined across the three content areas. Depending on the subject tested, the Transition Cohort lost between 3 and 38 points each year. In contrast, across math, reading, and writing, comparison students typically *gained* about 10 points each year. Two test administrations after the closure announcement, the score gap between the Transition Cohort and Other District stood at 69 points in reading, 106 points in writing, and 64 points in math. Similarly, the gap between Transition Cohort and Historic Jefferson stood at 70 points in reading, 93 points in writing, and 46 points in math.

Graduation and dropout rates also showed the negative impacts of the closure. At each grade level, those who had experienced the closure showed increased odds of dropping out compared to similar prior populations of students who had attended Jefferson. As dropout probability increased, graduate rates fell. Whereas Jefferson students had a 71 percent chance of graduating in the preclosure years, they had a 49 percent chance of graduating after the closure.

The qualitative data gathered by students, which identified social and academic challenges in the transition year, provide some insight into the declines in graduation rates and the increase in dropout rates. One of the biggest factors was the disruption to students' relationships with students and peers, which made their adjustment to new schools difficult. Although most respondents reported that they were treated well by the teachers in the receiving schools, the quality of their relationships with these teachers was weaker than what that they had experienced at Jefferson. The closure cut students off from adult school personnel to whom they felt connected and displaced them from a school that had deep symbolic meaning because of its history in their community. When these relational ties were severed, an important protective factor for students disappeared, which we think contributed to their lower graduation rates and higher dropout rates.[22]

The decline in test scores, which began after the closure announcement in 2006 and continued in 2007, is harder to explain. Some students may have purposefully not made an effort on the tests, particularly the 2006 one that was administered roughly one month after the closure announcement. With regard to 2007 performance, about half of the survey and interview respondents reported that the new school classes were harder. For students for whom this meant higher expectations and more intellectually engaging curricula, this was a positive outcome. Some students expressed their appreciation for access to AP classes, more challenging assignments, and other learning opportunities. Many students, however, said that they were accustomed to a high level of personal support and flexibility that was not met in their new schools. The combination of academic challenge and a decline in individualized support may explain the aggregate declines in academic performance.

These results suggest that forced mobility due to closure aggravated rather than alleviated academic challenges facing students who, prior to closure, lagged behind same-district peers of similar background. The decline in graduation rates and increase in dropout rates is particularly troubling, given that closure is touted as a remedy for students attending failing schools.

Implications for Youth Participation in School Reform

From a distance, closing chronically low-performing schools may appear to be the rational decision. If a school has been failing for several years, why not close it down and start over from scratch? And wouldn't students be thankful for the opportunity to leave a "failing school" behind? What might make sense from outside, however, makes little sense for those who are part of those schools, particularly schools that provide strong social and emotional support. Schools—their histories, their place in a community—hold symbolic meaning. The message to a school community conveyed by closure, particular when the decision is made without grassroots support, only further marginalizes students.[23]

These problems stemmed from an absence of robust structures for participatory democracy. This is where a mix of normative and empirical arguments come into play: Students ought to be viewed as stakeholders and partners in the efforts to turn around their schools. They have a right, according to the United Nations Convention on the Rights of the Child, to give their input into decisions that affect their lives. But it is also an empirical argument, derived from this study, whose findings lend support to political and developmental justifications for youth participation. By *political justification*, I mean that youth articulated interests that were discounted in the decision-making process and that challenged prevailing assumptions about school quality. By *developmental justification*, I mean evidence that young people were ready to participate under conditions of support, which counters discourses about youth as immature or unprepared.

Political Justification

Jefferson students articulated collective interests that were overlooked or discounted in the closure decision. Most significant of these was students' articulation of a broader view of school quality that encompassed academics, caring relationships, and connection to place. Students valued going to a school where they could maintain ties to a community that nurtured and supported them. Although Jefferson was not meeting its academic mission, its problems were not the same as those of many failing urban schools, where students experience feelings of alienation or anonymity.[24] The stories we heard about Jefferson echo descriptions of high quality community organizations, where youth experience a sense of belonging, support for cultural or racial identities, and connection to caring adults.[25] These social and emotional supports were especially important to those with a more fragile connection to school, as suggested by the experience of students who dropped out after the closure.

The combination of weak academic preparation with high social support at Jefferson presents a more complex view of a school than one that merely labels it as failing because of low test scores. Efforts to address the problems facing struggling schools should take into account their broader development function for youth.[26] When addressing a struggling school, for example, it would be useful to know whether most students experience it as an anonymous, hostile environment or a supportive one. Considering estimates that only 53 percent of students in America's largest cities graduate from high school,[27] it is important that we understand why Jefferson students fought for the opportunity to attend their struggling school. Doing so would enable stakeholders to capitalize on the positive aspects of a school while simultaneously working to eliminate its weaknesses.

The counternarratives articulated by students were also politically significant because they challenged the normative ideological climate in Riverside.[28] Members of the Tracing Transitions team articulated a competing vision of what it would mean to support Jefferson students. According to this view, fairness demanded that Jefferson get the proper resources that it needed to thrive as a neighborhood school serving African American and Latino students. Students and community members attributed its recent underperformance to a pattern of diminishing resources and disinvestment from feeder schools in their neighborhood. Consistent with arguments that reframe the achievement gap as an opportunity gap, these students argued that the public is accountable for ensuring that students have resources that enable them to reach high academic standards.[29] We do not know what impact these counternarratives made on the broader public, but they point to ways in which youth participation can broaden public discourse about the problems of underperforming schools.

Lastly, when young people are part of decision making, adult policy makers will be more likely to feel accountable to the students who are sitting around the table. Research on joint governance in youth organizations suggests that youths' presence contributes to fidelity to the mission and changed perspectives toward youth.[30]

Developmental Justification

The students demonstrated their readiness to participate in decisions about Jefferson's future in a few different ways. First, a critical mass of student leaders engaged in sustained efforts to participate in decision making. Many students' efforts to improve Jefferson began several years before the closure and continued after the decision. Members of the Tracing Transitions team studied the impact of the closure and discussed the findings and their implications in meetings with district leaders and national policymakers.

But my point is not solely about the active student leaders. I make a broader claim about the developmental readiness of ordinary Jefferson students to give input into the direction of their school. Students' anger signals the contradiction they experienced between their capacity for judgment, reflection, and agency and their limited opportunities to participate. It signaled a contradiction between the way they were positioned by the district and school board—as passive beneficiaries—and the way many of them saw themselves. Students wanted meaningful participation. I use the term *readiness* in a broad sense to include those who were new to public action. Readiness, from this perspective, means readiness to participate and learn under conditions of support.[31]

This begs the question, however, of identifying those conditions of support. Supporting student voice does not require adults to give up their decision-making roles, but instead to treat students as legitimate participants, with adults, in solving problems. Doing so is challenging because it defies taken-for-granted assumptions about age segregation between youth and adults.[32] How do young people learn to participate in public settings where consequential decisions are made? Where do they develop the self-confidence to claim space and the knowledge to speak persuasively? Just as important, how do adult teachers and policy makers learn how to step back and share the floor?

The kinds of activism practiced by Luis and Gabriela, the DREAM Activists, *Jóvenes Unidos*, and Jefferson students demonstrated a repertoire of civic practices that included political analysis and critique, strategic thinking, mobilizing peers, and sustaining their vision despite setbacks. These skills neither spring forth spontaneously nor do they result from sequestering youth in civic education classrooms. They unfold in learning ecologies that are saturated with tools, resources, and people. These learning ecologies have received limited scholarly attention and deserve more. The next two chapters examine research about these learning ecologies of youth activism in community organizations and schools.

PART II

Learning Ecologies of Youth Activism

4

Teaching without Teaching

People working in community settings that aim to mobilize, empower, or politicize young people face a vexing question: How does one—or better yet, can one—"empower" youth or "give them voice"? Most adults who work in this space readily acknowledge that posing the question in those terms gives too much agency to the teacher. Empowerment is not an entity that can be handed over to a person, ready-made. It requires the young person to exercise agency; to take risks and try out new practices.

Although insisting that empowerment cannot be done *to* or *for* a person places proper emphasis on the young person's agency, it leaves unexplained what if anything the older or more experienced person should do. I have observed program leaders—typically young adults in their twenties—enact a folk theory that their participation threatens the authenticity of a youth empowerment endeavor. Sometimes observers endorse a kind of purity test for youth voice initiatives, with the gold star going to those groups where young people are in charge and adults are absent. Such beliefs are preferable to hostility or indifference to youth voice, but they rest on misconceptions that can undermine youths' political development and power.

The first misconception, rooted in constructivist theories of learning, fetishizes choice and intrinsic motivation. Some youth groups, in an effort to equalize power relationships between adults and youth, aim to limit adult involvement so that project goals reflect youths' interests and viewpoints. The fear is that too much adult involvement might undermine youths' motivation or corrupt a youth-driven process. However, this emphasis on independence from adult influence can be counterproductive if it limits youths' access to expert practices or networks of power. Youth-led initiatives that limit adult involvement unwittingly reproduce their own forms of age segregation.

This critique is rooted in situated and sociocultural learning theories, which argue that learning is best supported when novices gain access to a practice, so that they can see themselves becoming part of a community of activists and researchers.[1] Veterans model expert practices, introduce resources and tools, and facilitate access to social networks. Given the prevalence of age segregation in the United States, intergenerational groups represent an important venue for youth to gain access to sophisticated research methods and political change strategies. In such contexts, motivation might in fact stem from the chance to work alongside adults, or to learn by being part of a sophisticated campaign that has a heightened chance of impact and where youth experience meaning, purpose, and mattering.

A second misconception pertains to youth voice. Calls for youth voice, by invoking the special insight that youth have by virtue of their status as youth, embodies a form of strategic essentialism.[2] Proponents strategically appeal to people's status as youth, as if this status holds a fixed or essential meaning, in order to confer legitimacy on young people's claims for power or voice. Because it is sometimes strategic, I often participate in this discourse about youth voice. But in essentializing youth voice this discourse fails to acknowledge the ways that "voice" is mediated by existing discourses in the culture at large.[3]

Mediation is a term central to sociocultural psychology.[4] The notion that human cognition is mediated by cultural tools and signs—that people make sense of the world by using language and interpretive frames that preceded their arrival on the scene—has important consequences for young people's sociopolitical reasoning. For example, social scientists have documented a pervasive discourse of individualism and self-reliance in the United States. One of its properties as a discourse is that it is viewed as self-evident or natural, rather than historically or socially produced.[5] My own experience as a program leader and researcher tells me that people don't arrive "naturally" at a particular set of insights about the social world, but instead draw on the explanations they have been exposed to among peers, with family members, or in popular media.

Recognition of the ways in which narrative frames mediate political meaning making creates new questions and dilemmas. Adults may struggle with how to share their sociopolitical views with youth. On the one hand, a principled commitment to youth voice could lead adults to adopt a neutral, detached stance, where they encourage students to develop their own ideas about the origins of and solutions to societal problems. Such an approach would be consistent with some strains of constructivism that emphasize peer interaction and student-centered inquiry and that strive to avoid the teacher's exercise of power and authority.[6] It also reflects a tenet of deliberative democracy, which aspires for people to form their own opinions and ideals.

On the other hand, research on social movements shows the vital power of *framing* when it comes to mobilizing people. How members frame the causes of problems shapes the kinds of solutions they develop.[7] The conflicts over Jefferson High School's closure reflected a conflict over narrative frames: was it a technical decision or a political one? Were Jefferson students in need of a "rescue mission" or were they capable of participating in solving the problems at their school? Settings that catalyze youth voice and engagement can help young people to critically assess available narrative frames and construct alternatives. Campaigns to improve neighborhood schools, for example, will be strengthened if they can be linked to broader frames related to equity and racial justice.[8] Such framing may require some type of exposure to curriculum, whether reading, discussion, or film. From this perspective, a "youth voice" discourse that treats youth perspectives as pristine, off-limits for criticism, or unmediated by ideology, limits young people's learning and power.

Where program leaders and adult staff find this balance generates lively dilemmas, which show up often in research about civic education and youth empowerment. Drawing attention to how adults manage these dilemmas—how they "teach without teaching"—has important payoffs for understanding the learning ecologies of youth activism. To do so I discuss evidence from a comparative ethnographic study of youth groups engaged in activism.[9]

Dilemmas of Guidance in Youth Activism

I performed two years of ethnographic research in the San Francisco Bay Area with three multiracial youth activism groups engaged in social justice-oriented, youth-driven campaigns. Each of the groups was racially diverse; most participants identified as African American or Asian American, and some identified Latino/a or white. These groups were different from the DREAM Activists in that they were not part of a social movement with overlapping policy goals and human rights claims. They acted as discrete groups with a local focus. But they shared with the DREAM Activists, as well as Padres & Jóvenes Unidos, an emphasis on sociopolitical critique and the exercise of collective agency.

The three groups emerged in different institutional contexts and pursued different campaigns. Youth Engaged in Leadership and Learning (YELL) was initiated by Stanford University's John W. Gardner Center in partnership with a high school in Oakland, California. YELL participants conducted research about stereotypes and organized a campaign to change the images of West Oakland youth in print and television news. After conducting focus groups with students and teachers about the origins and consequences of stereotypes, they created alternative media, such as a website, video documentary, and magazine, to combat stereotypes and tell richer stories about their lives. The campaign culminated in a community forum where youth presented their work to the school board president, journalists, students, and community residents. They also met with editors from a local newspaper to discuss ways to improve media coverage and presented their work to younger children in the neighborhood.

Kids First was a youth organizing group housed in a community-based nonprofit agency whose mission was for "youth to become visionary leaders capable of transforming their schools and communities." Participants were called "youth organizers" because they were expected to build power among youth by organizing their peers based on shared interests. Their Student Power campaign sought to improve student engagement in schools by providing students with greater voice in evaluating their teachers and governing their schools. As part of this process over 950 students, representing three high schools, filled out "report cards" assessing specific features of their schools. Youth organizers analyzed these data with the support of program staff and developed a Student Power resolution, which outlined new guidelines for student leadership in high schools. The resolution was endorsed by Oakland's school board but was not implemented after a state-appointed administrator was given governing authority for the district.

TABLE 4.1. Group Profiles

	YELL	Kids First	TRUE
Organizational context	University research center focused on youth development founded in 2000	Nonprofit youth advocacy organization founded in 1995	Nonprofit environmental justice organization founded in 1998
Campaign	Don't Believe the Hype: Reduce negative portrayals of youth from West Oakland through advocacy and creation of alternative media	Student Power: Persuade high schools to increase student input in school governance and improve counseling for students	Youth Conference: Inform youth about effects of war and persuade politicians to limit military recruitment in public schools
Campaign actions	Youth-produced 'zine, website, and video; Presentations to community members and journalists	Student voice resolution and report; Rallies, press conference, and presentation to school board	Conference for over 200 students and political officials; Resolution to limit military recruitment
Duration of campaign	9 months	9 months	7 months

Teens Restoring the Urban Environment (TRUE) was a nonprofit organization, based in a working class, primarily African American community, focused on educating young people to confront environmental injustices in their neighborhoods. TRUE ran multiple programs, which included park restoration and efforts to improve the availability of healthy food in the neighborhood. In 2002–3, during the lead up to the U.S. invasion of Iraq, a group of youth and adults decided to plan a one-day conference for students about the consequences of war for the local environment. The purpose of the conference was to raise awareness among local youth about the impact of the U.S. military on their neighborhood and also to promote interaction between elected representatives and youth.

I learned the routines of these groups by attending weekly or biweekly organizing meetings over the course of each group's campaign. I wanted to get behind the scenes to understand how youth developed the complex skills required for political action. Consistent with the method of "participant observation," I did not hide in the back writing notes on a clipboard but instead became part of each group in varying ways, while disclosing my role as a researcher. (For a full discussion of the methodology of the study, see the Methodological Appendix.)

Early in my fieldwork I was intrigued by shared patterns in the way groups talked about the categories of "youth" and "adult." First, consistent with the American focus on age as a metric for development,[10] participants used age-based language to refer to each other. The terms "youth" and "adults" took on similar fixed meanings across the three groups. "Youth" were those who were of high school age. "Adults" were those who were over 18 and worked as staff members for the organization. With the exception of executive directors, most "adults" were under 24. (To underscore the strangeness of this effort to differentiate people in their early twenties from people in their late teens, consider that the category "youth" extends to age 25 in Ireland and 35 in South Africa.)

Second, across all groups adult staff members expressed their desire for campaigns to be youth-driven; this was reflected in the names of the groups and their organization missions. Staff members wanted youth to take ownership of the campaigns, in the sense that they would care about the campaign goals and take the initiative to carry them out. However, some campaign tasks, such as formulating a long-term strategy or speaking persuasively to policy makers, were new to most youth. This raised questions for program leaders: Should youth be left to figure out these skills on their own, or should adults teach them? If the latter, how? These dilemmas showed up in all the groups and program staff responded to them in different ways.

In YELL program staff raised questions about their roles throughout the year. For example, after the first YELL meeting, Korina, an AmeriCorps volunteer helping with the project, sought clarification about "the definition of a teacher in YELL"—she feared that adults were not offering enough guidance to youth. Michelle, the program director who had just graduated from college, explained that she saw her role as supporting youth in making decisions but not making decisions for them. Two months later the adults continued to struggle with questions about their roles—one conversation revolved around the shared observation that youth deferred too much to the adult facilitators in small groups. The adults decided to leave the small groups to facilitate themselves so that youth would take more ownership.

Program leaders in Kids First and TRUE also deliberated about how to foster youth's sense of ownership. Alonzo, the Kids First coordinator, told me that he wanted organizing to be an attitude that youth brought

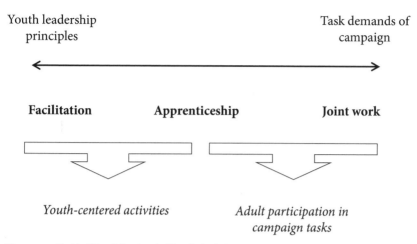

Figure 4.1. Guided Participation in Youth Activism

to their peer interactions outside the program and not just something they did when they were at Kids First. Vanessa, the executive director of Kids First, said that she felt pressure for groups like hers to appear "youth-led," but that this was sometimes unproductive because youth need support to develop certain skills necessary for political action. Both the adult coordinators in TRUE, Dave and Earl, told me that they found it challenging to balance the need to organize a successful conference with their wish for youth to lead the effort.

Although these dilemmas about how to empower youth were experienced by all three groups, they tended to manage them in different ways, which I describe as *facilitation, apprenticeship,* and *joint work.* These approaches were differentiated first by the relative priority they placed on youth leadership principles versus campaign quality, second by the extent to which activities were structured for youth's interest and skill levels, and third the extent to which adults participated in the campaign. Figure 4.1 provides a conceptual illustration of these distinctions. An overview of key differences between these forms of guided participation is presented in Table 4.2.

In terms of the tension between youth leadership and campaign task demands, in the facilitation approach the adults sought to be neutral facilitators of a youth-led process. This goal corresponded to the indirect kinds of guidance that the adults provided; they facilitated youth's

TABLE 4.2. Guided Participation in Three Youth Activism Groups

	Facilitation	Apprenticeship	Joint Work
Most typical in . . .	YELL	Kids First	TRUE
Relative importance granted to youth leadership versus campaign success	Emphasis on youth leadership	Roughly equal emphasis on youth leadership and campaign success	Emphasis on campaign success
Adult role	Neutral facilitator	Coach	Senior colleague
Division of labor	Youth select and implement projects; adults support through facilitation	Youth implement projects with some adult participation; adults support through coaching and feedback	Youth and adults make decisions and implement projects together
Boundary between "youth" and "adult"	Well-demarcated	Quasi	Not demarcated
Kinds of youth participation	Facilitate meetings and implement projects with limited adult assistance	Implement projects with guidance of adults; recruit other youth to join campaign	Plan conference collaboratively with adults

conversations, introduced routines to help groups work productively, and provided resources such as computers or video cameras. In contrast, in apprenticeship and joint work the adults demonstrated a vested interest in the sophistication and success of the campaigns. This interest corresponded to the kinds of roles that the adults performed, which included indirect support at some times but also more direct participation in decision making and tasks.

A second dimension that distinguished facilitation, apprenticeship, and joint work was the extent to which program activities were youth-centered. Here youth-centered refers to learning environments that are designed to engage youth by being responsive to their skill level and interests.[11] Youth-centered activities include team builders designed to foster group belonging, workshops designed to improve youth's skills or understanding, and participant structures, such as small-group activities, designed to foster participation from all members. Activities in facilitation and apprenticeship were typically youth-centered, unlike in joint work.

I observed these different approaches, to varying extents, in all three programs. For example, in situations where youth were preparing for public presentations or interactions, the apprenticeship pattern was common. Adults tended to provide coaching and feedback, presumably because of the higher stakes of public interactions. Also, within each organization I observed discussions that followed the facilitation pattern, in which adults refrained from offering their own views and instead solicited the opinions and perspectives of youth participants. In one group—TRUE—the modal pattern of interaction shifted from facilitation to joint work after a turning point in the planning process.

Despite these examples of internal variation, in each group there was a typical form of guided participation that characterized interactions between youth and adults. Adult guidance in YELL was best characterized as *facilitation*. As self-described "outsiders" to the high-poverty community where YELL was located, adults believed that youth participants had greater insight into the nature of the problems there and how to approach them. They argued that the project would be more authentic if it represented the interests and desires of youth. As one adult said, to a chorus of agreement from the other adult staff, in a debrief meeting, "I'd prefer for us to be like referees, help youth come to their own beliefs, rather than prod them towards ours."

In contrast to YELL, the adults in Kids First did not attempt to act as neutral facilitators for a youth-led project. Instead, they shared their political views with youth, pitched in to complete campaign tasks at key points, and participated in most decisions. In this apprenticeship approach the adults were veteran activists who participated in the same endeavor as the novices, while nevertheless structuring activities in ways that were sensitive to youth's skill levels.

The division of labor in TRUE shifted from facilitation to joint work about halfway through the project. In the early stages the group members worked on a funding proposal to host a youth conference about war and the environment. After the proposal was accepted and the planning process became increasingly complex, the dominant division of labor shifted to joint work. Joint work was a form of collaboration where the adults participated alongside youth, like apprenticeship. But unlike apprenticeship or facilitation, in joint work the environment was not youth-centered. Instead, the division of labor looked more like people working together, with little time set aside for training or team building.

Guidance Strategies

Consistent with the tenets of experiential learning, lessons were rarely taught prior to doing the work. Instead, learning happened opportunistically as the work unfolded. Learning scientists call this "just in time learning," in reference to the notion that people learn what to do when they need to, in the situation that demands it.[12] In recognition of this pattern in youth activism groups, I discuss adult guidance strategies in terms of three phases of campaign development: problem framing, sustaining the campaign, and public action.

Framing the Problem

Activism campaigns often start by diagnosing the "roots of the problem" and developing a plan to address those roots. There is a rich community organizing literature showing multiple phases of problem identification, including the important step of converting what can be a complex problem, such as failing schools, into a more targeted and "winnable" campaign, such as pushing to limit class sizes in high-poverty schools.[13] I observed a difference in approaches to problem framing, which varied between fairly "hands-off" brainstorms about kids' everyday experiences and more focused lessons aimed at framing problems in particular ways.

In YELL the adult staff wanted youth to select a problem that truly mattered to them. Although they shared historical readings to foster student understanding of local history, the adults refrained from teaching an explicit political stance and did not vote when it came time for the group to identify the most "popular" problem to address. Instead, they facilitated discussions in which youth were expected to initiate and evaluate each other's ideas with limited input from the adults. Consider the following example from the program's third week, when youth worked in small groups to generate possible campaign topics. This discussion followed from a meeting where the group read and discussed the Black Panthers' "Ten Point Program" first drafted in Oakland in 1966.

Small Group Discussion about Possible Campaign Topics (YELL)
[Unless noted with quotation marks, these excerpts represent paraphrases of statements.]

Beth, a college student and AmeriCorps volunteer, starts the discussion by saying this is a continuation of the lunch meeting yesterday when they talked about the Black Panthers. She says, just like the Black Panthers did, we are going to identify issues you care about. What are some issues that you care about?

MALCOLM: Thievery, reduce thievery.
BETH: Can you say more about that?
MALCOLM: Students are stealing from each other, we need to reduce it.
CEDRIC: Don't just reduce it, eliminate it.
BETH: What are some solutions?
GUILLERMO: Don't bring stuff to school.
BRIAN: Keep an eye on your stuff.
CEDRIC: People steal books, everything. Not just nice stuff, it could be a used book or a mouse wheel that they can't even use.

Beth then redirects the conversation toward possible solutions.

BETH: What are some solutions to this problem?
CEDRIC: They need they butt beat.
BETH: YELL won't really be able to do that. Are there other kinds of solutions?
JOCELYN: Guidance counselors. We should increase guidance counselors or let people know they are available.

The discussion continues.

Beth's approach to facilitating this discussion was common in YELL. She asked questions, tried to generate conversation, and redirected the conversation if she felt it was going off-topic. She did not offer problems or solutions of her own, nor did she define what it would mean to develop an effective solution. Instead, youth generated the ideas. Beth's approach, consistent with some forms of constructivist pedagogy, implied that youth would generate solutions to problems they cared about through discussion with each other.

As it turned out, the issue of theft from that small group discussion did not come up again in the large group YELL discussions about what problems to focus on. After a series of deliberations, the group decided, based on a majority vote, to design a campaign to combat stereotypes about youth. Youth chose the campaign strategies, which involved a mixture of research about the problem such as focus groups with their peers, and youth-produced media such as a video and magazine, to promote alternative stories.

Kids First demonstrated an alternative approach to the problem selection part of the campaign, which is best illustrated by an episode early in my research there. The associate director had asked me to help the staff think through different ways to use surveys in their upcoming campaign. In order to show them an example of research conducted by youth, I shared a report published by YELL from the prior year, which I had helped to edit. The report was far-ranging, drawing on the results of focus groups, interviews, and a survey filled out by more than half of the students and teachers at the school. The research addressed the topics of school safety, student behavior, attendance, and teaching and learning.

The two Kids First coordinators, Alonzo and Elsa, did not like what they saw. Alonzo said that seeing this report helped him get an idea about what he *didn't* want Kids First to do. He was concerned by the presentation of certain results that appeared to blame students for problems at their school and that could justify punitive policies. He told me that certain responses to the survey were a sign of "colonized minds"; he felt that it was wrong to give a survey without providing education at the same time. Alonzo told me, "There is a war on youth" going on; he wanted Kids First's research to be part of an effort to enlist young people in a broader campaign for social justice.

Alonzo's comments challenged a naïve version of youth voice, which holds that when given the opportunity youth will generate opinions that represent their best interests, or that youth gain insight merely from everyday experience. From Alonzo's perspective, however, the minds of many youth of color are colonized by rampant racism and sexism, which leads to self-blame and self-hatred. Consequently, youth voice, while ultimately important, must be accompanied by education so that it reflects a more liberated social identity rather than reified and fixed identities propagated in popular media.[14] When faced with an apparent contradiction between the liberal educational impulse to solicit youth voice and the radical political impulse to organize youth to change the system, Alonzo and Elsa advocated the latter.

This viewpoint was consistent with the approach to problem framing I observed in subsequent meetings, which was to encourage youth to see problems in a sociological context. When talking about the dropout rate in the Oakland Schools, the group considered contextual factors such as inequities in school funding or lack of access to guidance counseling. The adults planned activities such as interactive skits, board games, discussions, and even didactic lectures, which were intended to educate youth about the broader sociopolitical context for the dropout rate. I observed one meeting when Vanessa, the executive director, asked the youth to get out "their binders" and "something to write with." After youth had opened their binders she commenced a fifteen-minute lecture, interspersed with questions and comments from youth, about school finance policies that enabled schools in a neighboring town to have better facilities. This kind of political talk was new for many youth. As one youth leader put it, comparing Kids First to school: "The school is going to teach you the good side of everything, but up in here, they going to show you the good side, the bad side. They going to show you all four corners of everything."

The contrasting approaches to problem framing in YELL and Kids First suggested by the examples above had different strengths. Facilitation could boast of offering an open space for young people to construct explanations about social problems in conversation with one another. Although sometimes circuitous, the YELL group ultimately selected a problem, stereotypes, that was personally relevant and emotionally rich for most of the members. The apprenticeship approach, while also focused on a personally relevant topic for the youth organizers, offered an explicit ideological framework to young people that called into question familiar narratives about meritocracy and individual self-reliance. This approach broadened the interpretive repertoires that young people brought to their analysis of issues and activism.

Sustaining a Campaign

Once groups agreed upon the campaign focus they transitioned into the hard work of completing tasks related to the campaign. As other researchers have observed, motivation can flag during this long phase if members lose sight of the end goal or get bored by the execution of mundane details.[15] And mundane details there were: Members of TRUE needed to find out how to register students for the conference and locate a site that they could afford. YELL participants performed a content analysis of newspaper stories about young people in their neighborhood. Kids First members entered results from 956 surveys into Excel spreadsheets. All these tasks—central to the success of each campaign—posed risks for the group if they were not completed. Here too I observed variation in the strategies adults used to sustain the campaign.

The facilitation approach to sustaining the campaign emphasized the creation of systems and rules that shifted power and authority from adults to youth. For example, one of the first decisions in YELL had to do with ground rules for behavior. Youth defined unexcused absences, spelled out how many warnings students should receive for absences, specified the consequences of disrespecting others, and differentiated acceptable curses (directed toward oneself) from unacceptable curses (directed toward others). These deliberations, which the program director facilitated without giving input, took several afternoons. Some students found the whole exercise foreign. During a conversation at the beginning of the first year, one student said, in frustration at the slow pace, "I think ya'll [the adults] should make the rules." Over time, however, the group agreements became a resource that allowed adults to deflect authority from themselves to a more impartial set of rules. As one youth participant, Marlene, said in an interview, "If we break the rules, we couldn't get mad because we were the ones that put them in force." Marlene viewed the rules as a product of youth's labor rather than something imposed upon them arbitrarily. Dolores, a YELL veteran, endorsed this division of labor in an interview at the end of the year:

> *Now that the year is over, how do you feel about how it went?*
> This year I think it was harder, because last year [*year one*] the adults were more involved with the groups. . . . And this year it was more like,

"We're gonna let them do everything and we're just gonna sit back and watch and if they need help we'll be there but we're not really gonna take charge of the situation." And I think that's good though, 'cause that's what YELL's about: you making your own choices, you getting your things done.

Dolores observed that the adults made room for youth input and owner-ship by detaching themselves from the project and letting youth make key decisions. The adults reinforced this division of labor to youth par-ticipants by saying things such as, "This project is up to you," "You chose the topic," or "It's supposed to be the youth making the decisions." They shaped each other's behavior too by pointing out if one of them was interfering too much. Youth also contributed by placing constraints on adult roles, as in a collective decision midway through the year that adults should not supervise the different small groups.

What this meant was that young people gained a great deal of practice regulating their own work and behavior. Youth participants routinely initiated the meetings, explained the agenda, and helped keep the group on task. Relative to Kids First and TRUE, youth participants in YELL had more opportunities to facilitate large group activities.[16] Everyone facilitated at least once; five youth did so multiple times. In addition to facilitating group meetings, youth in YELL routinely worked in small teams with limited guidance from adults. The following episode, taken from a meeting five months into the year, shows youth working collab-oratively with limited supervision from adults.

Youth Leadership in YELL

The YELL meeting starts with Ellie (a 10th grader in her second year) reviewing the agenda and facilitating a brief game to reinforce the group ground rules. When the game is over, Ellie announces, "Now we're work-ing in research groups. Remember to pick a facilitator and note taker. You guys have to do that every single time."

After Ellie's instructions, youth assemble in their four groups: maga-zine, video, website, and research. Adults pursue other tasks: The pro-gram director is fixing the internet connection on a computer; another is working in the office. I go with the magazine group, which is comprised of four youth.

The first thing the magazine group does is pick a facilitator (Arun) and a note taker (Marlene). Arun asks, "What are our goals today?" They refer back to the timeline they had completed last week to identify their goal, which is to decide on the magazine's purpose and content. Members begin brainstorming ideas for stories to include. At one point Marlene starts asking questions to the group and Arun says, "You're trying to take my job away." Another youth adds, "Arun's the facilitator." Marlene smiles and says, "I'm sorry, I'll stop," and the group resumes its work.

In the above excerpt Ellie, a youth participant, initiated the large group meeting, facilitated an opening team builder, and then directed people to their "small groups." She reminded each group to designate a "facilitator" and a "note taker." In keeping with the decision about adult roles, adults worked on tasks separately from youth. The magazine group went to a corner of the room and after allocating roles, proceeded with its task. When one member, Marlene, overstepped her role, others reminded her that it was Arun who was facilitator on that day.

The magazine group distinguished itself for its ability to work collaboratively and stay on task. The other small groups, particularly those working on the video and website, struggled to stay on task. For example, there were several meetings where members of the video group did not complete steps they had planned, such as interviewing teachers and students at their school, which left little time for editing the footage. Similarly, the website group left much of its work until just prior to the culminating event. Adults anticipated that this would become a problem but did not intervene because they feared that it would undermine youth's feelings of ownership. One staff person defended this decision by arguing that youth would learn best if allowed to make mistakes.

Joint work, most common in TRUE, looked quite different from the careful systems and roles typical in YELL. During this phase of the project there appeared to be little effort to position youth as leaders of the project, distance adults from the project, or operate as if one group or another was supposed to be in charge. Adults participated alongside youth in carrying out the campaign; everyone was expected to pitch in.

The following excerpt, from a planning meeting two months prior to the conference, reflects salient qualities of the joint work approach. Three adults and four youth were present.

"Next Steps" Discussion (TRUE)

The meeting is almost over. The adult facilitator, Beatrice, suggests we figure out what to work on next. She asks everyone to suggest an item that is most pressing. Soon we have a list of eight tasks written on poster paper:

1. The logo.
2. Basic information flyer.
3. T-shirt design.
4. Food, donations.
5. Push to get teachers to turn the event into a field trip.
6. Workshop specifics.
7. Identify target participants.
8. Contact politicians.

Beatrice says, "I want to challenge us, who would be willing to do what before the next meeting?"

To get us started she volunteers to work on "outreach" to teachers. Anthony, a youth participant, says he will work on "workshop specifics." Dave, an adult staff member who has already prepared some ideas about workshops, offers to share these with Anthony. Then Sam, a youth participant, volunteers to work on the logo, saying, "I know some artists." Beatrice says to Dave, "We can do the flyer together."

She then says, "Octavio and Marvin? What about you?" Marvin responds by volunteering to type up information for the flyer, adding, "I've got some nice fonts on my computer." Octavio says that he will talk to some teachers at his school about bringing their classes to the conferences.

Beatrice then adds, "Ben, don't think I don't see you over there." I volunteer to work with Anthony to brainstorm ideas for the workshops, because I think that is most pressing. Anthony and I agree to communicate by email.

In the above excerpt an adult staff member, Beatrice, facilitated a discussion about next steps. Both youth and adults suggested tasks to be completed, ranging from designing a logo to inviting politicians to attend the accountability session. They made decisions together about how to prioritize tasks. Then Beatrice asked everyone to volunteer for a task. Unlike at YELL and Kids First, I was expected to contribute my labor alongside the other members of the group. No instruction was offered in how to do a particular task; it was assumed that people would volunteer for what they knew how to do or learn how if needed.

This example illustrates several features of joint work. First, the adult staff members participated in the project. They designed the agendas for meetings, sent out reminder emails, and kept track of the tasks that needed to be completed. The adults facilitated 90 percent of the activities where there was a designated facilitator. Also, they tended to complete tasks that were more time-consuming or that required access to certain social networks. For example, Beatrice secured permits from the opera house where the event was held. Dave recruited several of the workshop presenters from other nonprofit agencies in the city. Earl negotiated with a local hip-hop artist that he knew to speak at the event.

Second, unlike either facilitation or apprenticeship, joint work rarely included elements of a "youth-centered environment," such as skill-building workshops or efforts to foster group belonging. Aside from periodic check-ins at the beginning of meetings, there were no team-building activities. The TRUE project resembled what one might expect a planning process to look like in a workplace or community group, in which the primary goal is to complete the project successfully rather than to teach, mentor, or counsel certain members. One youth participant, Marvin, conveyed this task-oriented atmosphere when I asked him to tell me about the ways it felt different from school:

> It was an all-work environment.
> *"All-work environment"? What does that mean?*
> It was just all work, no playing.

Marvin saw this project as *more* work than he faced in school, because of the predominance of time devoted to planning and preparing, with few breaks or opportunities to socialize.

Similarly, the adults rarely organized workshops for youth or set aside time to coach them. I observed only one activity whose explicit purpose was to train participants in a particular piece of information or skill: Youth and adults watched a video documentary that critiqued the military's effort to target high school students of color for recruitment.

By contrast, adults in YELL and Kids First offered workshops in a variety of topics, including: public speaking, how to facilitate, and how to do research (in YELL) and conflict resolution, racial justice, and the political economy of public education (in Kids First).

The adults attributed their high levels of involvement to the complex demands of the conference, which not only required expertise in planning but also multiple tasks that needed to be completed while the youth were in school, such as placing phone calls and dealing with permits. Dave, one of the adult staff members, told me that initially he had hoped that it would be a "youth-led process," but that he came to realize "it didn't seem feasible for how much of a huge vision that we were trying to bite off." Earl, another adult staff member, made a similar point: "The adults didn't want the young people to mess up, so they definitely took an active role and shaped everything with a skeleton, with an outline." Both Dave and Earl made a pragmatic decision to prioritize the success of the conference over a youth-led process.

The apprenticeship style enacted by the adults in Kids First fell somewhere between YELL and TRUE. Apprenticeship shared with facilitation an effort to be "youth-centered," in the sense of organizing activities to cultivate a sense of belonging and trusting relationships among the youth organizers. They accomplished this through a combination of activities, including team builders at the beginning of meetings, discussions about behavior ground rules, and role-play scenarios where they acted out how to resolve interpersonal conflicts. But as in joint work, the adults were also likely to participate alongside youth in key campaign tasks. Alonzo and Elsa justified their participation in the campaign by referring to the principle, "It's about the work, not the worker." Vanessa, the executive director, thought it was vital that youth experience adequate support to ensure a successful campaign. Alonzo exemplified this approach in a pep talk he gave to youth as they prepared to lead organizing meetings at their schools:

> I got faith in ya'll . . . you guys are ready. At Franklin, I'll be right there with you, so anything you forget I can say. Also, I don't want you to think that having hella [a lot of] people is the goal. We just wanted to be sharing our energy, wanting to resist. Even two people will be successful if they keep coming back.

Alonzo signaled his commitment to the campaign by saying, "I'll be right there with you" to pitch in if youth struggled.

Public Action

The campaign work of each of the groups culminated in public actions. During a dizzying two weeks in May, I observed eight public events that addressed issues such as the high school dropout rate, environmental justice, and stereotypes of urban youth of color. Youth participants sought to educate other youth, communicate political views to adults, and influence public policy. On a Wednesday members of Kids First held a press conference and rally to build support for student voice in school governance. Two days later, TRUE implemented its daylong conference addressing the "toxic legacies of war" on the environment. In the morning students attended workshops about different environmental issues in their neighborhood. The day ended with an "accountability session" with a panel of politicians, including a representative for Nancy Pelosi. I observed more events during subsequent days. Two members of YELL spoke at a press conference where they discussed their concerns about the statewide exit exam. Organizers from Kids First went back to the school board (after the prior meeting was canceled) and proposed their resolution to improve student governance in district high schools. Members of YELL organized a meeting with local journalists to talk about the adverse impact of negative coverage of youth in their school and neighborhood; they hoped to generate ideas for stories that weren't just focused on homicides and violence. YELL followed this up the next day with a "community forum" during which youth leaders presented their research and facilitated discussions among neighborhood residents, local leaders, and other students.

There was a fairly consistent pattern across all the groups during this time. When interactions with adult policy makers neared, adults provided coaching and instruction more typical of apprenticeship. In order to help youth organizers learn how to speak persuasively, adult staff members engaged in modeling, coaching, and fading. The modeling and coaching parts took place behind-the-scenes, in rehearsals for the upcoming presentations. Fading occurred, across all three groups, during the public actions themselves, when young people took center stage and adults were more likely to be in the audience or on the side. Even YELL, which had been more facilitation oriented, shifted toward apprenticeship as meetings with adult policy makers approached. Michelle organized a role play, made suggestions about what should be included, and gave constructive criticism on public speaking.

An example of this kind of modeling and coaching took place in an afternoon activity toward the end of the year in Kids First, when youth organizers prepared for a meeting with school board members. The students hoped to persuade the school board to adopt their new student power resolution to give greater voice to student councils. Lisa and Denise, two youth organizers, practiced making their pitch to Vanessa, who played the role of a school board member:

Field Note Observation: Role Play Prior to Meeting with
School Board Members
Lisa states Kids First's recommendations: counselors should meet with students once per semester to help students develop a plan to fulfill high school graduation requirements. Lisa concludes by saying, "If we have more student voice in the schools then we could ask our student councils to meet with counselors and let them know our concerns."

Vanessa, posing as a school board member, says, "So that's what you want us to vote on?"

Lisa says, "Yeah."

Vanessa says, "Counselors?"

[Here it appears that Vanessa is trying to trick Lisa, because the school board is only supposed to vote on the student council resolution.]

Denise, who is sitting next to Lisa, whispers "no" in her ear.

Lisa says, "I mean, no."

Vanessa says, "Oh, so you want the student council resolution and then once you get that they can work on improving the situation with the counselors. I see . . ."

In this example Vanessa played the part of a school board member who misinterpreted what Lisa was trying to say. After the exchange, Vanessa returned to a point she had communicated earlier: It was important that the students stay "on message," a key skill for advocates and activists who need to control their communications in the public arena and not get sidetracked by members of the media or skeptical politicians.

After Lisa's turn was over, Denise, another youth organizer, made her pitch. In this example Vanessa tried a different strategy to distract her:

Field Note Observation: Role Play (Continued)
Denise starts her speech next, saying, "Seventy-seven percent of students surveyed want to evaluate their teachers to help them improve . . ."

Vanessa interrupts her: "I'm sorry, what is your name?"

Denise, who hadn't introduced herself at the beginning of her speech, says her name and tells Vanessa her high school.

Vanessa says, "I want to ask you about your school, you know, because that's . . . in the neighborhood that I represent, and there have been some problems with the plants behind the school . . ."

[As in the prior interaction with Lisa, Vanessa appears to be trying to divert Denise from the message about student councils.]

Denise says, in her attempt to stay on message, "We'll get to that."

By this time both Vanessa and Denise are smiling; they appear to be having a good time playing these roles. Others are laughing because they see that Vanessa was trying to trick Denise into getting off message, but Denise has successfully parried Vanessa's diversion.

Like her interaction with Lisa, in this example Vanessa tried to get Denise to digress. But Denise had mastered the principle that Vanessa hoped to teach; she discerned Vanessa's efforts at manipulation and stayed focused on the student voice resolution.

These examples suggest that Vanessa sought to prepare youth to be seasoned advocates, rather than just hope that the adult policy makers would go easy on them because they were young. The youth organizers appeared to enjoy the activity, perhaps because Vanessa's efforts to alter their words or trip them up resonated with prior experiences with adults.

Summary

The adults in each group sought to foster youth leadership and civic engagement. At the same time, most youth participants were new to organizing campaigns or engaging in political action. The adults managed the tension between youth empowerment goals and the complex demands of social action campaigns in varied ways, which I describe as facilitation, apprenticeship, and joint work. Although each of these forms of interaction could be observed across the groups, one pattern was predominant in each group. In the facilitation pattern, common in YELL, the adults sought to be neutral toward youth's decisions and be a resource for youth to plan and implement the campaign. In the apprenticeship pattern, common in Kids First, the adults were more likely to coach youth in campaign strategy and they participated in campaign tasks within the context of a youth-centered environment. The third form of guided participation, joint work, took shape in TRUE after the group received a small grant to organize the conference. Joint work was similar to apprenticeship in that the adults participated alongside youth. It differed from both apprenticeship and facilitation because the adults rarely set time aside for coaching or instruction and did not draw distinctions between adults and youth as a basis for delegating tasks or participating in decisions.

Comparing Learning Opportunities across Groups

Did facilitation, apprenticeship, and joint work promote different kinds of learning? Yes and no. On the one hand, I don't want to overstate the differences attributable to the styles of adult guidance. Other factors that were different across groups, such as the kinds of campaigns and youth's prior experiences, likely played a role. Also, it is useful to step back and note certain similarities in learning opportunities across groups. The campaigns in each group required youth to grapple with problems whose solutions were ill-defined and subject to the constraints of the real world. For example, YELL's decision to battle stereotypes identified a problem but did not dictate the solution—how does one take on such a diffuse issue? Kids First participants had to create a new strategy after their initial target—the school board—lost its decision-making authority. Members of TRUE sought to organize a conference with limited funds—their $3,000 budget constrained what they could do and forced them to continually reevaluate their priorities. Experiences such as these, which require youth to respond to contingencies and sustain their commitment over an extended period of time, help youth develop initiative and resourcefulness.[17] Another shared feature of the groups was their intensive collaborative atmosphere. In end-of-year interviews a majority of youth across the groups reported that they learned about making decisions and working with others.

On the other hand, I did observe differences in learning opportunities across the groups. Facilitation created opportunities for accelerated participation by novices; youth—even those with little prior experience—assumed responsibility for key decisions and tasks. In YELL, where facilitation was the predominant pattern throughout the year, youth reported in interviews that they gained extensive practice in a variety of group process skills, including peer collaboration, facilitating meetings, and public speaking. I observed several youth become adept at managing group activities and facilitating decisions. Some of the lessons from such experiences, such as awareness of the pros and cons associated with group decision making, are not directly observable as "skills," but may prepare these youth for future educational or work environments where they are granted autonomy to plan and regulate their activities.

A unique element of Kids First's apprenticeship approach was its focus on sophisticated skills related to civic participation, such as persuasive speech and campaign strategy. Kids First program leaders modeled effective strategies, performed role plays with youth, and coached them on how to stay "on message." These practice sessions were routinely followed by public events where youth took center stage to advocate for their positions to policy makers. Through this mixture of sheltered practice and actual performance youth developed the ability not just to deliver a scripted speech, but also to respond to challenging or unanticipated questions. Youth also learned about sophisticated strategies for organizing and carrying out a campaign. This included analyzing social problems to get at root causes and generating policy recommendations that would address the problem. Also, they developed skills for mobilizing youth to take action. In end-of-year interviews, in addition to describing group collaboration, a majority of youth described learning how to make an impact on social issues that they cared about.

As in the apprenticeship approach, in joint work youth were exposed to mature strategies used by more experienced activists. In this case the focus was on planning and carrying out a conference. But because so much of the work was performed collaboratively with adults, youth had fewer opportunities to practice and master skills on their own, which makes it challenging to draw inferences about their learning. This does not, however, mean that they did not learn. Developmental psychologist Barbara Rogoff, for example, has shown that the opportunity to observe an activity, initially as a peripheral participant, is a common route from novice to expert, particularly in community settings.[18] Opportunities to observe, listen to conversations, and engage in shared endeavors with adults were significant even if they did not lead to independent performance within that setting. In interviews youth reported that they learned how to plan a conference and how to make an impact on social issues. Although changes in youth's participation or skill levels were not evident during my fieldwork, such changes would likely become evident if observed over a more extended timescale.

Conclusion

What does this mean for the dilemmas raised at the beginning of this chapter? What should teaching look like in settings aimed to encourage political agency and voice? How should program leaders conceive of their roles? There is a place for each of the three approaches. Embedded in facilitation are important tools for supporting a group's democratic decision-making and collective governance. Apprenticeship is called for when preparing youth for sophisticated organizing strategies or linking them to a social movement. And joint work may be an optimal interaction style once participants have achieved a certain skill level with each other.

What is most important, from the perspective of building young people's agency and power, is to embrace the potential of *intergenerational*, cross-age collaborations. The facilitation approach can be counterproductive if it segregates youth from adults. Certainly there is a need for teen-only spaces, but young people are likely to find these whether they are officially sanctioned or not. The bigger problem is the absence of *intergenerational* spaces where young people are taken seriously as thinkers and actors engaged in collective action alongside older people.

To contribute to productive intergenerational spaces adults need to recognize their age-based privilege. They need to practice certain habits of allies, such as knowing when to stop talking and start listening, or when to vary participation structures so that young people feel safe and engaged, as was observed in YELL. Several researchers have described youth participation initiatives that went off track because adult leaders made decisions on behalf of youth without consulting them or adopted paternalistic rather than collaborative roles.[19]

But once adults have mastered some of these basic (if challenging) precepts, they need to share their insights and knowledge rather than withhold them, particularly when it comes to youths' political participation. This represents a more conservative interpretation of empowerment because it emphasizes adaptation to and participation in adult norms and practices rather than autonomy and choice. But it is justified to the extent that people need certain kinds of skills or knowledge in order to be effective in the political arena. For example, to be persuasive with policy makers, young people may need to support their opinions with empirical evidence. Or when speaking with legislators, they may need to frame their proposals in terms of bipartisan goals, such as reduced dropout rates or improved student test scores. More experienced activists play an important role when they help make discourse practices of the domain visible to youth.[20] Moreover, through interaction with veterans, newcomers not only learn the cognitive dimensions of a task but they can also begin to envision their future participation.[21]

Access to veterans is also important when it comes to the process of problem framing. Adult mentors can play an educative role by asking critical questions or sharing sociopolitical analyses that depart from dominant cultural narratives about individualism or color-blindness. The adults in Kids First, for example, said that they needed to explicitly combat internalized racism and sexism among youth organizers. Youth voice would be an empty promise if not accompanied by critical social analysis.

Recognition of this complex issue of voice does not provide easy answers for adult leaders. There is a difference between challenging people's common sense about sociological topics and imposing a particular frame in a dogmatic or orthodox way. Talented educators engage in dialogue with youth in ways that respect their dignity and autonomy as thinkers. Knowing how to foster open exchange of ideas, such as sharing everyday experiences in schools, deliberating about the causes of social problems, and inquiring about the political economy of local schools, takes support and practice.

This chapter has proposed a more fluid conception of youth and adult roles, which puts static definitions of *youth* and *adult* aside in favor of broader concerns about social justice and opportunities for young people to "matter" in the public realm. Doing so challenges naïve conceptions of empowerment and gives permission to practitioners to engage in more collaborative, intergenerational work with young people. This collaborative work involves "teaching," but not the kind found in most school classrooms. Such an approach builds on the expertise and social capital of adults to facilitate meaningful and competent participation by young people.

Schools as Sites of Struggle

Critical Civic Inquiry

Consider two important images from the struggle for educational justice in the United States. The first, in 1957, shows Elizabeth Eckford, an African American 15 year old, walking bravely, with sunglasses on, holding a notebook against her chest.[1] Behind her is a white 15 year old, Hazel Bryan, with her face contorted in hatred, alongside other white spectators and police.[2] Ms. Eckford was one of the Little Rock Nine, whose act of defiance was to enter Little Rock Central High School, which had formerly been reserved for white people.

Flash forward to 1968 and a different photograph: Chicano/a high schoolers are walking *out* of a high school in East Los Angeles to draw attention to problems at their schools.[3] This action was part of the LA blowouts of March 1968. First 125, then 500, then 1,500, then 4,500 students walked out of their schools to protest, among other things, their remedial education, whitewashed curriculum, racist teachers, and decrepit school facilities.[4]

Both images illustrate the central role of schools in social justice activism among the young, in which the object of activism is to make the promise of education more real. The first image reveals a hopeful view of schools as a vehicle for progress and justice: the problem is being locked out of school and the solution is to get inside. The second photo reveals a different situation: the problem *is* the school; the solution is to get out. What are we to make of this competing imagery—are American schools a vehicle for equity or an apparatus of an unjust society?

These different tendencies in high school student activism are captured today in protests against high school closure. Jefferson High was not the only school where students walked out to protest high school closure. Thousands of Philadelphia teachers and students walked out of school and protested closures in 2013.[5] An estimated 1,000 students walked out of schools in Newark the same month.[6] About 180 students were suspended from school in Detroit after walking out during the school day to protest upcoming school closures.[7] Walking out is one of the most potent tactics that students have to communicate their frustration and their power.

Contemporary school walkouts symbolize the dual meaning of public schools for social justice movements. Students walk out of schools to protest the failed promise of public education. But we must also remember that the purpose of the walkout is to keep their schools open. In these protests the neighborhood school is not the enemy, but instead a cherished institution that, despite its problems, is seen as an essential part of a community.

These examples capture a guiding assumption of this chapter: Many urban public schools are deeply flawed places, and sometimes toxic to the aspirations and dignity of students of color. But hopes for a more equal and vibrant democracy depend on public schools. Young people and their families fight to keep them open—even when they are flawed—because public schools are guardians of the democratic promise of America. As tempting as it may be to criticize American schools, they are one of the few public goods in an increasingly market-driven and commercialized society.

In order for them to realize this potential, however, schools need to become places that nurture democracy and student voice. They need to treat young people as partners in school change rather than just as targets of remediation. They need to scaffold opportunities for students to participate in critique and collective agency.

What would it take for schools to become hospitable to—and even encouraging of—these practices? Could the learning ecologies of youth organizing groups outside school take root inside schools? What are the challenges to activism in public schools and how can they be overcome?

Critical Civic Inquiry in Schools

In 2008 I received a phone call from Shelley Zion, a sociologist of education from the University of Colorado Denver, whose dissertation research about student voice had identified a troubling phenomenon. In her focus groups with urban high school students, Shelley found that students in the poorest and most marginalized schools articulated an analysis of education inequality but tended to report that there was nothing that they could do to address the situation. Although their schools had succeeded in cultivating a deeply held belief in meritocracy, they had failed to cultivate a sense of civic empowerment. Shelley's work echoed prior research on youth "resistance," which identifies the varied ways in which young people may resist the injuries of toxic schools without necessarily channeling their desires and fears into organized collective action.[8] Shelley invited Carlos Hipolito-Delgado, who studies ethnic identity and school counseling, and me, because of my work on youth organizing and student voice, to develop a collaborative project. Carlos brought his prior research on issues of internalized racism and ethnic identity development in Chicana/o and Latina/o communities, as well as a sharp critique of the limits of typical school counseling practice. Over several conversations we developed a project that we called Critical Civic Inquiry (CCI).

The intent of CCI was to create opportunities for critique and collective agency in schools serving students of color from low-income communities, thereby fostering school reform as well as youth sociopolitical development. The approach was informed by prior work on youth organizing outside school and participatory action research projects such as Tracing Transitions. We would partner with teachers to facilitate a cycle of participatory action research with their students: Students would reflect on their school experiences, identify a problem, study it through systematic research, and then develop an action plan to raise awareness or change a policy. The term "civic" is a bit of a misnomer in that we did not intend the class to study the three branches of government, how a bill becomes a law, or the U.S. Constitution. The course's content was rooted in the discipline of sociology because of its focus on social conditions that shape educational success and failure. We kept the word "civic," however, because of our emphasis on engaging youth in action to solve problems in their everyday lives. This focus is consistent with recent calls for an "action civics" that enables students to practice civic participation through authentic projects.[9] We were inspired by groundbreaking work happening in places like Tucson, Los Angeles, and San Francisco where youth discuss issues of social justice, document their experiences through systematic research, and develop proposals and solutions for educational change.[10] A grant from the Spencer Foundation gave us the time and resources to put our ideas into practice.

One distinct aspect of CCI's design was our effort to integrate it into a range of academic classes during the school day, including literacy, science, math, and traditional civics. Rather than an after-school program or university-based summer institute, we wanted to reach students inside typical urban high schools who might not opt into such an opportunity of their own accord. Could CCI classes deepen students' engagement in learning by embedding content in an action research project about an issue relevant to kids' lives, such as clean drinking water (science), college matriculation rates (math), or race relations at the school (literacy and social studies)? We embraced a spirit of experimentation to see how this might work. If we could get this right, show what it looks like in practice, and document evidence of engagement and learning, we would be making a real contribution to changes in secondary schools.

In this chapter I focus on the experiences of teachers in our second year of CCI, when we expanded from three teachers to seven. Year 2 marked a shift in the project because we decided to embed CCI in a graduate seminar for secondary school teachers. Doing this created an intellectual context to read, discuss, and reflect together, and when appropriate, for Shelley and I to offer coaching and feedback to participating teachers.

In terms of the demographics of the schools, all but one were schools where Latino students were the majority, which is a reflection of demographic trends in Colorado schools serving low-income families. All the teachers were white native English speakers; 5 were female and 2 were male. Five out of the seven reported coming from a middle-class or affluent socioeconomic background; two from working class backgrounds. Most taught high percentages of kids in poverty for whom English was not the language spoken at home. Two of the teachers (Nancy and Jim) were veteran teachers of more than ten years who had heard about the project and wanted to participate. The other five were in their second or third year as Teach for America fellows who opted into the course and received credit toward their Masters in Education program offered by UC-Denver. Table 5.1 summarizes the kinds of

TABLE 5.1. CCI Schools during Year 2

School	Teacher	Grade level	Type of School	Subject	CCI Project Focus
Jane Addams	Nancy	11	Alternative school for pregnant and parenting moms	Civics	Enhancing safety for children of students
Roosevelt	Jim	11–12	Comprehensive high school	ESL	Building awareness and celebration of cultural differences
New Collegiate	Bryan	7	No excuses charter middle school	Literacy	Stronger support and advising for undocumented students
Pathways	Jane	10–12	Continuation (second chance)	Science	Strengthening teaching and learning
Central	Mary	7	6–12 school	Literacy	Reducing bullying
View Crest	Sarah	7	No excuses charter middle school	Science	Awareness of funding inequities and funds for new gym
Springs	Megan	5	K-8 charter	Integrated	Promotion of project-based learning

variability in participating classrooms, including grade levels, philosophy, and content area. Given this variability, CCI projects by necessity varied as well, but they were guided by three signature practices: sharing power, critical conversations about educational equity, and participatory action research.

Sharing Power

Sharing power draws considerably on what research has found about productive youth-adult partnerships in community youth programs. It is based on recognizing that students have interests, skills, and knowledge that ought to be productively brought to bear on the learning processes. Sharing power means that teachers make an effort to learn about students' lives and the kinds of knowledge they develop outside school. It means periodically asking students for their opinions about what is and is not working in the class. It means that students experience some choice related to curriculum and classroom activity.[11] Sharing power is fundamentally a relational approach to teaching. This means that teachers also share something of themselves: they locate themselves for their students and aim to be an ally for their students' development.

Critical Conversations about Education and Identity

The second practice, *critical conversations*, is aimed at creating classroom spaces where students feel safe discussing topics related to race and ethnicity, power and privilege.[12] We had found—in our first pilot year—that without an explicit invitation such conversations tended not to happen inside classrooms. Critical conversations recognize that current features of the social order are not natural or inevitable, but instead are socially produced. Such conversations open up the possibilities for what kinds of problems students select to work on and feel comfortable discussing in a classroom setting. Acknowledging and discussing experiences related to racism and inequality can also contribute to stronger teacher-student bonds.[13] Students who are aware of racial tracking at a school, for example, might lose faith in the moral credibility of a teacher who doesn't acknowledge it. As education philosopher Meira Levinson argues in *No Citizen Left Behind*, patterns of racial segregation and injustice all but demand that young people have guided opportunities to ask questions about the origins of current social relations and to imagine alternatives.[14]

Participatory Action Research

These efforts to share power and interrogate social conditions at the school culminate in a *participatory action research (PAR)* project.[15] In PAR, students identify a relevant problem, collect data about the problem, analyze those data, and develop strategies to address the problem in partnership with adult school personnel. In theory, the activities and learning objective of PAR line up with those of schools: PAR emphasizes academic skills, such as data collection and analysis, and twenty-first century skills, such as teamwork, public speaking, and initiative. Certain types of PAR practices, however, such as calling attention to racial inequities or engaging in inquiry-based learning, can clash with normative school practices.

The second year CCI teachers facilitated a range of PAR projects. All seven of the schools completed projects that included critical conversations about their schools, research about the problem, and interactions with relevant policy makers ranging from state congressional representatives to school board members to principals. Students at Roosevelt, as discussed in chapter 2, studied their peers' perceptions of Cinco de Mayo and used their findings to advocate for changes to the school climate. Seventh graders at View Crest visited and compared resources at three schools: their own, one located in a nearby affluent suburb, and one on Oglala Lakota land in Pine Ridge, South Dakota. They developed a proposal for a gym, which their school did not have, and pitched it to their school board and local policy makers. Students at a school for teen moms came to the conclusion that they did not feel their school provided adequate safeguards for their children, who were looked after in day care during the school day. They met with staff and board members from their school and developed solutions. These are just three examples: All seven of the teachers, as summarized in Table 5.1, facilitated sustained projects that enabled students to perform original research, develop tangible policy proposals, and assert their ideas on a public stage.

Highlighting these accomplishments, however, is not the purpose of this chapter. We researchers have a terrible habit of telling "victory narratives" about our work. By victory narratives I mean accounts that focus on putting the project in the best possible light. The problem with victory narratives is not necessarily that they are untrue but that they are often unhelpful. I've encountered this problem numerous times in working with teachers. We read an article or book about an impressive project, but we don't understand the challenges or failures along the way. This leaves ordinary teachers feeling dispirited or inadequate: Why can't I be just like the heroic educator I just read about? As one of the CCI Year 2 teachers said: "I don't want another *Freedom Writers*. I'm tired of always talking about the exceptional."[16] Another said, "I want to have a life while teaching." And these were hardworking, dedicated teachers! What they meant is that they wanted examples of transformative work with students that was sustainable. They wanted to be able to develop and teach CCI as part of their ongoing practice—and most of them, including some of the Teach for America teachers, intended to be teaching for more than just two years.[17]

So sustainability is important. But of course so are impact and quality. There is no point in sustaining something that aspires to mediocrity. And the more impactful one gets, the more pushback comes with it. One can imagine that if CCI were to "succeed" in that students began to challenge entrenched patterns of racial inequity, then new barriers would emerge. One can see this in examples from the Mexican American Studies program in Tucson, Arizona, which state officials shut down despite evidence of strong academic impact, because of its allegedly un-American values.[18] So this is a two-pronged challenge: What conditions facilitate sustainability *and* quality? How do we develop an approach in CCI that is sustainable while also holding on to its focus on critique and agency?

The remainder of this chapter gets at these questions by identifying the most persistent and frequent challenges to sustainability and quality voiced by teachers. Doing so is meant to provide a useful look behind the curtains of the CCI project for educators who may want to do similar work. Whereas the prior chapter focused on social interaction patterns in community groups, this chapter looks at the broader ecology of schools that shapes opportunities to learn for students. Only by understanding the nature of these barriers can we then develop an action civics that is impactful and sustainable. Data are all based on teacher comments in online discussion threads, papers, or interviews.[19]

Threats to Sustainability and Impact

In the course of trying to enact the three signature practices of CCI, teachers encountered a range of challenges and barriers, which they vocalized in their online participation in the graduate course. Their comments were offered not as excuses for inaction; they emerged because they were trying to take action with their students. I view these challenges as inevitable when one is doing something that diverges from, or clashes with, cultural and institutional inertia. One teacher wrote that she was "going rogue" with her CCI project while others talked about feeling at odds with the norms and practices at their school. Several felt that facilitating a PAR project called for far more work than if they were just to teach their regular curriculum. This section aims to unearth the various forms these challenges took.

Structural Challenges

I use the word structural reluctantly, because structures—such as class size, school accountability policies, or the length of class periods—are intertwined with cultural norms and assumptions. Structures don't exist if there is no cultural apparatus to tolerate or support them. But "structure" is useful to the extent that it signifies a force that is relatively distant from the control or manipulation of a local actor. The structures discussed here were ones that were relatively outside the control of the CCI teachers.

"TCAP ATE ME AND THE SCHOOL ALIVE"

TCAP stands for Transitional Colorado Assessment Program. TCAP, formerly called CSAP (Colorado Student Assessment Program), was (as of 2013) the reading, writing, and math test that determined a school's status on the state accountability framework. Although there was some variation in the way schools chose to implement this test, most allocated two weeks to administer it to the whole school. Aggregated across separate testing sessions during those two weeks, students were in testing for between 9 to 10 hours. According to the CCI teachers, some schools released early when the day's testing was over, while others held class but allowed students to relax or have fun.

Although all schools had to take these tests, they were a particularly fraught time period for those schools that had been identified as underperforming. Principals' and teachers' jobs were on the line. (One of the three schools in our first year of work was closed due to patterns of low performance at the school and our partner teacher lost her job.) During the 2011–12 year, three of the schools scored very low compared to district averages and were in various stages of turnaround status. Two schools, which served a population of more than 90 percent of students on free and reduced lunch, scored relatively well, with more than 60 percent of 7th graders scoring at or above grade level in math.

A lot was riding on those two weeks in March 2012. This meant that it was not just the specific days of testing that were lost to other kinds of instruction, but several days leading up to testing that focused on preparation. This showed up in the CCI teachers' weekly updates, such as "Unfortunately, we were not able to do much research for our project this week due to TCAP prep," "[TCAP] prep basically sapped the entire week," and "Teachers are overwhelmed with TCAP preparation and unable to participate in research efforts at this time." Teachers also talked about needing time to "recover" from TCAP after it was over. Mary wrote, "We had a few days to get back into CCI after recovering from TCAP." Bryan wrote:

> TCAP ate me and the school alive. Almost no movement on CCI this week. I lost two instructional days and had almost zero planning time thanks to proctoring. I think this week will be much better, and the remainder of the year should be staunchly focused on the project.

Standardized tests are not by definition hostile to the kinds of learning sought by CCI. The one teacher in our group who designed a natural experiment—by teaching CCI in only two of his four classes—showed dramatically higher testing gains in the CCI classes and boasted the greatest performance gains in his school. My interpretation of the above quotations is more concerned with the narrow ways test preparation is defined and the climate of pressure and stress that accompanies them. In a system where the teacher is held to account for her students' performance there is a great deal of pressure to conform to the instructional routines believed to contribute to success, which in most of our schools was remedial instruction that relied on decontextualized worksheets and drills. Teachers did not see how this instructional regime could be integrated into their CCI work.

"THE GIRLS ARE ENJOYING THE PROJECT, BUT WE SIMPLY DON'T HAVE THE HOURS IN THE WEEK TO PUSH IT FORWARD QUICKLY *AND* MEET THE STANDARDS I NEED TO MEET"
Whereas "testing" refers to the high-stakes tests I discussed above, "standards" refer to district-defined curricular objectives tied to each subject.

The two science teachers, Sarah and Jane, felt this problem of alignment between CCI and standards most acutely. Although both teachers recognized that certain aspects of the inquiry cycle of CCI were theoretically aligned with scientific thinking and practice, they did not see a way to integrate the open-ended CCI project with their earth science (Sarah) and biology (Jane) classes. Instead, they sought permission from their principals to allocate some time from science class for CCI. This adaptation posed its own challenges because both feared that they were shortchanging their students. Jane, for example, wrote:

> I gave my Bio 2 kids their unit test today and it became pretty clear that something is not working. I am starting to feel a little concerned that this is partially related to CCI Tuesday. They LOVE the CCI stuff and I think it may be eclipsing the science stuff.

Sarah reported a similar challenge:

> One of the major barriers to this project is that I am having an incredible difficulty linking it to science. I am teaching CCI and civic engagement as a second part of my class; one that is relegated to the outskirts of teaching instructions. The civic engagement part of my classroom happens on Fridays and whenever we have a weird bit of extra time in the schedule. The project requires about 500% more time. There are so many learning opportunities I am missing in both science and civics as a result of the half-time commitment.

Nancy, a civics teacher, also reported this shortage of time due to non-alignment between the district's civics standards and the action research project called for by CCI. Given her personal investment in her students, this caused her great distress: "It's been a real struggle the past six weeks and I feel as if I am letting everyone down . . . this class, my students, my school, and my own expectations." I categorize this issue of alignment as *structural* because these teachers felt accountable to either a curriculum supervisor or district standards that were not flexible enough to accommodate integration with the more experiential and open-ended inquiry goals of CCI.

The other teachers—literacy, ESL, and interdisciplinary—found it easier to align their content standards with CCI. The two literacy teachers—Mary and Bryan—generally were the most confident about the substantive connections between CCI learning objectives and their literacy curriculum. Both teachers, for example, built their students writing skills by having them write persuasive essays about the issue that they wanted their class to address. They read and dissected texts that raised topics such as racism, xenophobia, and the politics of language. Bryan felt he could only do CCI if it were closely matched to the standards: "Going off the grid isn't an option."

"WE NEED TO SLOW DOWN ANY FURTHER ACTIONS"

Two projects elicited opposition from upper administration. The first was one where students tried to raise public awareness about their school's need for better facilities, which they framed in a broader narrative about school funding inequities. After presenting their argument to the school board and being politely ignored, the students wrote letters to reporters and politicians. To the surprise of many of the students a local television news station showed up one day, without notice, to do a story about their issue. After the visit, senior administrators wished they had had more advance warning and worried that the airing of the news story might jeopardize their ongoing efforts with the district to secure more funding for the school. They expressed support for the work and the importance of "honoring student voice" but felt that in this case it would work at cross-purposes with the long-term goal of bringing in more resources. So they told the teacher, "We need to slow down any further actions," meaning that they wanted her to hold back from publicizing the issue in the news.

This example illustrates how a student voice project can mess with business as usual. The request to slow things down created a set of dilemmas for the teacher, who felt caught between her subordinate role in her school and her loyalty to her students. As Sarah wrote, "Right now, I am trying to work within the system and be true to the students and their project. It is a maddening, political space to exist."

Sarah's experience reveals a basic dilemma of teacher-guided student voice projects: The more potent the project, the greater the risk to the teacher. If CCI, for example, is carried out in a quality way, it should eventually challenge entrenched systems, but this has the potential to create trouble for the teacher employed by that system. This is one reason why much of the most impressive youth organizing is rooted in independent organizations outside school.

A second project, in which students called attention to racism at Roosevelt High, did not receive explicit pushback but met passive resistance. The principal initially told the students that she did not want to hear about the issues of race and ethnicity. According to the students, then she was polite but ultimately did not follow up on their proposal to create opportunities for learning about cultural and ethnic diversity at the school. As the teacher, Jim, said: "I think she just wanted to sweep it under the rug and hope for the best."

Five of the seven CCI projects did not rise to the level of public controversy or institutional opposition. I attribute this primarily to the fact that all these teachers and the CCI projects were in their first year of this work; their projects had not reached a level of public awareness that would elicit push back. It was also the case that some of the projects, such as reducing bullying and improving safety for the children of teen parents, were aligned with the core values and mission of the administration. CCI action projects such as these can make a big impact without taking an oppositional stance toward teachers or administration.

Instructional Challenges

Testing, curricular standards, and institutional resistance were in many ways beyond the control of the teachers. They were based on the structural conditions of different schools and districts rather than the personal capacities of the teachers. Even the most talented teacher would be unable to sustain the work if they persisted in going rogue. In contrast, the following three "instructional challenges," although also tied to structures of schooling, were tied to people's capacity and expertise.

"WOWZA, THAT REALLY SUCKED TO HEAR ALL OF THAT": SHARING POWER IN THE CLASSROOM

About three months into the year teachers administered a feedback survey to their students asking for their perceptions of the teacher and classroom climate. Reading the results was difficult for several of the teachers. As suggested by Mary's "Wowza" comment, one of the biggest challenges of sharing power can be the emotional vulnerability that comes with it. It is far easier to go about your teaching without leaving space for students to comment on your instruction. It wasn't just Mary who found this difficult. Megan wrote:

> Students can be brutally honest, and sometimes I'm afraid to hear what they have to say. While I love being able to use their feedback to improve my classroom practices, it hurts when students share negative feedback.

Bryan talked about losing the "joy" of teaching after receiving criticism from his students. Mary, on another occasion, wrote, "The extremely mixed feedback I got from my Student's Maps surveys put me in a slump yesterday."

Sharing power, of course, is not just about asking for feedback every couple of months, but also finding ways to shift from a one-directional, banking model of education to a more dialogic and relational approach. To enter into dialogue means eliciting and learning about the kinds of skills and interests that students bring to school that can be leveraged for academic learning. While teachers endorsed this dialogic approach, they expressed uncertainty about how to do it. After hearing Mary raise questions about how to build on student expertise, Jim, a veteran teacher of fifteen years, agreed:

> You're not alone, Mary. A number of my boys are skilled in mechanics or some aspect of the construction trade. Short of doing some kind of project, it's hard to incorporate these strengths in the classroom. . . . I'd love to use them if I only knew how.

Sarah also felt inadequate to the task of sharing decision making with students. Comparing herself to the example posed in a book we had read as a group, she wrote: "I think I am the weakest at authentically doing this. Given the limited time, I do a lot more directing than what we read about in the Schultz book."[20]

Teachers' uncertainty about how to build on students' funds of knowledge and share decision making was compounded by the absence of examples in their current schools. Two teachers taught in No Excuses schools, which utilized strict behavioral codes such as walking silently in single file between classes, raising one's hand before speaking, and holding one's body in particular ways. Bryan tried to reconcile the practice of sharing power to the specific behavioral demands of his school and found it difficult. As he wrote in another post,

> I am nervous and curious about turning over too much or enough power to my students. I'm not totally sure how to do it best in an authentic way. It runs counter to our school model, but I see the value in making it work. I think it will be an ongoing process of feeling the students out—of giving and taking power where it's applicable. Still, it makes me nervous.

Even teachers working outside No Excuses schools felt unprepared to share power by their own schooling experiences or teacher training. Megan wished she had received more training and support for the shift that she was trying to make in her teaching. She wrote, "It can be difficult to incorporate more non-authoritarian means of teaching because students, at least in my class, act up when I give them too much freedom." Mary felt that Teach for America, in particular, had not prepared her for balancing her own authority with cultivating student voice and input:

> I don't really feel that I have been given many, if any, models for this type of teaching. . . . To be honest I am not really sure what this balance looks like and I am certainly working to achieve it.

As teachers worried about their ability to manage the art of sharing power, they also received mixed signals from students, who sometimes responded to the invitation to participate in classroom decision making with passive resistance. Sometimes teachers encountered apathy when they expected engagement. The high school teachers, in particular, reported being surprised or disappointed at students' apparent lack of excitement about giving input into classroom norms or choosing a CCI project. Nancy wrote, for example, "For many of my students finding a voice, even anonymously, is extremely challenging. Until recently, even when I've asked for feedback, I'd hear much more frequently from the vocal students with whom I have built a strong relationship." Throughout the year Jim ruminated on the reasons why some of his students did not appear to respond to the opportunity to "make a difference" with the gusto that the middle school teachers were reporting and that our readings suggested would happen.

> I'm finding, at least with my current group, that choice is something that they really don't want. Giving them choice is only creating confusion and anxiety about what it is they are supposed to be doing. Most of my students are looking for the easiest way around this project and they want me to be the decision maker and the chief designer of the project. They tend to be more "task oriented" and will do, for the most part, what they are told to do.

Jim, Nancy, and others interpreted students' hesitance as an artifact of their prior experiences with schooling. Mary wrote:

> Overall, I think the apathetic trend we are seeing with even our most capable students is a result of years in a school system where their ideas, feelings and identities are often squashed in return for compliance.

Jim too saw this as a compelling explanation, particularly for his students who were in ESL, who he felt were too coddled with low expectations and were not taught to "express creativity or analytic thinking." He wrote that the juniors and seniors in his class "have felt so powerless and down-beaten by the system for so long that they no longer care to fight the system." Jim pointed out that undocumented students in particular would understandably shy away from the request to select a CCI project:

> To make change you have to put yourself out there. I think many of my students have a real fear about standing up and being recognized, even in school. This is particularly true for undocumented students. They have been taught to live in the shadows and to keep a low profile for fear of the consequences that await not only them, but their entire families.

The students in these classes did not have the opportunity to learn by observing other activists, as is typical in community organizations outside of school. They were being asked to take on new roles in an accelerated fashion, with few examples or models to emulate.

"IT'S WEIRD TO THINK ABOUT RACE, BECAUSE IT'S NOTHING THAT I EVER REALLY HAD TO THINK OF"

Racism. Oppression. Power and privilege. Drawing on theories of critical pedagogy and antiracist education, teachers tried to encourage conversations about the social context of their students' lives. They discussed articles about anti-immigration legislation and racial microaggressions, such as the purposeful mispronunciations of Mexican names. These *race-conscious* conversations invariably implicated not just distant political issues, but also the social identities of the people in the room. What does it mean for a white teacher to talk about white supremacy with a class of students of Mexican, Salvadoran, and Vietnamese descent? How do the personal experiences of white teachers from middle-class backgrounds became relevant in discussions about the root cause of schooling inequities? Like people's discomfort about sharing power, teachers voiced a sense of vulnerability or insecurity about these issues. Here the discomfort was deeper, I would argue, because it called forth not just unfamiliar teaching strategies but also their own raced, classed, and gendered identities.

Teachers' comments early in the year indicate their discomfort shifting from either a "color-blind" or "color mute" ideology to one that recognized racial positionality or cultural difference. Megan said, "I was uneasy about the thought of engaging my students in difficult conversations about race and discrimination as a white woman." Jane wrote: "I knew I was white but . . . I never had to really think about what that meant for me or try and feel it out as I feel some of my students do." Jim, in a discussion of a text on white identity, wrote:

> In the past I've never referred to myself by my race or my "whiteness." I've always considered myself as color blind. After reading "The Development of White Identity," I've realized that I'm ignoring the fact that race identification is important and I should recognize diversity, including my own. I now occasionally refer to myself as the "old white guy." I feel a little uncomfortable doing it, but the fact remains that I am the only white

person in the room. I want to bring an awareness of race identity, without the use of these microaggressions and insults.

Bryan recounted his first impressions of being called "Mister" by his students of Mexican or Central American descent: "My response was always the same. I'd tell them my name wasn't mister. I'd refer to them as "student" in return. I'd tell them to try it again." It was not until a Chicano colleague explained to him that "mister" was a variant of "maestro," which was a sign not only of respect but endearment, that Bryan changed his response. He later wrote:

> That's a specific and seemingly small incident, but it illustrates how out of touch I am with my students' culture norms and vice versa. It makes me wonder what else I'm missing. A lot, likely.

Just as the challenges of sharing power with students was heightened for teachers in school contexts that were inhospitable to it, so too were conversations about race. The cohort of CCI teachers were for the most part willing, and in several cases eager, to explore issues of race with their students. But adopting a race-conscious approach was new for most of them, and even in cases where teachers felt comfortable talking about their own identities and privilege, most of the schools were places unaccustomed to this kind of talk. Teachers are not socialized or trained to engage in antiracist pedagogy; nor is it part of the routines of the schools or society at large. Bryan wrote: "It's strange to me that . . . if I frankly address race, many call me racist for simply bringing up the topic." Jim wrote:

> We spent three days this week discussing, reading, and writing about race, power, and privilege. We've had some interesting discussions in class and it's been a bit uncomfortable for me and for some of my students to discuss this issue. Some students considered the topic to be somewhat racist.

Some of the teachers also encountered pushback from fellow teachers, particularly teachers of color who were skeptical about their ability to facilitate a conversation about race with students of color. Sarah, after hearing a story about this from Bryan, voiced a similar experience:

> I have heard that push back too. I think it's important to acknowledge that in the past white people teaching about race was working towards eliminating that culture. For example, when white people were educating the Lakota tribe it was in boarding schools designed specifically to erase their culture. This is the legacy I am fighting against as a white teacher but I understand the deep skepticism that my colleagues of color have brought up.

The CCI teachers faced a challenging task. On the one hand, they were being encouraged to be race-conscious in their interactions with students. On the other hand, some of them encountered colleagues who had well-justified skepticism about their efforts to discuss race and students who interpreted the conversations as racist.

A factor that exacerbated these challenges was teachers' limited expertise in this kind of teaching. They sometimes stumbled in figuring out the right language or activities to catalyze race-conscious discussions. For example, when teachers presented data about differential academic performance by racial and ethnic groups, to some students it sounded as if they were perpetuating racial stereotypes. Teacher comments at the end of the year testify to the importance of personal growth around their racial identities. Jane wrote that her "greatest learning" centered around her identity development and awareness of her biases. This personal growth contributed to greater skill in her interactions with students: "This has extended to the development of my ability to speak with students . . . and approach situations with a more open mind and a greater ability to speak about my own opinions and hear those of others." Jim, a veteran teacher, reported, "My own ethnic identity and the strength to explore that issue with my students was my big learning curve." Jim achieved greater understanding of his students precisely because of his new understandings of himself:

> I see a lot clearer why my students often make the kinds of decisions they do. This is not based on a better understanding of their culture,

but a better understanding of my culture and the power structure I am a part of.

Megan wrote that early in the year "I was uneasy about the thought of engaging my students in difficult conversations about race and discrimination as a white woman." Now, however, "I . . . find myself having these complicated conversations with students regularly and with great honesty." She acknowledged that it still can make her "uncomfortable" but not enough to cause inaction. This is a domain where teachers can gain expertise and become more skilled. It may be counter-normative, but with practice, feedback, and reflection one can get better at it.

"WHY CAN'T I SHAKE THE FEELING THAT I AM FAILING THEM IF NOTHING HAPPENS?"

Finding ways to facilitate a project that would include a culminating action proved difficult for the teachers. As with issues of power sharing and critical conversations, the challenge was partly one of unfamiliarity: It was not something that these teachers were trained to do or that schools are designed to support. One of the first concerns that came up was teachers' fear of how students would react if the project did not achieve its goals. Jane wrote:

> The more I think about implementing this project, and using the resources that we've been given, etc., the more I worry that this will become demoralizing for students instead of inspiring. . . . I will need to be very sure to present the CCI curriculum in a way that empowers my students and does not serve to make them feel even more powerless.

Bryan echoed Jane's comment: "I've wondered about that, too, Jane. What if they take on an issue, put in all of this work, and nothing happens. Nothing changes. I guess that's a life lesson, but it makes me cringe." Sarah too worried about how students would feel and about her moral responsibility to her students:

> Are they going to feel like everything we tried this year is dumb and worthless because nothing happened?? Is it worth it to try to create

some sort of "fake win" so they trust and believe in using their voice in the future? Why can't I shake the feeling that I am failing them if nothing happens?

These teachers suspected, with reason, that it would be difficult for their students to achieve tangible policy victories or culture change. There are so many reasons for this: limited teacher power, absence of structures for substantive student voice in decision making, accountability structures that limit school autonomy, political opposition, disinvestment in public education. . . . I could go on. Given that it is a challenge for the most seasoned community organizers to accomplish meaningful changes in the culture or policies of schools, it is no surprise that it would be difficult for a classroom of students and their teacher to do so, particular if the teacher's job is dependent on the people who are targets of the students' campaign.

What I call attention to, however, is what these statements reveal about the common sense of schools. In schools, "learning" is assumed to have happened if a person is successful on a test or gets a good grade on a project. In everyday life, however, deep learning often comes from some combination of failure and reflection on that failure. Proponents of experiential learning know this, which is why organizations like Outward Bound emphasize the importance of challenge, debriefing, and reflection. Teachers' doubts about the outcome of projects, although laudable for their concern and commitment, reveal this clash of ideologies between a school paradigm and an experiential paradigm.

After overcoming their fears of letting down their students, teachers faced the practical challenge of formulating a set of action steps that would make a difference at their school. Social change is hard. Finding ways to identify the right target and define an issue in a way that is "winnable" is an expert skill. This is particularly true in schools whose political organization tends to more closely resemble feudalism than democracy. Youth councils, although common in many American high schools, are kept separate from the work of governing, and instead focus on fund-raisers, dances, or spirit days. None of the CCI schools had existing channels for students to share and discuss their action projects. Instead, teachers worked with their students to organize opportunities to present research findings and proposals to school personnel who were not accountable in any formal way to the presenters. This is why I call it feudalism: It depended on the goodwill of the person in power rather than any sense of democratic accountability. Student presentations get framed as requests or recommendations rather than demands. Community-based organizations can respond to this problem by building power through numbers; by doing what groups like Padres & Jóvenes did to implement their campaign to end the school-to-jails track. Structural factors make this more difficult for school-based programs led by teachers.

In CCI Year 2, half of these requests were, to the best of everyone's knowledge, ignored. I was present for a school board meeting where Sarah's students made a presentation asking for more resources for their school. In a telling contrast, Sarah's students followed a presentation by the official Student Board of Education, who wanted to push back the start day of school by a few days. Sarah's students stood out: They were younger, they were Latino/a, and they framed their presentation around education inequity. After citing examples of overcrowding in their schools, including the use of hallways for gym class on cold days, they shared data contrasting their facilities with a neighboring middle school in an affluent neighborhood. They concluded their presentation by saying:

> STUDENT 1: We have a dream. We dream of having equality of every-one. . . . We're a school of future inventors engineers and doctors. Every student deserves to go to a good school and as we know this is not true for many children. We are taking first step to do this by coming to talk to you.
> STUDENT 2: Thank you for listening; what we are asking for is a soccer field, a new building, and a gym.
> STUDENT 1: Any questions?

After a brief silence, there was one. One of the school board members asked, "What makes you guys so cool?" Applause followed and the students were ushered off the stage. Friendly? Yes. Respectful? No. To use a metaphor from theories of framing in social interaction, the students were engaged in what they thought was a political interaction: They shared evidence, made arguments, and put forth a proposal. The school board member's response flipped the frame from a political interaction to something more akin to a children's theater performance: It's so cool that you're doing this (but I'll ignore what you said). This is a major problem in student-led efforts at taking action in public settings such as city councils and school boards. Those who are fortunate not to encounter hostile decision makers must still confront condescension. Too often adults interpret the presentation as a child development exercise rather than a political exchange.

The impact of CCI projects was also weakened by the problem of time. Administrators can outwait their students. Several of the projects advanced substantive proposals to their school leadership at the end of the year, but then the following year the students were dispersed and there was no institutional mechanism to check for follow-through. In three cases (Megan, Jane, and Sarah), the teachers had switched schools or careers.

Successful campaigns may achieve an initial policy victory, such as a change to disciplinary codes or how students are counseled into college prep classes, but then the real work must begin of monitoring implementation and holding decision makers to account. Padres & Jóvenes's campaign to end the school-to-jail track, for example, lasted for more than five years and is ongoing. This is why it helps to have an institutional structure that enables someone or some people to "hold" a campaign beyond the timescales of an academic semester or year. This is a structural challenge that we, as designers of CCI, still grapple with.

Sustaining Change from the Inside

In the long term public schools need to create structures, policies, and incentives that encourage student voice and participatory action research in schools. Students need opportunities to help govern their schools. Teachers need resources and coaching to become skilled professionals who can flexibly plan a curriculum. Schools need more autonomy in the way they assess student learning. Districts and states need more money to put in place the necessary infrastructures that support learning. But in the short term, while teachers try to carve out room for action civics, what are some ways to make it sustainable and impactful?

Cultivate Allies

Few teachers prefer to work in isolation or worse yet, "go rogue." It's not sustainable. If your job status is linked to how your principal assesses your work, you need to figure out a way to get her support. CCI teachers sought this in different ways. Sarah and Jane, the two science teachers, both asked and received permission to use some of their science time to "teach CCI." Bryan, who was on shakier ground as a new teacher because he did not agree with many of his school's approaches to behavior management, struggled initially to get his principal's support. He made sure, however, that his curriculum was aligned with standards. And after his students showed the greatest growth of any class at the school, his principal's views of him shifted.

Cultivating allies might also mean seeking political support from colleagues in your building for an action project that is controversial or threatening. Teachers need to learn to think like organizers: Map out who has power in your school (the real power, not just the principal!); anticipate whose interests are likely to be affected; invite those people to visit your class, and hear their feedback before the project goes public. In our first year we spent a lot of time talking about the power of the "lunch ladies" at one school, because students had chosen to focus on the poor nutrition in the school lunches. Framing the project in a way that did not antagonize the women working in the cafeteria was important for its success. In another example, the young moms who Nancy taught encountered a setback when the school secretary, while making copies for their presentation, read the contents and felt personally attacked by the presentation. Nancy recounted:

> Rather than wait for the presentation to hear the students defend their work, the secretary took the criticism to heart, cried openly, and then shared the content of the presentation with her student assistants. As a result, before the presentation even began, the students began receiving criticism from their peers and our class was labeled as "trouble makers." The secretary then refused to attend the presentation.

This example shows the importance of cultivating allies in the school, particularly those people—secretaries, lunch ladies, custodians, safety and security guards—who are essential to the climate and operations of the school. Get to know them.

Connect with Critical Friends

Building a base of support is not just about making sure you will not get in trouble with your colleagues or your boss. It also means seeking out critical friends with whom you can share ideas, challenges, and stresses. This work calls for too much risk and vulnerability to do it alone. The CCI teachers were fortunate to be part of a seminar that met weekly online and once per month in person. They could share when they felt overwhelmed or frustrated. They could ask people to share lesson plans and assignments. One can see in their online exchanges the spirit of collaboration and sharing they developed:

> I really like the twist of creativity you put on the project. Can you share what the 9 groups are? (Mary to Bryan)

> I like the idea of having a pamphlet as the end product of your school report card. (Jim to Bryan)

> Keep us posted on what works and what doesn't. You can be our guinea pig. (Bryan to Jane)

> I am curious if everyone thinks that this is enough time or too little? (Mary)

> As I was reading through the roles you use, I was already thinking of students who fit your descriptions. Can't wait to try this out in my classroom! (Megan to Mary)

Sometimes these exchanges went beyond the sharing of resources to including constructive criticism or differences of opinion. Creating an intellectual community where this is a norm and doesn't lead to personal injury is not easy. We only partly got there with the CCI class. But the discussion threads were places where teachers felt safe sharing their struggles and personal vulnerability. At the end of the year Sarah wrote about how valuable the chances to engage in safe but challenging conversations about race, power, and privilege were and how this showed up in her interactions with students:

> During CCI adult class, I learned further how to speak about the subject of oppression and empowerment while keeping race, class and other forms of oppression at the forefront. In the white community, there is a trend to try to discuss these topics without naming them but it has been nice to "try out" different conversations within the confines of the classroom or wiki in order to get feedback on them. It also allowed me to hear different ways in which to speak about them. I would then take this into my classroom and my own comfort/vulnerability allowed my students to be equally adventurous and vulnerable with their language.

The CCI teachers had the advantage of an institutionally recognized structure for these exchanges, in the form of a graduate class. But there are other ways to form these kinds of small learning communities, whether during time set aside for teacher collaboration in some schools or by taking advantage of online social networks with like-minded teachers.[21] There is a growing and strong body of curricular resources designed for classroom teachers. In our work developing resources for CCI we found several publicly available resources with high quality lesson plans and resources for teachers.[22]

Become a "Tinkerer"

To tinker is to experiment; to try things out; to adopt a playful orientation to learning that involves risk and self-correction.[23] Tinkering is often associated with practical work with one's hands, but it is useful as a metaphor for all sorts of learning, particularly ones where setbacks and mistakes are common. Part of the challenge for CCI teachers was the pain or self-criticism that followed from low-energy lessons or negative student feedback. Self-criticism is productive in moderation, but it is not an emotion on which to build a movement. In large doses it stifles courage and innovation. Tinkering suggests an approach to self-reflection that encourages attention to failure or mistakes without wallowing in them.

Without adopting this openness to mistakes and learning, teachers will freeze up or be reluctant to experiment. Michael Nakkula, an education and counseling scholar, calls this process of learning by teachers and mentors reciprocal transformation.[24] It requires a shift in orientation that is fundamentally dialogic: I learn from you as you learn from me. It can be uncomfortable, especially if you hear things you don't want to hear about your teaching or your treatment of students. It goes against the typical way we position teachers: in control and always three steps ahead of their students. But if you shift to a learning mind-set, then setbacks are no longer indictments of your core being or a sign that you should get out of the business. They lose their emotional sting. They are expected. Messing up becomes productive. Each action project offers an opportunity to learn, go back to the drawing board, and build on experience with new insight.

Champion Your Work to Colleagues

Just as teachers need to be prepared for failure, so too do they need to champion their work when they see engagement and learning by students. Doing so will build a base of support that enables critical inquiry and action projects to become sustainable. We saw evidence of this support after teachers championed their students' work to their colleagues and principal. At View Crest, for example, Sarah presented at her school's professional development about her work with CCI. She reported later that she was pleasantly surprised to find that her colleagues were "moved" by the "radical" approach and several came up afterwards and wanted to take the class. Sarah acknowledged that it is hard to "brag," but that it is "an important part of drawing attention to the work." Sarah's principal, in a separate and private interview, said that Sarah's work "was noticed by teachers and other students. There was a positive ripple effect through the culture of engagement." I asked him to say more about what was "noticed."

> For example, Sarah was very vocal about making known what the CCI group was working on when the project became more tangible. When they visited the school in [an affluent town], there was staff chatter about that. Then the students came back and there was student chatter about

that. . . . When the students came to talk in front of the school board, many teachers went to support them. Our staff watched the screening of the video and there was excitement that our students were stepping forward and looking and finding ways to make their voices heard.

Sometimes the most compelling evidence comes from seeing students get animated and engaged. Word spreads. In this case, the faculty didn't need to see test scores to make inferences about what the students were learning.

But seeing strong test score gains doesn't hurt. In Bryan's school, which was part of a network also working under the No Excuses model, his CCI students' performance caught the attention of school leaders. (His two CCI classes grew in their writing scores by 2.9 and 4.6 grade levels in just one year, compared to his non-CCI classes that grew by 1.6 and 2.1). The next year an administrator from Bryan's network contacted me about leading a professional development session related to CCI principles; we had to change the location because of the "overwhelming number of people" who signed up for it. A few months after that I heard again that there was going to be a curriculum committee working on "how our move to the Common Core Standards can support the CCI model." And this was from the school network that had initially been the least hospitable to core features of CCI's work.

Megan too saw change at her school. Her students focused on quality of instruction: They wanted to see more "project-based learning" rather than worksheets. In reflecting on the possible impacts, Megan wrote: "Teachers and students have seen the work my students are undertaking and have begun wanting to participate in similar projects of their own." Her principal asked her to be a Service Learning Teacher Leader to "implement this type of learning" and "pledged to provide teachers with professional development in the use of project-based learning." I don't know how much of this was actually sustained at the school the next year because Megan left to assume a position at a bigger school to lead their civic engagement efforts.

These examples suggest that the culminating action of classroom projects is just one small way of generating support for sustainability and impact. What was most compelling in these schools was when other teachers saw what the students were doing. When they saw their excitement and engagement; when they saw them staying afterschool to make phone calls or prepare posters; something clicked. In Bryan and Sarah's schools the demand from teachers played a key role. In Megan's, there was also a demand from students. This suggests a different way to think about sustainability and focuses on a key principle of organizing: building power through numbers.

* * *

Fostering critique and collective agency inside schools faces a set of challenges that are different from those that community organizations face. The CCI action projects revealed key differences from groups like YELL, Kids First, and TRUE. Whereas the culture of the community programs was to privilege and prioritize youth voice, the teachers operated in school contexts where teacher authority was taken for granted as the norm. They also worked in a context where there was an overwhelming priority placed on academic standards and testing, which limited the space and time for student-centered learning.

However, schools also have advantages over community-based organizations as spaces to organize and mobilize young people. Compulsory enrollment means that there are large numbers of youth who show up on a reliable basis. The expectation of academic work—including homework—is compatible with the rigors of participatory action research. And a great deal of evidence suggests that students crave the opportunity to work on personally relevant projects. This focus on purpose and meaning was one of the things that most stood out to the CCI students, when asked to compare it to typical classes. As a female student from Mary's class said, "It was more unique, 'cause we did more . . . productive things, like, we actually tried to solve something in our school instead of just . . . focusing on reading and writing."

The CCI teachers showed that academic rigor and action civics go hand in hand. Even in the most behaviorally strict urban middle schools, they carved out space for dialogue with students and experiential learning. Their work demonstrated the promise of public schools as sites for young people to develop as political actors and contribute to change in the climate and policies of their schools.

Conclusion

Activism, Dignity, and Human Development

In June 2007, after nine months of work, the time to meet with district administrators had arrived. Our group—a participatory action research team formed after the closure of Jefferson High School—prepared a forty-five minute presentation called *Tracing Transitions: Displaced Jefferson Students Speak Out.* Five displaced Jefferson students and two recent Jefferson graduates delivered the talk, which drew on historical records, news articles, and a combination of interviews and surveys from 117 Jefferson students. One student, reluctant to speak, participated by being responsible for the slides. The talk highlighted successes and challenges experienced by Jefferson students after the closure, as well as recommendations for the district.

In a refreshing departure from common discourse patterns in student voice presentations, when the talk ended the audience members did more than just politely applaud or ask students what they had learned from the experience. Instead audience members engaged with the material and posed challenging questions about the findings: *How do you reconcile the theme of students feeling successful with the number of challenges they experienced? Could you expand your recommendations slide for other schools going through closure or turnaround processes? How did you, as student researchers, manage the tension between looking at data with an open mind and bringing passions to the project?* The student members of the Tracing Transitions team spoke up with answers and ideas.

When the meeting ended I approached Lucy, one of the Tracing Transition team members, to ask how she thought it went. Lucy said, "We did a good job and showed them." Then she lowered her voice to a whisper and said, "These people didn't expect us to be able to do it, they didn't think we could do it, they think we're dumb like the stereotype."

The next day, during a debriefing with the whole group, another participant, Cheryl, said something similar: "That presentation was really good; it showed we're actually smart." Another student interjected, using humor typical of the group, "because Jefferson students are dumb." Cheryl responded: "No, not like that. A lot of people stereotype Jefferson students so it felt good to see."

Lucy and Cheryl's comments surprised me. It did not occur to me that their intelligence or insight was in doubt. I had been focused on the policy implications of our meeting: Would it lead to actual changes in the way the district handled schools in turnaround status? I was frustrated that we had not specified clearer next steps for administrators. But these policy questions, although important, were not the first priority for the students. Their primary goal had been to show that they were smart, to assert their dignity. They were motivated by the idea of defying stereotypes about Jefferson. A few days later I told another member, Bianca, a Jefferson graduate who was in college, about Lucy's comment and asked if it surprised her. She said, "No that doesn't surprise me at all because I feel like . . . I have to prove that every day."

I walked away thinking about these comments. It perhaps reflected my privilege as a white male that I had been focused on policy proposals and not existential claims for dignity and respect. Growing up, I had not experienced ubiquitous messages assembled to tell me I was intellectually inferior. What I was hearing from Cheryl, Lucy, and Bianca was that their intelligence was cast into doubt by others because they were young people of color from Jefferson High School.

Looking again at the data we had collected, I could see why the Tracing Transitions project had become as much about disproving deficit stereotypes as it was about achieving a specific policy victory. The word "dumb" showed up throughout our surveys and interview notes. Jefferson was closed "because the students were dumb." The curriculum in new schools was "dumbed down" for Jefferson students. People at the new schools said Jefferson students were "slow or dumb." "We want to prove we're not dumb," said one member of the group in a discussion about our goals.

This story illustrates a central claim of this book: In a context where racial inequality reigns and the fundamental dignity of youth of color is undermined by a politics of dispossession, the exercise of voice in the public square is essential for human development. It is not a nice bonus or add-on to other necessities such as academic performance or emotional intelligence. It is central because it enables young people to change a system of relations whose deficit orientation threatens their dignity.

Changing deficit talk may seem like a simple task, but it is so persistent and protean.[1] Just when you thought you had it beat, it shapeshifts. Consider the evolution of the phrase "youth at risk." One of the early uses of this term was in the Carnegie Council on Adolescent Development's 1992 report, *A Matter of Time*.[2] Read the document closely and you will see an earnest effort to turn the reader's gaze to structural problems, such as in its reference to deteriorating public schools and decreasing financial support for public facilities and programs for young people. The term "at risk" was intended to capture the fact that youth from low-income families were not inherently bad or promiscuous, but instead at risk, from a structural perspective, for lower educational attainment, greater rates of illegal substance use, and incarceration.

The term has changed in its meaning and implications, however. Now the phrase "at risk youth" has taken on the discursive properties of a deficit label, which acts as a proxy, in urban contexts, for poor African American and Latino youth who are in need of intervention.[3] Most who still use the term do so in quotes, signaling a self-conscious recognition that it has become associated with pathology.

Deficit assumptions are remarkably resilient and tend to show up even when we try to change the language or frames. It can be tinged with a sense of danger and fear, evoked in the infamous 1990s formulation of young superpredators, which justified the turn toward zero tolerance and increased prison terms for youth.[4] But it can just as easily accompany innocence narratives, in which young people are cast as the victims in a drama where they do not play a leading role. The superpredator imagery at least endows youth with agency, whereas the innocent child frame leaves them mostly being passive objects.

These deficit frames, so inaccurate yet so deeply embedded in discourses about race and class in the United States, are a problem. This we know.[5] And have known.[6] What's the alternative?

One argument that has gained increasing currency since the turn of the twenty-first century is the shift toward assets and strengths, epitomized by the Positive Youth Development (PYD) movement. This approach emphasizes a turn toward young people's capacities rather than their pathologies. It tries to depart from a century of adolescence research that takes for granted storm, stress, crisis, and risk, to a focus on productivity and resilience. It is captured in a synergistic mix of research communities, public policy initiatives, and program approaches. Emphasizing the strengths and assets of youth from nondominant cultural or class backgrounds is a valuable intervention in such a context.[7]

Although PYD represents a productive step for the research community, the asset-based language is not our best alternative. It tends toward euphemism. Instead of talking about risk factors we talk about the absence of protective factors. We replace talk of preventing problem behaviors with talk about cultivating strengths. But substantively we're talking about the same phenomenon. Youth studies scholars Mayssoun Sukarieh and Stuart Tannock call it "old wine in new bottles":

> [W]hether the one or the other is emphasized, each serves equally well to signal a particular set of institutional and ideological expectations "about whom we should, as adults, become." (p. 678)

From this perspective, deficit frames occupy the flip side of a binary, but we have not escaped the binary. We have merely replaced one-dimensional negative stereotypes with one-dimensional positive ones.[8] Scratch the surface and deficit perspectives show through. This kind of dilemma was documented in a 2014 study of youth workers in an organization for African American and Latino youth. Despite efforts by the staff to focus on youths' strengths and funds of knowledge, the organization based its fundraising appeals on "saving" the youth or preventing a range of undesirable behaviors.[9]

Even when educators embrace the asset-based alternative, it can be just as flat and brittle. It makes it difficult to testify to situations when a child really is missing something crucial, whether material resources or academic skills. It can divert attention from structural contradictions that youth of color face. It lends little guidance if a young person engages in cultural productions that communicate racist or sexist or homophobic practices. To respect young people means to engage with them critically.[10] The asset-based approach is an improvement on the deficit approach, but it still risks becoming a caricature that does not offer a useful guide to practice.

Rather than replace negative stereotypes with positive ones, this book forwards a *political account of youth* that locates their interpretations, actions, and learning in a material and structural context. They do not wait until age 18 or 21 to grasp political systems, but, consistent with developmental theory, begin constructing their understanding and perspectives in childhood.[11] Political beings identify and act on self-interest. Just as people of voting age recognize political interests, whether for lower taxes or access to health care, so too are young people capable of recognizing self-interests that arise due to their particular material and social location, such as for high quality schools, access to college, or safe routes to school. Sometimes they identify collective interests motivated by concerns about social justice or human welfare, such as in youth organizing groups. Regardless, this political account strives to avoid binaries that govern how youth are typically described: as vulnerable or resilient, dangerous or prosocial, impulsive or responsible.

Political beings are capable of agency and action; they make sense of and participate in fashioning their social and political worlds. Acknowledging young people's status as political beings counters deficit-based viewpoints that cast them as less than or other. This political approach answers anthropologist Ray McDermott's call for research that shows how "people adjust to tight circumstances with passion and ingenuity. . . . It can deliver portraits of what people in trouble can do, rather than cannot do, and it promises research better tuned to the work of democracy."[12]

Activism among youth of color is one such portrait "of what people in trouble can do." McDermott's statement would, I am guessing, resonate with the Jefferson High School students who carefully studied the consequences of school closure while laboring under the burden of deficit stereotypes. The experience of the Jefferson students illustrates my argument that *activism is human development*, felt most acutely by young people growing up in a world toxic to their dignity and aspirations. James Baldwin said something akin to this in his 1963 *Talk to Teachers*: "One of the paradoxes of education was that precisely at the point when you begin to develop a conscience, you must find yourself at war with your society."[13] As those concerned about human development have said for decades—Carter G. Woodson, Paolo Freire, Carol Gilligan—the project of growing up calls for questioning and transforming social structures, rather than merely accommodating to them.

When young people engage in social critique they begin to denaturalize inequality and question attributions that locate the source of failure inside the person. They begin to change the narrative about the intelligence and worth of young people of color. They construct increasingly complex and more adaptive explanations for and responses to their social environment.

When paired with the kinds of collective action found in youth organizing, the developmental changes that ensue are not merely inside the head. Action in the public square is significant because it can catalyze a shift in *social relations*. The interactional space, for example, where Bianca and Lucy spoke back to the district officials who closed their school, much like the space where Denise addressed the Oakland School Board and Luis and Gabriela patiently reasoned with their principal, was powerful because of their claims to be seen and heard. This rests on a view of development that privileges one's roles and visibility within a community, where identities are produced by the way people position themselves and are positioned by others.[14]

The shift toward understanding youth as political beings is not just about their own development, but also about what it can catalyze for broader changes in society. This book's case studies of young people and their organizing campaigns demonstrate the interdependence of youth development and democratic renewal. Part I showed how youth and institutions benefit when youth experience intentional opportunities to critique their sociopolitical worlds and take action to address problems. The case of Luis and Gabriela documented their experience of a classroom project where the goal was to denaturalize the social order of Roosevelt High and invite students to change that social order. Luis and Gabriela jumped at this opportunity with enthusiasm and articulated a critique of the racism and cultural myopia that existed at the school. Case studies of DREAM Activism and Padres & Jóvenes Unidos showed the broader kinds of impact young people can have when sustained in the context of social movements. Campaigns for immigrant rights and to end the school-to-jail track show contemporary examples where youth of color build power that changes the cultural and political landscape. Later, in a kind of reverse case, I discussed the kinds of problems that ensue when young people *are not* at the table for high-stakes school reform decisions. Although the closure of Jefferson High School motivated activism by a cadre of students, it also had damaging consequences for many of their peers. Taken together, the case studies lend empirical evidence to the argument of this book: Young people are political beings who, when offered the right opportunity structure (and sometimes even when not), can marshal their political critiques into sustained action that is good for the actors and good for society.

Part II of the book drew on empirical research to explore ecologies of learning and development. Reframing youth as political beings is not meant to deny that they—like all of us—benefit from training and support to be capable political actors. What does teaching and learning look like in community programs that engage youth in action campaigns? Can learning processes in community settings take root inside contemporary public schools? How do teachers navigate barriers, such as the immense pressure to boost test scores, in their efforts to foster critique and collective agency among their students? Although we looked at two different institutional contexts, they produced similar findings about learning ecologies for youth organizing and activism. Effective learning spaces tended to be intergenerational: People of varying ages pitched in based on their experience and skills. Educators—whether in the community or at school—were ready to take risks alongside their students, both in terms of exploring their own personal identities and also in positioning themselves as part of the team rather than a neutral facilitator. Learners came together around shared experiences and issues that affected their dreams for the future. Taking part in high-stakes activity motivated youths' desire to master the needed skills and knowledge. This was learning by doing, not solely learning as preparation for future activity.

In sharing these case studies I want to normalize the view of youth as political beings. It is all too easy to adopt a heroic frame when talking about youth activism or civic participation. Its exceptionality gets laminated with a moral quality. This book would be misinterpreted, however, if it were seen as case studies of exceptional people. It's not. We did get to glimpse some exceptional opportunity structures—unusual organizations and classrooms that invited young people to talk with each other about their political experiences and interests and mobilize around social dreams—but the key distinction is the setting, not the person.

The novelty of these settings is, on the one hand, a limitation of this book. The settings discussed here were not representative of the kinds of learning ecologies that the broader population of youth in the U.S. experience. Similarly, we are talking about a small number of youth across the pages of this book; and these young people were not randomly selected to participate. In that sense we cannot treat the perspectives of people such as Denise, Luis, and Gabriela as representative of African American or Latino/a youth.

But the fact that the empirical cases discussed in this book are uncommon is also why they are important to tell. Empirical research is not merely about describing main effects and aggregate trends, but also documenting powerful spaces that inspire innovation. Social scientists famously failed to predict the Arab Spring because they were blind to the democratic capacity of ordinary Arabs.[15] Indeed, a truly representative study would find that those youth who participated in Tahrir Square represented a tiny percentage of Egyptian youth. Although there is a place for identifying trends and averages, there is also a place for carefully selected cases that document an unusual phenomenon that resonates with people's dreams and values.

Some readers may also be concerned that the case studies in this book reflect a particular agenda about education policy or what civic engagement ought to look like. Guilty as charged. I readily acknowledge that the selection of cases was in part driven by normative values about the kinds of opportunities I believe young people ought to have. The UN Convention on the Rights of the Child, for example, is a statement of values. Sometimes we social scientists forget this when we are intent on proving that a particular intervention leads to positive outcomes. Although there is good evidence of the developmental outcomes of civic engagement, this argument is not merely an instrumental one. Consider a hypothetical randomized trial that assigned half of a town's children to a school modeled on Athenian democracy and the other modeled on Spartan discipline. If it turned out that the Spartans boasted higher graduation rates or higher feelings of empowerment, does this mean it is the "better" school? Empirical results are interpreted in tandem with a set of moral values, whether explicit or opaque. I have tried to be explicit about that normative argument in this book. Some readers may privilege other virtues in adolescent development or disagree with my description of the structural dispossession facing youth of color in poor and working class urban neighborhoods. Making my beliefs and frames explicit is intended to facilitate the reader's critical interpretation of this book's claims.

What Next? Implications for Youth Development and Educational Equity

Democracy demands active participation by all. Electoral voting is just one small part of how people can participate in democratic self-governance. There are many other ways that institutions and policies can address the *developmental contradiction* that confronts young people as they grow into their teen years. The young people discussed in this book were mature enough to vocalize their aspirations and recognize their interests but not old enough or privileged enough to have clear channels for political participation. One can see this in the experience of Gabriela and Luis, who articulated solutions to social divisions at Roosevelt High but were not on the student council or in a position to participate in realizing those solutions. One can also see it in the Jefferson High students who fought back against a decision made "for them" but not "with them."

There are multiple ways that youth development programs and schools could broaden the entry points for voice and participation. These are purposefully incremental. Think of them as democracy-building incubators. They themselves will not solve the problem of structural dispossession facing youth of color but they will create more compelling learning environments for youth and build skills that produce the capacity for participation in future struggles.

Recommendations for Youth Development Programs

Traditional youth development programs or after-school spaces do not need to transform themselves into community organizing groups.

Not all youth are drawn to political contestation. Nor do staff necessarily possess organizing skills or activist goals. But without departing from core missions around mentoring, academic support, or the arts, youth programs can do a better job of treating their target populations with dignity and practicing democracy. It is not enough to tell youth workers to use asset language or avoid deficit orientations. Instead we need to design practices and routines that, through their regular enactment, support "developmental alliances" between young people and program adults.[16]

CHANGE THE PREMISE

Too many interventions that target students of color—despite decades of critiques of deficit-based approaches—continue to be designed without their input and to be based on carefully elaborated accounts of what they lack. Youth development agencies work in a landscape where they must justify their work by appealing to what is missing in their target population: social skills, academic achievement, grit.[17] This creates problems, particularly for programs targeting older youth. As teenagers experience more autonomy and agency in their everyday lives, why would they want to participate in an organization whose premise defines them as being in need of saving? Transformational educators like Paolo Freire and Myles Horton, who both started their careers working with adults, recognized this. Many front-line youth workers, who hone their craft trying to create spaces that young people want to be part of, have also figured it out.[18] The key is to change the deficit premise.

Putting this core belief into practice so that it is woven into organizational roles, approaches to decision making, and program activities is best accomplished through the framework of youth-adult partnerships. Community psychologists Zeldin, Christens, and Powers define youth-adult partnerships as

> the practice of: (a) multiple youth and multiple adults deliberating and acting together, (b) in a collective [democratic] fashion, (c) over a sustained period of time, (d) through shared work, (e) intended to promote social justice, strengthen an organization and/or affirmatively address a community issue.[19]

Youth adult partnerships shift the relation from one of mentor and mentee, or case manager and client, to one of joint work where both parties are working together to get something done. This opportunity to work on a third thing—rather than on the young person—can shift the relationship toward respectful and collegial joint work.

Effective youth-adult partnerships tend to embrace the idea that every participant brings particular skills and knowledge; age is not the primary dimension upon which expertise is distributed. When framed this way, participants begin to see how young people bring certain kinds of relevant expertise to the table that others do not. For example, students may be aware of the reasons why their peers are not showing up to certain kinds of programming or what kinds of technologies are most engaging. Some youth, particularly those with prior experience, may be more skilled in facilitating group decisions than the adults or more knowledgeable about state law.

Although it is important to recognize insights that younger people bring to the table, successful partnerships also build in some forms of developmentally responsive scaffolding that create pathways to participation for less experienced members. If groups do not take certain purposeful efforts to recognize differences in skill and knowledge, young people may not know how to participate or bring their knowledge to the group. Here the research on learning outside school boasts agreement about what developmentally responsive scaffolding looks like: It is a dynamic relationship in which more experienced others support the participation or problem-solving of novices in ways that progressively change over time as the novice assumes greater mastery or skill.[20] The notion here is that people with less experience will learn through participation in the ongoing activities of a group, particularly if they have opportunities to observe and enact practices they see performed by more skilled members. Such joint work may periodically require "just-in-time" coaching around a particular skill or knowledge—to pause during the activity in order to explain or demonstrate a skill—but much can also be done by learning through shoulder-to-shoulder participation.

This kind of joint work also calls for support or training for adult members of the group. For youth-adult partnerships in particular, scholars recommend that older members of the group receive training around how to share the floor and unlearn deep-seated deficit perspectives of youth.[21] Some partnerships set out to recruit "youth" but end up excluding the most vulnerable or marginalized youth within a community.[22] Any initiative to engage young people needs to develop an inclusive space that attends explicitly to differences in power and privilege.

INVITE DISCUSSIONS OF RACE, POWER, AND PRIVILEGE

Take a look at various PYD frameworks that guide program development and evaluation. You'll see consistent articulation of desired outcomes such as academic competence, leadership and purpose, and positive social relationships.[23] You will see careful and empirically based elaboration of what it means to create a safe environment and supportive relationships in the National Research Council's report about features of community programs that support youth development.[24] You might encounter the new excitement about grit and other noncognitive skills that predict educational attainment. Similarly, look at training documents for youth workers that lay out key elements of what practitioners need to know.[25] Knowledge of developmental change tends to be prioritized, as well as some of the mechanics of building relationships with youth and delivering programs. Most will agree that it is a good idea to hire youth workers who are representative of the communities from which the target population comes.

You will be less likely, however, to encounter youth development frameworks that emphasize critical analysis of race and inequality as either a program activity or a learning outcome. Nor will you see adequate attention to cultivating staff members' awareness of their own power and privilege.

These are areas where youth development practice can improve. It might begin by making use of freely available self-assessment tools that facilitate reflection about program practices related to equity and diversity.[26] These kinds of self-study tools can make the familiar strange and catalyze discussions about existing organizational culture. Making power and privilege visible in youth work can also be integrated into other common features of youth worker training, such as the techniques of relationship building. It would be time well-spent, for example, to facilitate staffers' reflections on their own histories with power and privilege. There is a compelling literature in the teacher education research literature about how white teachers learn to be allies for youth of color growing up in neighborhoods of concentrated poverty.[27] A major finding from this work is the importance of reflecting on one's own experiences and gaining greater insight into one's own structural location. Teachers who are able to locate themselves for their students can begin to develop candid and more trusting relationships. Nor are power and privilege solely the domain of white practitioners. Adults of color, who may bring advanced education degrees or be from a different class background, bring their own assumptions based on their life circumstances.

The examination of race, power, and privilege is also valuable for young people. It does not have to be didactic. In fact, it shouldn't be![28] One genre of programs that deserve greater attention are those that focus on identity-based rites of passage, such as Brotherhood/Sister Sol in Harlem, New York. But even programs without an identity-producing focus can offer youth-centered activities that raise social issues for discussion. In an after-school program this might mean, for example, carrying out a project to map the social dynamics of the school. Where do kids of different races and ethnicities hang out? How did that come to be? If this particular program is for Latino youth, why is that? What is the reputation of the program? How do you feel when you walk in the door? These are questions that encourage reflection and attention to the broader systems and discourses in which the program sits. They might call for some forms of action, but they don't need to become full-fledged organizing campaigns. What they will do, however, is create a space for young people to talk about their experiences and for staff members to witness the participants' insight and knowledge.

These two practices—youth-adult partnerships and making discussions of power and privilege visible—can be done in all sorts of youth programs. They can be incorporated into after-school settings that focus on digital media or the arts, just as they can be built into the design of mentoring programs. They call for a shift in organizational practices but not a change in mission. They represent important steps toward shifting the premise in youth work—away from the alleged lack of skills or self-control or motivation of the target demographic—toward joint work that fosters collective learning and development.

Advancing the Democratic Mission of Schools

There is a long-standing tension between the vocational and democratic aims of American schooling. Today's efforts to fight for the democratic soul of public education are occurring on many fronts, including racial segregation, school closures, the gap between rich and poor in opportunities to learn, and increased privatization of schools and school districts. Here I focus on curricular and institutional changes that can strengthen the democratic mission of schools. The first kind is curricular and focuses on student learning. The second is institutional and addresses the social organization of relationships and power arrangements between youth and adults.

ACTION CIVICS

Democratic education scholars such as Meira Levinson, Peter Levine, and Beth Rubin articulate the rationale and mechanics of action civics.[29] According to Levinson:

> Through this model, students do civics and behave as citizens by engaging in a cycle of research, action, and reflection about problems they care about personally while learning about deeper principles of effective civic and especially political action.[30]

Action civics is well-aligned with the Common Core State Standard's emphasis on "making well-defended claims," and developing the "ability to inform and persuade."[31] The emerging evidence suggests the value of action civics for student learning and engagement.[32] Participation in this kind of cycle enables students to see the social relevance of academic material while pursuing challenging academic tasks.

Action civics can be seen in the work that Luis, Gabriela, and their classmates did at Roosevelt High School. After observing and hearing from students about race relations at the school, the teacher encouraged students to do further research about the topic. They wrote reflective essays about their own experiences, identified themes in those essays, and then used those themes to design a survey that went out to several hundred students. Findings from the surveys revealed divisions in the school that called for intervention, which students designed and proposed to school leadership.

Another example can be seen in a 7th grade Critical Civic Inquiry (CCI) class whose teacher focused his literacy unit on persuasive public writing. Students voiced their concern that many of the students targeted by the school's ubiquitous pro-college messages would be ineligible because of their status as undocumented residents. They wanted the school staff to understand this contradiction and the broader educational policy community to do something about it. Consistent with CCI practices, these students researched the topic and used that research to write persuasive letters about the issue to state legislators. Students did not have to take a uniform position on this; what they needed to do was to take a position that they believed in and argue it persuasively.

Both the CCI examples underscore Freire's maxim that action must be accompanied by analysis and reflection. As I illustrated in the CCI cases discussed in this book, schools tend to discourage controversy; school-based action civics may experience pressure to avoid political topics or topics that upset local relations of power.[33] Quality action civics, therefore, should include not just action but sustained opportunities to question the social order and imagine alternatives: What kind of education do we want and deserve? Who has power in this situation and how did they get it? What kinds of solutions would get at the root causes of the problem? These are questions that may not arise spontaneously and instead call for explicit invitation from the teacher.

APPRENTICESHIPS IN PARTICIPATORY DEMOCRACY

Beyond these curricular opportunities, schools need to experiment with the way they organize relations and decision making among students, teachers, and administrators. Schools can offer more and better ways for young people to develop skills for community and collective self-governance by working alongside school personnel in decisions that matter.

Rethinking Student Council

There are two fundamental problems with existing efforts at student governance in American high schools. First, they almost invariably restrict youth leadership to school spirit activities, such as planning dances or raising money for a class trip, which do not challenge age segregation or engage youth in governance Second, when the school does depart from these bounded roles and a visionary principal or teacher tries to establish a student council that consults with administration or weighs in on policy or climate issues, it is often restricted to high-achieving students or those who have time and encouragement to engage in voluntary, resume-building activities.

To fulfill their civic potential, schools need to encourage and support opportunities for all students to engage in decision making and take on meaningful governance roles. This can be done by drawing on insights from emerging research about deliberative democracy with young people.[34] For example, groups should refrain from making decisions until people have had the opportunity to listen, explain their reasoning, and develop a sense of shared or public interests. Groups need practice in accountable talk and taking the perspective of others. Without this the process will reward those who come into the deliberation with greater prior knowledge or certainty about their positions.

Second, and just as important, we need to rethink who gets to participate in student councils. Instead of restricting access to those with high grades or popularity, we should instead ask how we can get as many people as possible to contribute to school governance. A guiding principle calls for attending to issues of power, diversity, and inclusion. There should be *low barriers to entry* in student council, which means that young people who do not already have well-crystallized interests can try out new opportunities and practices. For this we can learn from current research in creative media arts, which has found that few young people show up ready to "geek out" by investing in a long-term commitment to learn technical skills around digital production. Instead, the majority of youth tend to show up with friends and "hang around" digital media spaces, get to know people, and learn about the social norms.[35] A similar process should exist for youth around student governance. Too often I see schools treat student council as a reward for good behavior or high grades. Why is it a reward and not a right? When schools adopt a participatory culture, they would encourage everyone to join, see who shows up, see who keeps showing up, and let the council develop organically based on the interests of participants. This will be slow and sometimes complicated logistically, but ultimately more inclusive and sustainable.

Multiple Pathways to Participation

As accessible as we might make it, student council should not be the only kind of participation opportunity. Additional and varied structures that enable youth and adults to work together include strategic planning committees, student-guided neighborhood tours for teachers, student-led professional development workshops, and intergenerational participatory action research teams.[36] There could be weekly or monthly community forums for members of the school community to meet in larger groups to discuss pressing issues that affect everyone, such as bullying, the cafeteria, homework policies, or their educational futures. Take a lesson from the city of Boston's 2014 effort at participatory budgeting, which successfully identified issues that mattered to a large number of youth from across the city.[37]

Let's reframe remedial education too. Instead of relentless drills in reading, writing, or math, the remedial context can also be a place to learn more from students about what is working and what is not working at the school. During Critical Civic Inquiry's third year, a special education teacher designed a participatory action research project in which her students wrote about their experiences in special education. Many of her students were unaware of their federal rights to accommodations and resources; they also reported feelings of stigma.

These examples reflect design principles that encourage robust participation. When schools begin to reorganize their work to a partnership model, young people will benefit by having opportunities to speak in public, work alongside peers and adults, and exercise the range of skills called for in complex public work. At the same time, schools will benefit by learning from the experiences of their students and how the school can be most effective.

From Programs to Movements

Shifts toward greater democracy and partnership in PYD programs and schools are necessary. They will better engage young people; they also provide opportunities for young people to develop skills and repertoires that strengthen their ability to participate in democracy. Challenging deficit assumptions through new norms and practices in programs and schools will be a positive step forward.

It is less clear, however, how such changes disrupt deep-seated forms of structural and racial inequality shaping young people's lives. The structural contradictions that limit educational opportunity are not likely to be affected by even the most exemplary classroom action research project. For this we need a theory of change that gets beyond the bounded walls of classrooms or schools. Broader issues of educational equity called for by youth activists will remain unaddressed without attention to what education policy analysts have called "third-order change."[38]

Third-order change refers to education reforms that challenge power and entrenched interests. According to this viewpoint, equity-focused reform is not merely a set of technical challenges solved through rational deliberation by experts. Instead, substantive equity reform confronts normative and political barriers that emerge when middle class or affluent parents fear that a particular reform threatens their class advantage, such as desegregation or detracking.[39] Such reforms present technical challenges, for sure, such as the logistics of scheduling, or professional development for teachers to broaden their instructional repertoires. But they also give rise to political contestation and conflict. This is a more pointedly agonistic problem space where struggles over relative power shape outcomes. Youth-driven campaigns that remain isolated from broader networks and movements will have limited influence. Third-order change is brought about by social movements.

Consider the distinction between the kinds of accomplishments boasted by CCI classes or community programs such as YELL and those achieved by DREAM Activists or Padres & Jóvenes Unidos. Whereas the former are laudable for what they mean for the development of participants (with potential long-term consequences for democracy), the latter can boast tangible impact on opening up education opportunity in the United States.

One way to capture this distinction is the different resonances of *agency* versus *power*. To exercise agency is valuable; it connotes that a person—or group of people—acts on the social world and is not merely buffeted by it. Young people can exercise agency, however, without having power. Power has a stronger resonance: it suggests that a group's interests need to be taken seriously in the public domain. Research on youth civic engagement, including my own, tends to talk a lot about agency but less about power. Programs that engage youth in a one-time social action project may increase the sense of civic agency of participants; social movements build power.

Shifting the lens to the formation of political power means shifting the ways we think about *scale*.[40] First, timescales change. Instead of being governed by the length of the academic year or summer program, timescales are dictated by how long it takes to get traction. Equity struggles tend to take time. One can see it in the work of DREAM Activists, whose skills were cultivated in the early years of the immigration rights movement and who took several years before they engaged in public action. It may mean that engaging youth in an organizing campaign involves connecting contemporary topics to historic struggles.[41]

Second, spatial scales get broadened. As environmental justice theorists have pointed out, people tend to experience injustices at a local level; but often the solution to these injustices can only be found in a more geographically diffuse national or regional set of policies. This can be understood as a disjuncture between "scales of meaning" and "scales of regulation."[42] Scales of meaning refer to the everyday experiences that are meaningful to people; scales of regulation are spread across policy sectors and levels of government. For many youth, the scale of meaning is located in their school or neighborhood, which can pose challenges when trying to solve a problem that is regulated by state or federal policy. The local scale at which youth may experience problems, such as their school being closed down, feels remote from a diffuse set of policies whose origins are in the state legislature or federal department of education. This scale can be even more confused when the school decision-making authority, as in many U.S. cities, is appointed rather than elected.[43]

In such a context, social movements help connect discrete groups to each other across geographic or regulatory scales. Through their work to organize young people and parents they do the slow and steady work of building collective political power. The ubiquity of social media has changed, to some extent, core practices of social movements. It expands the number of people who can be reached and reduces the organizational infrastructure necessary to link geographically dispersed groups.[44] But social media still needs people doing face to face work in organizations, guided by a long-term strategy to address political barriers to equity-oriented reform.[45]

This shift can be supported by philanthropic initiatives that value youth civic engagement and democratic renewal. Debates reign about how such support should be given and if it should be accepted by social justice organizing groups. Some scholars caution that foundations will push organizations to prioritize the youth development side of their work and ignore or weaken the focus on third-order change.[46] As one group wrote, *the revolution will not be funded*.[47] These are valuable criticisms that deserve attention by program leaders, youth organizers, and philanthropists. But I think that the distinction between programs and movements is useful here. Foundations with strong interests in democratic renewal and grassroots participatory democracy can be educated about how to support broad-based movements. Evaluation requirements can focus on organizational learning and capacity building rather than merely assessing youth outcomes. Given the severe limits placed on political activity by federally funded civic engagement programs such as AmeriCorps, there is a pragmatic role for philanthropy in supporting groups engaged in movement building and youth organizing.

* * *

This book has offered case studies of youth activism that vary along several dimensions. Some were local in scale, carried out by no more than ten to twelve youth, and initiated by educators in school classrooms or community organizations. Others emerged in relation to national and international networks of young people linked by shared concerns for immigration rights. Some began as groups of young people and adult facilitators in search of a compelling problem to fuel sustained action. Others, such as the Tracing Transition students fighting school closure, arose in response to a crisis. The campaigns reflected a mix of procedural goals (to facilitate opportunities for youth voice) and issue-based goals (to defend immigrant rights or dismantle the school-to-jail track). This variation is productive. Different efforts to foster voice and action are not in competition with each other. Democracy needs more procedural opportunities for youth voice, particularly in school decision making. Democracy also requires equitable educational opportunity—a thriving ecosystem of issue-based organizations that build the power of young activists can make that a reality.

Despite their differences, the groups profiled in these chapters are united by their treatment of young people as political beings who interpret policies, make judgments about justice and fairness, and have a stake in the quality of institutions that shape their everyday lives. They cultivate practices of critique and social dreaming, in which youth question what is and imagine what can be. But they don't stop there: they help marginalized youth develop power to wage campaigns about issues that matter to them. They promote human development while renewing democracy.

Jefferson students, fighting the closure of their school, voiced two slogans. The first, "Nothing for us without us," communicated their desire to be part of democratic decision making about their schools. They demanded dignity and respect. The second phrase, "Not down with the shut down" conveyed their desire to save a neighborhood school that had nurtured the development of prior generations; they opposed a school reform that dispossessed them of an essential community resource. "Not down with the shut down," in my reading, was also a prophetic cry against the broader foreclosure of opportunity facing youth of color in neighborhoods of concentrated poverty in the United States. Democratic participation. Educational opportunity. In their words and actions young people are joining the struggle for quality education in an unequal world.

METHODOLOGICAL APPENDIX

Study 1: Ethnographic Research about Youth Activism (2002–4)

Findings from this study, discussed in Chapter 4: Teaching without Teaching, are based on an ethnography I carried out over the course of two years in the San Francisco Bay Area. Research took place in three different multiracial youth groups: Youth Engaged in Leadership and Learning (YELL), Kids First, and Teens Restoring the Urban Environment (TRUE).[1]

YELL, which met at an urban high school with high percentages of students eligible for free and reduced lunch, was funded and staffed by a research center at a nearby university that sought to build partnerships with neighboring communities to promote positive youth development. YELL's specific purpose was to help high school students develop leadership and research skills so that they could gather evidence about conditions in their school or neighborhood and advocate for change based on their findings. Because of YELL's university affiliation, research and documentation were central to its mission.

YELL was comprised of seventeen youth ranging in age from 9th to 12th grade. The adult staff included one director, Michelle, and two AmeriCorps members, Beth and Korina. (All personal names are pseudonyms.) In the program's second year, which I focus on in chapter 4, YELL participants developed a campaign, called Don't Believe the Hype, to challenge media portrayals that perpetuated stereotypes about violence and academic underachievement among youth of color in their neighborhood.

Unlike YELL, Kids First was housed in a grassroots advocacy organization, not affiliated with any university, whose purpose was to advocate for children and youth. Six years earlier the advocacy organization had led a successful ballot measure that allocated a percentage of the city's budget to youth programs. Funding for Kids First was provided by a combination of foundations, membership dues, and the city of Oakland.

Kids First described itself as a multiracial youth organizing group that created opportunities for "youth to become visionary leaders capable of transforming their schools and communities." They met two days per week after school. Two part-time staff members, both in their early twenties, coordinated the group's activities, with the support of a full-time executive director. In its second year the group developed a campaign to reduce the high school dropout rate by promoting greater student voice in school governance. As part of this effort youth organizers asked their peers to fill out "report cards" that evaluated their schools. They also enlisted their fellow students in the campaign by inviting them to monthly "membership meetings," where visitors learned about the campaign goals, talked about their experiences in Oakland schools, and socialized with students from across the city.

TRUE's mission was "to foster an understanding of the principles of environmental justice and urban sustainability in our young people in order to promote the long-term health of their communities." In 2002–3, during the lead up to the U.S. invasion of Iraq, a group of youth and adults decided to plan a one-day conference for students about the consequences of war for the local environment. Unlike the other groups, there was no selection process for youth who wanted to join; anyone who showed an interest could participate. The number of youth who attended meetings varied. At some meetings there were as many as ten youth and at others as few as four. Seven youth were part of the group for at least two months. Of these, five were veterans of other TRUE programs and two were new members who had been recruited to participate by a TRUE veteran.

The purpose of the conference was to raise awareness among local youth about the impact of the U.S. military on their neighborhood and also to promote interaction between political figures and youth. The conference had three main parts: in the morning, neighborhood groups led workshops about issues ranging from juvenile justice to food security. At lunch a DJ performed and people experimented with graffiti art. After lunch there was an "accountability session," whose purpose was to get local politicians and their proxies to answer questions from youth. TRUE asked for political support for a resolution to limit military recruitment in public schools, which members feared was contributing to disproportionate enlistment by low-income students of color.

Unlike YELL and Kids First, the conference planning group was an ad hoc offshoot of TRUE rather than a program with stable funding and dedicated staff. Two AmeriCorps members were the most consistent adult representatives at the meetings. The executive director of TRUE came to several meetings, as did a program manager.

Data Sources

The study relied on four sources of data: observations of program activities, observations of special events, semi-structured interviews with youth and adults, and program artifacts, such as newsletters written by youth or handouts prepared by adults. (See Table A1 for amounts and types of data collected in each program.) I observed more program meetings in YELL because I began my research earlier in the year and because YELL met more frequently. Differences in numbers of interviews with youth reflected the different sizes of the groups. Interviews were tape recorded and transcribed. All field notes and interview transcripts were subsequently entered into N6, a software program for qualitative, text-based data analysis.

My observations and interviews were informed by interpretive, ethnographic approaches.[2] My role in each group varied. For example, in YELL I helped design the project, routinely sat in on meetings among adult staff members, and co-led a conference presentation about YELL with two youth participants. In Kids First I participated in team-building activities, helped small groups with tasks when asked, and

TABLE A1. Amount and Types of Data Collection

	YELL	Kids First	TRUE	Total
Duration of fieldwork	10 months	9 months	9 months	
Program meetings	57 (> 95 hours)	27 (> 60 hours)	18 (> 40 hours)	102 (> 195 hours)
Special events	9 (> 25 hours)	6 (> 12 hours)	4 (14 hours)	19 (> 51 hours)
Taped interviews	17 youth	8 youth and 1 adult	4 youth and 2 adults	29 youth and 3 adults
Artifacts (similar across groups)	• Program brochures and grant applications • Flyers • Newspaper articles • Youth-authored documents			

contributed my ideas to an evaluation plan for the program. Unlike in YELL or Kids First, in TRUE adults and youth treated me as a regular participant in the conference planning process—I was expected to offer opinions, vote on decisions, and implement necessary tasks.

Performing these different roles informed my comparison of the groups in two important ways. First, by being part of planning meetings in YELL I gained an insider view of adults' goals and decision making. I compensated for this unique access by finding opportunistic moments in Kids First and TRUE to ask staff people about their goals and decision making. Second, how I was positioned by members of each group was relevant to my analysis. For example, the fact that people in TRUE expected me to contribute along with everyone else to planning the conference gave me insight into the shared division of labor among adults and youth there.

Data Analysis

During fieldwork I developed a set of descriptive codes with three colleagues who were engaged in qualitative research in another youth program. We developed a shared set of low-inference codes intended to capture types of activities, leadership roles, and kinds of talk that could apply across multiple types of groups.

Initially I set out to identify the strategies that adults used to turn responsibility for the group over to youth so that it would become youth-led. It quickly became apparent, however, that Kids First and TRUE did not share this goal with YELL. Therefore, instead of approaching my study as a technical question about how adults support youth-led activities I sought to document the variety of approaches to working with youth that I observed and how these related to broader group goals and contexts.

Two codes were especially relevant to understanding adult-youth interaction patterns across groups: "activity leader" and "activity purpose." Activity leader referred to the person who initiated the activity, facilitated it, and called it to a close. Sometimes youth played this role, sometimes adults, sometimes a youth and an adult, and sometimes there was no clearly designated activity leader. Activity purpose referred to the kind of activity taking place, such as workshop, team building, campaign-related tasks, announcements, or hanging out. Beginnings and ends of activities were defined according to the agendas that the groups used to organize their meetings. Typically there were three to five activities during a given meeting. The following excerpts from two of the youth groups provide examples of how I coded "activity leader" and "activity purpose."

YELL, 12/17/02

It is 3:35, and young people are entering the room to begin the meeting. I hear Dolores, a youth participant, greet people by saying, "Hello, I'll be your facilitator today." After a few minutes, Dolores starts the meeting by asking people to be quiet. She asks a volunteer to read the agenda and then asks if anyone has questions. She proceeds to explain the opening team-builder activity, called "Sound Track," in which we are supposed to write down five songs that represent a sound track to our lives.

This example illustrates two codes of relevance to this analysis. First, it is an example of an activity led by youth because Dolores, a youth participant, initiated the meeting and explained instructions for the activity. Second, it is an example of an activity whose purpose was "team building," because the goal was to help members of the group get to know each other.

I coded this second example, from Kids First, differently:

Kids First, 2/13/03

It is 4:30 and the meeting is getting started. Alonzo, an adult staff member, hands out a piece of paper titled, "Liberation, Healing, Resistance." Alonzo asks someone to read the quote at the top of the page, which says: "Be grateful for blessings. Don't ever change—keep your essence. The power is in the people and the politics we address. Always do your best, don't let the pressure make you panic—Tupac Shakur."

After Christopher, a youth organizer, reads the quote, Alonzo reads it again in a hip hop cadence. He then asks other youth to read the rest of the page, which discusses strategies for overcoming "internalized oppression." [*This is one of the goals outlined in Kids First's evaluation plan—to build student's understanding of oppression and responses to it.*] When the quotes have been read, Alonzo asks, What does this all mean? A discussion ensues among participants.

This excerpt is an example of an "adult-led" activity, because Alonzo, an adult staff member, facilitated it. (Note that "adult-led" means that an adult initiated and facilitated the activity—it does not imply a particular method, such as didactic or inquiry-based.) The excerpt is also an example of a "workshop," because the activity's purpose was to introduce a new concept to youth ("internalized oppression") and give them opportunities to discuss its meaning.

In addition to these codes based on observational data, I analyzed interviews and group conversations to understand how participants interpreted their roles, responsibilities, and goals. I also examined the broader organizational context of each group, such as its history and mission.

These analyses contributed to two broad dimensions upon which to compare the groups: the level of adult participation in campaigns and the extent to which the learning environment was designed to respond to youth's skill levels and interests. After I had generated coherent descriptions of forms of guided participation I met with adults and some youth participants in each setting to get their feedback about the credibility of my analysis.

Study 2: "Tracing Transitions": Participatory Research about School Closure (2006–8)

The Tracing Transitions project, discussed in chapter 3, was motivated by two broad goals that called for two strands of research.[2] The first strand, called Student Experiences, used qualitative methods to document students' narratives about the school and its closure and also how they navigated opportunities and challenges in their new schools. These qualitative data were collected as part of a participatory action research (PAR) project with former Jefferson students. The second strand, called Academic Performance, examined whether Transition Cohort students experienced a change in academic performance that could be attributed to the closure. Detailed versions of each of these studies have been published in peer-reviewed journals coauthored with Kristen Pozzoboni and Matthew Gaertner.[3] This appendix summarizes key features of the methodology but more details can be found in those articles.

Strand One: Student Experiences

RESEARCH PARTICIPANTS

Research participants were recruited from the population of youth who attended Jefferson at the time of the closure. I distinguish "youth researchers" from "research participants." Whereas youth researchers were former Jefferson students who designed and carried out the PAR project, research participants were former Jefferson students who responded to interviews and surveys, participated in focus groups, or spoke at public meetings. Because most of the data collection for this study took place in the year following closure, the study relied primarily on respondents who had been in 9th, 10th, or 11th grade at the time of the closure. In addition to students still enrolled in school, we recruited twelve former Jefferson students who stopped going to school after the closure to participate in focus groups.

DATA COLLECTION

Five sources informed our qualitative analysis: surveys, peer interviews, focus groups with nonattending students, field notes, and interviews with youth researchers.

Open-Ended Surveys (n = 95)

Youth and adult researchers designed a two-page survey that asked students to describe their experiences in new schools in their own words. Prompts asked about goals, feelings of success and adjustment, perceived support from adults, level of challenge in classes, transportation, social environment, and extracurricular activities. Bilingual team members translated surveys into Spanish, which were then edited by a professional translator. For recruitment, at most schools an announcement was made inviting Jefferson students to attend a lunch meeting, where pizza was provided, to share their experiences. Some youth researchers recruited students to fill out surveys between classes or on the bus to school.

Peer Interviews (n = 21)
Youth researchers completed 21 ten-minute interviews and typed summaries of each interview. The interview protocol asked students to describe what was best and worst about their new schools and what they thought people should hear about the closure.

Focus Groups with Nonattending Students
Along with Kristen Pozzoboni, I led two focus groups with 12 former Jefferson students (8 males and 4 females) who were not in school and had not graduated. Some of them were trying to get back into school. We recruited them through an organization whose mission was to help out-of-school youth return to school. We asked students to describe their experiences since Jefferson closed, the circumstances of their leaving school, and their feelings about the closure. We sought out nonattending youth because the surveys and peer interviews recruited students who were still in school and we knew that some displaced students were not attending.

Field Notes from PAR Research Meetings (June 2006–May 2007, 47 meetings)
We documented group discussions about Jefferson student experiences.

Newspaper Articles (February 2006–June 2007; 40 articles)
The Tracing Transitions team reviewed articles about the closure. This review helped to establish a timeline of events and identify narratives emphasized by the media.

DATA ANALYSIS
The Tracing Transitions team worked collaboratively to identify major themes. First, the youth and adults tallied survey responses to give the group a sense of the distribution of responses in the data. Next, youth and adults identified seven important codes: relationships with adults, relationships with peers, benefits of the transition, challenges of the transition, comparisons of Jefferson to new school, opinions about the closure, and attitudes about school in general. The group split into pairs; each pair was responsible for analyzing the surveys and interviews in terms of one of the seven codes. The pairs were instructed to

highlight any statements that they thought were examples of the code. Highlighted statements were then typed into separate electronic files, so that there was a long list of quotations for each of our seven codes. Next, the group reorganized into different pairs to analyze each coding file. Pairs were instructed to create subthemes by reviewing the specific quotations that had been selected. This constituted a second reliability check, because if the two analysts believed a quotation was not relevant to the code they discarded it. In consequence, only quotations that had been agreed upon by at least three people were included as examples of a particular code.

The Tracing Transitions team presented our results summarizing students' views of the closure and their experiences in new schools in two meetings—one with senior officials from the district and the other with community members. Consistent with PAR, these meetings represented our first "actions" where the group sought to link the research to policy recommendations. Feedback spurred further conversations among team members about the findings.

The second phase of data analysis built on the work completed by the youth researchers, but focused specifically on the closure, rather than students' experiences in new schools. Along with Kristen Pozzoboni and Matthew Gaertner, we reanalyzed the data because we had not yet gained a satisfactory grasp of its nuances. This required a time commitment for which the youth researchers were no longer available. In this second phase, we met several times to discuss stories about Jefferson using a narrative lens. Narratives refer to recurring stories in the data about Jefferson or the closure process, not specific kinds of data sources. After developing an initial list of codes we coded the same data sources and met to discuss our interpretations several times. This led to a revised set of 18 codes, each of which evoked a different story about Jefferson. These researchers, working independently, coded the same 61 text statements and achieved an inter-rater reliability rating of .68 using Fleiss's kappa for the coding system as a whole. We then split up the remaining data sources and coded them independently using NVIVO.

When this process was completed we were able to view frequencies of specific stories as well as matrices that showed intersections between them. For example, we looked to see which codes were often linked together. We also examined internal variation to test whether the views of focus group participants, for example, differed from those of survey respondents. It also enabled us to examine variation across ethnicity and grade levels. Once we had identified which stories about Jefferson were most robust we wrote conceptual memos describing central themes. For example, a prevalent story about Jefferson was that students felt a "sense of belonging." Each analyst independently read through relevant data excerpts and identified what contributed to this sense of belonging for students, and we discussed our interpretations.

In our final phase of data analysis we met multiple times with four youth members of Tracing Transitions and one adult community member to solicit their perspective on puzzles in our data, test the validity of our emerging claims, and discuss implications. We also discussed our findings and solicited feedback from four additional community adults, two former Jefferson students, and two school district administrators.

ADDRESSING THE VALIDITY OF QUALITATIVE DATA
Selection Threats

Our qualitative data did not permit us to link academic records to individual respondents, so it is possible that our qualitative sample was not representative of the full cohort in terms of academic performance. Also, unlike survey recruitment, which did not rely on personal connections, youth researchers chose to interview peers whom they already knew, which may have created a biased sample of peer interviewees. Comparisons of themes in peer interviews and surveys, however, did not show meaningful differences.

Managing Researcher Bias

First, we managed bias by treating surveys, peer interviews, and focus groups as our primary data sources, rather than field notes or interviews with Tracing Transitions members, so as not to overrepresent the views of the youth researchers in our analysis. Second, adult and youth researchers participated in activities where we stated our goals for the study and our personal views of the closure. Doing so helped us clarify our purpose and make our biases transparent to each other. Third, we addressed bias by collecting data that could disconfirm our personal views and by including codes for both benefits and challenges, so as to capture respondents' full range of experiences.

Strand Two: Academic Performance

We investigated patterns in students' academic performance using three metrics: standardized test scores, dropout rates, and graduation rates. Consistent with other forms of community-based research, our study was designed in response to an unexpected event. As such, we sought to make optimal use of available data and naturally forming comparison groups. Statistician Matthew Gaertner led the quantitative analysis of data.

STANDARDIZED TEST SCORES

For the analysis of test scores, we obtained five years of linked student standardized achievement scores (2002–3 through 2006–7) in three content areas (reading, writing, and mathematics) for all students from the district. The test publisher vertically aligned these scores to enable comparisons over time. These tests were administered in March of each year to students in grades 3 through 10. Student-level descriptive characteristics available in this data set include school attended, grade level, status as an English learner (EL), status as a racial or ethnic minority, and eligibility for free or reduced-price lunch (FRL). Status as a student with special needs (IEP) was not available in the test score data set. For the analysis of test scores, we specified discontinuous individual trajectories via multilevel models. Two-level models were utilized to account for the nested structure of the data (i.e., yearly test administrations were nested within students).

DROPOUT AND GRADUATION RATES

Student-level data on dropout and graduation were obtained separately from test scores. Dropout and graduation data pertain only to Jefferson students; we were not provided districtwide data for these variables. The district provided "exit" records for students attending Jefferson in the academic years 2003–4 through 2005–6, and for Jefferson students who had transitioned to other schools in 2006–7. We used these records to analyze Jefferson students' graduation and dropout patterns before and after the closure. Student-level descriptive characteristics provided by the district include grade level, IEP, EL, minority, and FRL status. Using binary logistic regression, we modeled the closure's impact on students' likelihood of graduating or dropping out, conditional on student demographics and academic achievement.

Comparison Groups

The "treatment" group, referred to as the Transition Cohort, represented students who were in 9th, 10th, or 11th grade when the closure was announced. Transition Cohort students who stayed in the district enrolled in 23 comprehensive and alternative schools. Seventy percent of them attended four comprehensive schools. To identify whether their postclosure academic performance changed in ways that could be attributed to the closure, we established two comparison groups: Historic Jefferson and Other District.

Historic Jefferson

Historic Jefferson comprised students who attended Jefferson prior to the closure, during the years 2003, 2004, and 2005. Including this group enabled us to identify baseline test performance, graduation rates, and dropout rates with which to compare the Transition Cohort. This helped us rule out an alternative explanation that trends we observed for the Transition Cohort were typical of preclosure Jefferson students.

Other District

Other District comprised all students in the district who never attended Jefferson. This group provided a second reference point to which to compare Jefferson students and enabled us to rule out the alternative explanation that changes in Transition Cohort performance reflected district-level events that may have taken place during 2006 and 2007. Because districtwide student-level data on dropout and graduation rates were not available, Other District was only used for analyses of test scores.

Although we estimated our statistical models using all available student data, when reporting any closure effect we restricted the treatment and comparison groups to minority students eligible for free and reduced-price lunch. This matched the profile of the modal Jefferson student at the time of the closure. Doing so helped us estimate a discrete effect of closure controlling for family background or poverty status, as suggested by the literature on student mobility.[4]

Study 3: Critical Civic Inquiry (2010–13)

Critical Civic Inquiry (CCI), a research project developed by Ben Kirshner, Shelley Zion, and Carlos Hipolito-Delgado, partnered with secondary school teachers to engage students from underresourced schools in participatory action research as a vehicle for learning and equity-based school reform. CCI research was organized in two interrelated strands. Strand One focused on sociopolitical development among CCI participants. We employed a triangulation approach to mixed-methods research, which gathers qualitative and quantitative sources concurrently.[5] Strand Two, which utilized a range of qualitative sources, focused on features of school context that support or constrain student voice and teacher autonomy.

Strand One: Civic Development

INTERVIEWS

We conducted interviews with 5–8 CCI participants from each school at the end of each CCI year. We recruited participants in an effort to maximize variation in GPA and engagement in CCI activities. Interviews focused on participants' prior civic experiences, their school experiences, and their experiences in the CCI project.

OBSERVATIONS OF CCI ACTIVITIES

Observations of meetings were carried out ten times per semester at each school. Narrative field notes were typed and entered into qualitative software. Field notes focused on two dimensions of CCI activities: (1) student engagement, as demonstrated through verbal participation, body language, and task completion, and (2) the content of discussions, in terms of students' civic attitudes, prior civic experiences, and perceptions of the school climate.

STUDENT-LED SCHOOL TOURS

Researchers spent a part of the school day with one or two students to observe daily routines and elicit their interpretation of the school. We recruited a subsample of three CCI participants from each school to lead researchers on a tour of their school. These student-led tours enabled us to learn about students' experiences at the school and key events in their recent history that were related to the CCI projects.

STUDENTS' WRITTEN WORK

The CCI projects generated a range of written work completed by youth that displays their reasoning about social and political issues and the kinds of topics that were relevant to them.

QUANTITATIVE SURVEYS

Students completed a survey at three intervals: at the start of the academic year, end of the first semester, and the end of the second semester. The survey was based on three sets of instruments: the Civic Measurement Models, the Multigroup Ethnic Identity Measure, and the Patterns of Adaptive Learning Scales (PALS).[6] We included an ethnic identity measure because it assesses self-awareness and sociopolitical awareness for students of color; we anticipated that ethnic identity would be related to civic identity. We included PALS in order to see if participants' motivational orientations shifted over the course of the project.

For Year 2 data, which is discussed in chapter 1, we administered validated surveys at three time points (beginning, middle, and end of the academic year) to CCI participants and comparison students from the same schools ($n = 177$). Carlos Hipolito-Delgado led the statistical analysis. A split-plot MANOVA was conducted and revealed a statistically significant difference in academic engagement between the experimental and control group (Wilks $\lambda = .97$, $F(4, 169) = 2.85$, $p = .038$, $\eta^2 = .015$, Observed power $= .72$). The CCI group reported increases in academic engagement over three time points, in contrast to the control group, which declined in academic engagement. Also, we detected a statistically significant difference between groups in civic self-efficacy (Wilks $\lambda = .96$, $F(4, 168) = 3.39$, $p = .01$, $\eta^2 = .019$, Observed Power $= .85$). CCI participants experienced a growth in civic self-efficacy compared to comparison students whose civic self-efficacy decreased. This analysis was presented at the American Educational Research Conference in April 2014 and is in preparation for a peer-reviewed journal.[7]

Strand Two: Contexts for Student Voice and Action Civics

We collected data about school contexts through multiple sources. Three sources used for Strand One also contribute evidence to Strand Two: case study interviews, student-led school tours, and students' written work. For example, by interviewing CCI participants we gained a deeper understanding of the overall supports and opportunities for civic engagement in the school.

One important additional source for Strand Two was the perspective of CCI teachers. In Year 2, the CCI project shifted to a hybrid graduate seminar offered by the University of Colorado-Denver. The online portion of the course included readings, discussion threads, and weekly updates about how the CCI project was going. The face-to-face portion of the course met monthly to discuss readings and adopt a "workshop" method for teachers to share their work and instructional dilemmas. Data for chapter 5 of this book were drawn primarily from teacher reflections and posts in discussion threads, but also from notes taken during face-to-face seminar meetings.

Data Analysis

We worked as a team of five graduate students and three coprincipal investigators over the course of two summers to develop and iterate a coding scheme that captured data excerpts pertinent to both strands of our research. The construction of the coding scheme included a mix of deductive and inductive strategies. The selection of deductive codes was guided by core features of our theoretical framework, which situates student learning in an ecological context of classroom, schools, and neighborhoods. Inductive strategies included open coding, multiple group discussions about interview and field note transcripts, and attention to unique features of school contexts that appeared to mediate opportunities to learn. Once we had settled on codes we spent several meetings clarifying definitions and decision rules. Initial files were jointly coded until the coders were confident in their shared application of codes to a range of qualitative data.

In developing claims for chapter 1 of this book, I focused on two types of codes: Classroom Activity and Talk. For example, we developed codes for each step of the action research sequence; codes for "problem selection" and "taking action" helped me describe with precision the process by which Mr. Monteith's classroom implemented their project. With regard to Talk, key codes included "representing issues of power, privilege, and difference" and "talk about the school."

In developing claims for chapter 5, I relied primarily on codes describing instructional practices, such as "Sharing Power" and "Teacher Vulnerability." These codes were initially developed by a graduate student, Carrie Allen, as part of her effort to understand how CCI teachers carried out a democratic pedagogy in school contexts that had a strong focus on behavioral discipline and compliance.[8] They proved useful for locating examples of core instructional practices for CCI and how teachers enacted these in varied school contexts.

NOTES

INTRODUCTION

1. Watts and Flanagan (2007).
2. Seif (2004).
3. James and McGillicuddy (2001); Ginwright and James (2002).
4. James and McGillicuddy (2001), p. 2.
5. I use the term education "inequality" instead of "inequity" in the title primarily because of its resonance with the familiar term "income inequality" and I wanted to avoid technical language in the title. But I agree with the important distinction drawn by education scholars between *equality*, which connotes sameness, with *equity*, which connotes fairness. For example, equity demands that children growing up in poverty be supported with resources that enable them to thrive, which may exceed those needed by affluent children. Equality, to some people, means ensuring that all children receive the same resources. Although in places I use the terms interchangeably, the *equity* frame informs my analysis in this book.
6. Kwon (2013).
7. Checkoway and Richards-Schuster (2006).
8. Schneider and Ingram (1993); Vadeboncoeur (2005).
9. Akiva (2012).
10. Youniss and Hart (2005); Zeldin, Christens, and Powers (2012).
11. Youniss and Yates (1997).
12. United Nations (1990); Zeldin, Camino, and Calvert (2003).
13. Summaries of the methods for each study are presented in the Methodological Appendix.
14. Anyon (2005); Carter and Welner (2013); Gonzales (2011); Warren and Mapp (2010).
15. Lederman (2009).
16. Tough (2006).
17. Carter (2000).
18. Gonzales (2011).
19. Weis and Fine (2012); Ceballo, Huerta, and Epstein-Ngo (2010).
20. Oakes (2004).
21. Carter and Welner (2013); Noguera (2003).
22. Lee (2006).
23. Bonilla-Silva (2014); Reardon (2011); Rothstein (2013).

24. Reardon (2013).

25. Gabrielson, Jones, and Sagara (2014).

26. Coates (2014).

27. Hoytt, Schiraldi, Smith, and Ziedenburg (2002).

28. Hall (1904); Mead (1928).

29. Knox (2010); Cloud (2009); Friedman (2014).

30. Valencia (2010).

31. Skiba and Knesting (2001).

32. Rubin and Jones (2007).

33. Lesko (1996).

34. Mead (1928).

35. Rogoff et al. (2003).

36. Rogoff (2003).

37. Burton, Obeidallah, and Allison (1996).

38. Orellana et al. (2003).

39. Huisenga (2011).

40. Larson (2000); Lerner et al. (2005).

41. Kuhn and Franklin (2006).

42. Fielding (2004).

43. Kirshner, Gaertner, and Pozzoboni (2010); Kirshner and Pozzoboni (2011).

44. Kahne and Middaugh (2009); Levinson (2012); McFarland and Starmanns (2009).

45. McFarland and Starmanns (2009).

46. American Political Science Association (2004).

47. See Rubin (2007).

48. Bonilla-Silva (2014).

49. Library of Congress (2004).

50. Gutiérrez (2008).

51. Griffen-El (2014).

52. Levinson (2012); Rubin (2011); Cammarota and Romero (2014).

53. Cole (1996); Rogoff (2003); Weisner (1998).

54. Wortham (2005).

1. CRITIQUE AND COLLECTIVE AGENCY IN YOUTH DEVELOPMENT

1. Pseudonyms are used to protect the identity of the school, the teacher, and the students.

2. Interviews with Luis and Gabriela were carried out by Elizabeth Mendoza, who at the time was a doctoral student in Educational Psychology and Learning Sciences at the University of Colorado, Boulder. Certain parts of this interview were left out of the excerpt so that it would be more concise while preserving the meaning.

3. Weis and Fine (2012).

4. Microaggressions are brief and commonplace putdowns, sometimes unintentional, that communicate hostile or derogatory messages based on race or ethnicity.

See Balagna, Young, and Smith (2013); Ceballo, Huerta, and Epstein-Ngo (2010); Irizarry (2011); Solórzano, Ceja, and Yosso (2000); Sue et al. (2007).

5. Gonzales (2011); Ginwright (2010).

6. Ginwright, Noguera, and Cammarota (2005).

7. Watts, Williams, and Jagers (2003).

8. Kirshner, Mendoza, & Allen (2012).

9. Rogoff (1997).

10. Kahne and Westheimer (1996); Watts and Flanagan (2007).

11. Skiba and Knesting (2001); Skiba (2010).

12. Gregory (2014).

13. Greenberg et al. (2003); see also the Collaborative for Academic, Social, and Emotional Learning at http://www.casel.org.

14. Durlak and Weissberg (2011); Payton et al. (2008).

15. Duckworth and Eskreis-Wingler (2013); Tough (2012).

16. Duckworth (2013).

17. Sharkey (2009); Winship (2011).

18. Rose (2013).

19. National Research Council (2002); Larson (2000); Lerner et al. (2002).

20. See, for example, Cammarota and Romero (2014); Duncan-Andrade and Morrell (2010); Pacheco (2012); Rubin (2011); Stovall (2006).

21. Ginwright and Cammarota (2002).

22. Cole (1996).

23. Gramsci (2010).

24. Purcell (2012).

25. Prilleltensky (2008).

26. Baldwin (1963/2008); Biko (1980); Hipolito-Delgado, Gallegos Payan, and Baca (2014).

27. Baldwin (1963/2008).

28. Freire (1970/2002).

29. Cammarota and Fine (2008); Gutiérrez (2008).

30. Collatos et al. (2004); Rubin (2007).

31. Diemer and Hsieh (2008); Diemer and Li (2011).

32. Pollock (2008).

33. DeMeulenaere (2012); Duncan-Andrade (2007).

34. Kirshner, Hipolito-Delgado, and Zion (2014).

35. See Methodological Appendix for a description of methods.

36. Pollock (2005).

37. These interviews were carried out by Erin Allaman, who at the time was a doctoral student studying Educational Foundations, Policy, and Practice at the University of Colorado, Boulder.

38. Rose (2004).

39. I have not edited this text. "Mexicans/Americans" means, in this context, Mexicans and Americans.

40. Student Relations is the term for the office where school security handles disciplinary problems.

41. National Research Council (1999).

42. Kirshner, Hipolito-Delgado, and Zion (2014).

2. MILLENNIAL YOUTH AND THE FIGHT FOR OPPORTUNITY

1. Ndlovu (2010).

2. Wilson (2012), p. 111.

3. Primary schools were for grades 1–7, secondary schools for grades 8–12.

4. Ellis and Sechaba (1992).

5. Apartheid Museum (n.d.).

6. Wilson (2012).

7. Cohn (2010).

8. Flynn (2012).

9. Levine (2013).

10. Flanagan and Levine (2010).

11. Commission on Youth Voting and Civic Knowledge (2013).

12. Commission on Youth Voting and Civic Knowledge (2013), p. 24.

13. Levinson (2012), p. 14.

14. Hyman and Levine (2008).

15. Commission on Youth Voting and Civic Knowledge (2013).

16. Levinson (2012); Cohen (2010).

17. Bandura (1999); Flanagan and Faison (2001); Levinson (2012).

18. CIRCLE (2007).

19. Hyman and Levine (2008).

20. Commission on Youth Voting and Civic Knowledge (2013); Sullivan (2014).

21. Cohen (2010).

22. Hyman and Levine (2008); Cohen (2006).

23. Gonzales (2008).

24. Lopez and Marcelo (2008).

25. Perez et al. (2010).

26. www.gsa.network.org

27. www.gsaday.org

28. James and McGillicuddy (2001).

29. Ginwright (2003); Warren, Mira, and Nikundiwe (2008).

30. Torres-Fleming, Valdes, and Pillai (2010).

31. CIRCLE (2012); Robillard (2012).

32. Westheimer and Kahne (2004).

33. Watts and Flanagan (2007).

34. Cohen (2006); Hyman and Levine (2008); Levinson (2012)

35. Zuckerman (2013a).

36. In addition to my own analysis of newspaper articles and observations of presentations by DREAM Activists, I draw on five main scholarly sources for this

account: William Perez is one of the first researchers to tell the story of undocumented youth and their high levels of civic engagement. Roberto Gonzales has published several studies on the role of youth in immigration activism as well as the sociology of adolescence among undocumented youth. Hinda Seif published studies of the role of youth in immigration activism. Robert Nicholls published a book about the role of undocumented youth in the immigrant rights movement. Arely Zimmerman worked with a team of researchers from USC to study how DREAM Activists used social media to advance their efforts.

37. Perez (2009).

38. Perez (2009).

39. Perez (2009).

40. Wexler Love (2010).

41. Tracy, Coronel, & Martinez (2010), p. 10.

42. Discussed also in Gonzales (2011).

43. The version of the DREAM Act voted on in the House and Senate in 2010 would have provided conditional nonimmigrant status to undocumented immigrants under the age of 30 at the time of the bill's enactment who (1) arrived in the United States before the age of 16; (2) lived in the United States for at least five years; (3) have no criminal record; and (4) demonstrate good moral character. Those meeting the eligibility criteria would be granted conditional nonimmigrant status for ten years, during which time they would have to graduate from a U.S. high school (or equivalent), and complete an associate's degree, or two years toward a four-year degree, or serve two years in the military in order to apply for permanent residency.

44. Nicholls (2013); Zimmerman (2012).

45. Zimmerman (2012), pp. 42–43.

46. Corrunker (2012) wrote a helpful analysis of the global dimensions of this phenomenon, including the Sans Papiers movement of immigrants in France and related efforts by undocumented people in Montreal.

47. Nicholls (2013); Zimmerman (2012).

48. National Immigrant Youth Alliance (2010).

49. Nicholls (2013).

50. Flanagan, Levine, and Settersten (2009).

51. Cahill (2010); Corrunker (2012); and Gonzales (2008).

52. Cohen (2013).

53. Perez (2009); Zimmerman (2012); Vargas (2012).

54. Quoted in Nicholls (2013), location 1076-1077 (Kindle).

55. Quoted in Nicholls (2013), location 1087 (Kindle).

56. Abrego (2008).

57. *New York Times* Editorial Board (2010).

58. Robbins (2005).

59. Kwon (2006).

60. Contrast the kinds of police responses documented by the Advancement Project with a little-known story from Vermont. A group of teenagers held a party in the

empty former home of poet Robert Frost. They broke windows, consumed alcohol, and damaged property. The punishment? A series of classes on Frost's poetry taught by Middlebury College teacher and Frost expert Jay Parini (National Public Radio, 2008).

61. Hoytt et al. (2002).

62. Schiff (2013), p. 5.

63. Hoytt et al. (2002), p. 11.

64. Hoytt et al. (2002), p. 10.

65. Schollenberger (2013).

66. Stanley and Weaver (2014).

67. Data for this case study are primarily drawn from news articles available on the Internet. Some details about campaign events were documented through qualitative fieldwork carried out by Erik Dutilly, who was at the time a doctoral student in Educational Psychology and Learning Sciences at the University of Colorado, Boulder. Erik was employed as a graduate research assistant for an international youth organizing (IYO) research study led by Dr. Roderick Watts (principal investigator) and Ben Kirshner (coprincipal investigator). Because data collection for the IYO study was just getting underway at the time of writing this book, the findings from the IYO study, which focus on young people's learning, are not discussed here.

68. http://www.padresunidos.org

69. Rice (2013).

70. The report was called *Education on lockdown: The schoolhouse to jailhouse track.*

71. Restorative justice refers to a paradigm that aims to repair relationships between the offender, the victim, and the community at large, through mediation, dialogue, and accountability to each other. http://www.ojjdp.gov/mpg/progTypesRestorativeJustice.aspx

72. Its other main campaign effort has been immigrant student rights, in alliance with groups fighting for immigration reform and in-state tuition equity.

73. http://www.ed.gov/blog/2013/03/the-time-is-now-students-talk-school-and-community-safety-with-secretary-duncan/

74. Urie (2010).

75. Pease (2012).

76. Engdahl (2012).

77. Other members of this coalition included Alliance for Educational Justice, Dignity in Schools Campaign, Labor/Community Strategy Center, Youth United for Change, and the Gay-Straight Alliance Network.

78. Su (2010).

79. Su (2010), p. 377.

80. Jenkins et al. (2005), p. 3.

81. Schutz and Sandy (2011).

82. Renee, Welner, and Oakes (2010).

83. Nicholls (2013).

84. Levine (2013).

85. Sirriani (2005).

86. Gilman (2014).

87. Levine and Nierras (2007).

88. O'Connor, Hanny, and Lewis (2011).

89. Nicholls (2013).

3. "NOT DOWN WITH THE SHUT DOWN"

1. See Kirshner and Pozzoboni (2011), Kirshner, Gaertner, and Pozzoboni (2010), and Kirshner, Pozzoboni, and Jones (2011).

2. For particulars about the process of working in partnership with the Student Leadership Council, see Kirshner, Pozzoboni, and Jones (2011).

3. Cammarota and Fine (2008); Cook-Sather (2002).

4. Framing refers to a process in which people coordinate and mobilize certain narratives about their joint activity. A frame defines the meaning of a situation for participants interacting within it. See Benford and Snow (2000); Goffman (1974); Hand, Penuel, and Gutierrez (2012).

5. Lipman and Haines (2007); Maxwell (2006); Olson (2006).

6. Quaid (2009).

7. Carter and Welner (2013); Darling-Hammond (2004).

8. Maxwell (2006).

9. Briscoe and Khalifa (2013), for example, who analyzed the closure of a majority African American high school, found that district officials framed their decisions in technical or bureaucratic language that emphasized fiscal efficiency, enrollment data, and statistics about student performance. Chicago's mayor, for example, defended the school closures by pointing to an alleged looming deficit of $1 billion and data suggesting that many schools were underutilized. See Ahmed-Ullah, Byrne, and Chase (2013).

10. See Kirshner and Jefferson (in press) for a discussion of this evidence. See also Schott Foundation (2013); Huron (2013); Valencia (2008).

11. Galletta (2012).

12. Lipman (2004).

13. Herold (2011).

14. Kirshner (2010).

15. National Research Council (2002).

16. Cahill, Rios-Moore, and Threatts (2008); Horton (1990); Torre and Fine (2006).

17. Ginwright (2003).

18. Bamberg (2007); Howard (2008).

19. Hursh (2006).

20. For a full discussion of the methodology for this study, see Kirshner, Gaertner, and Pozzoboni (2010).

21. Rumberger (2003).

22. Croninger and Lee (2001); Lee and Smith (1999).

23. Rumberger (2003).

24. National Research Council (2003); Rubin and Silva (2003); Valenzuela (2005).

25. Deutsch and Hirsch (2002); McLaughlin (2000).
26. Eccles, Wigfield, and Schiefele (1998); Klem and Connell (2004).
27. Swanson (2009).
28. Hursh (2006).
29. Lipman (2004); Torre and Fine (2006).
30. Zeldin et al. (2000).
31. Kirshner (2008); Larson and Hansen (2005).
32. Zeldin, Camino, and Calvert (2003).

4. TEACHING WITHOUT TEACHING

1. Lave and Wenger (1991); Rogers, Morrell, and Enyedy (2007); Rogoff (2003).
2. Pollock (2005).
3. Soep and Chavez (2010); Wertsch (1998).
4. Gutiérrez (2008); Vygotsky (1978); Wertsch (1998).
5. MacLeod (1987); Way (1998).
6. Perlstein (2002); Piaget (1965).
7. Hunt, Benford, and Snow (1994).
8. Ginwright and James (2002); Tejeda, Espinoza, and Gutiérrez (2003).
9. This analysis is based on findings presented in Kirshner (2008).
10. Rogoff (2003).
11. McLaughlin (2000).
12. Brown, Collins, and Duguid (1989).
13. Schutz and Sandy (2002).
14. Freire (1970/2002); Kilgore (1999).
15. Larson and Hansen (2005).
16. Youth facilitated 53 percent of activities in YELL, 24 percent of activities in Kids First, and 10 percent of activities in TRUE. I calculated these percentages by dividing the number of activities facilitated by youth (either alone or jointly with an adult) by the total number of activities for which there was a designated facilitator in the notes. Activities without a designated facilitator were not counted in the analysis. They are based on coding a random subsample of 114 activities in YELL, 41 activities in Kids First, and 30 activities in TRUE. (YELL meetings had a higher number of discrete activities than Kids First or TRUE.)
17. Larson (2000).
18. Rogoff et al. (2003).
19. Hogan (2002); O'Donoghue and Strobel (2006).
20. Nasir et al. (2006).
21. Packer and Goicoechea (2000).

5. SCHOOLS AS SITES OF STRUGGLE

1. The photo, by Johnny Jenkins for UPI, can be viewed at: http://en.wikipedia.org/wiki/Elizabeth_Eckford
2. Margolick (2011).

3. Photographer not identified; images can be seen at http://blogging.la/2005/09/16/east-la-walkouts and http://www.pomona.edu/magazine/pcmsp08/FSmaninthemiddle.shtml.

4. Rosales (1997); Solorzano and Bernal (2001).

5. Lattanzio (2013).

6. *Al Jazeera* (2013).

7. Thomas (2012).

8. Tuck and Yang (2014).

9. Levinson (2012); Rubin (2011); Schultz (2008).

10. For Los Angeles, see Rogers, Morrell, and Enyedy (2007); for Tucson, see Cammarota (2007); for San Francisco Bay Area, see Ozer and Wright (2012).

11. Cervone and Cushman (2002); Rubin and Jones (2007).

12. Cammarota (2007); Gutiérrez (2008); Morrell (2008); Torre and Fine (2008).

13. Pollock (2008).

14. Levinson (2012).

15. Ozer and Schotland (2011); Rubin (2011).

17. Two years later, as of this writing, six of the seven people are still working as teachers in Colorado schools. One person is in law school.

18. One can see that in the state of Arizona's decision to terminate Tucson's Raza Studies program because of its alleged "anti-American" tendencies. In January 2012, bowing to pressure from the state of Arizona, the Tucson Unified School Board closed its Mexican American Studies program. The state argued that Mexican American Studies was contrary to American values of individualism and color blindness. Supporters marshaled evidence that participation was linked to better graduation rates and academic learning. Students testified that learning about Mexican American culture and history promoted the relevance of school and their identity development; Ceasar (2011a, 2011b).

19. See appendix for a discussion of research methods utilized in the CCI project.

20. The teacher was referring to *Spectacular Things Happen Along the Way*, by Aaron Schultz (2008).

21. See, for example, http://www.edliberation.org/

22. See John W. Gardner Center for Youth and their Communities (2014); Sabo Flores (2008); Center for Education in Law and Democracy (n.d.). Additional resources can be found at http://generationcitizen.org/, http://www.mikvachallenge.org/, http://actioncivicscollaborative.org/

23. Voussoughi et al. (2013).

24. Nakkula and Toshalis (2006).

CONCLUSION

1. McDermott (2010); Valencia (2010).

2. Task Force on Youth Development and Community Programs (1992).

3. Baldridge (2014).

4. Becker (2001).

5. Valencia (2010); Ladson-Billings (1997); Noguera (2008); Valenzuela (2005).

6. Baldwin (1963/2008).

7. Nasir et al. (2006).

8. Prout (2005).

9. Baldridge (2014), p. 462.

10. Paris and Alim (2014).

11. Flanagan (2013) describes this well: "(T)eens' political theories are built up over time as they negotiate power and privilege in their relationships; as they encounter discrimination and wrestle with exclusion; and as they interact with fellow citizens from diverse backgrounds, reflect on the different perspectives they bring to the table, and try to find common ground" (p. 13).

12. McDermott (2010)

13. Baldwin (1963), p. 18.

14. Holland et al. (1998); Wortham (2005).

15. Adi (2013).

16. Nakkula and Toshalis (2006).

17. Baldridge (2014).

18. Baldridge (2014).

19. Zeldin, Christens, and Powers (2012).

20. Brown, Collins, and Duguid (1989); Li and Julian (2012); Rogoff et al. (2003).

21. Camino (2005); Zion and Petty (2014).

22. Campbell and Erbstein (2012).

23. See, for example, Heck and Subramaniam (2009).

24. National Research Council (2002).

25. See, for example, Vance (2012); Stone and Rennekamp (2004).

26. California Tomorrow (n.d.).

27. Duncan-Andrade (2007); Jean and Zion (in preparation); Nakkula and Toshalis (2006).

28. Pollock (2008).

29. Levine (2013); Levinson (2013); Rubin (2011).

30. Levinson (2012), location 3550 in Kindle.

31. Common Core State Standards Initiative (2014).

32. Levinson (2012); Pope, Stolte, and Cohen (2011).

33. McDevitt and Caton-Rosser (2009).

34. Fung (2007); Hanson (2013).

35. Ito et al. (2013).

36. Mitra (2008).

37. Gilman (2014).

38. Welner (2001).

39. Oakes and Lipton (2002); Renee, Welner, and Oakes (2010).

40. Jurow et al. (2014); Kurtz (2003); Nespor (2008).

41. Kirshner (2014).

42. Kurtz (2003).

43. Howe and Meens (2012).

44. Zuckerman (2013b).

45. Anyon (2005); Bonilla-Silva (2014); Oakes and Lipton (2002); Oakes and Rogers (2006).

46. Sukarieh and Tannock (2011).

47. INCITE: Women of Color against Violence (2007).

METHODOLOGICAL APPENDIX

1. Becker (1998); Spradley (1979).

2. Creswell and Tashakkori (2007).

3. Kirshner and Pozzoboni (2011); Kirshner, Gaertner, and Pozzoboni (2010).

4. Rumberger (2003).

5. Creswell and Plano-Clark (2006).

6. Flanagan, Syvertsen, and Stout (2007); Midgley et al. (2000).

7. Kirshner, Hipolito-Delgado, and Zion (2014).

8. Allen and Kirshner (2012).

BIBLIOGRAPHY

Abrego, L. (2008). Legitimacy, social identity, and the mobilization of law: The effects of Assembly Bill 540 on undocumented students in California. *Law & Social Inquiry, 33*(3), 709–734. doi:10.1111/j.1747-4469.2008.00119.x

Adi, L. Z. (2013, May 8). Does it matter that Middle East studies failed to predict the "Arab Spring"? | Al Qawl. Retrieved from https://blogs.commons.georgetown.edu/alqawl/2013/05/08/does-it-matter-that-middle-east-studies-failed-to-predict-the-arab-spring-2/

Ahmed-Ullah, N. S., Byrne, J., & Chase, J. (2013, March 21). Chicago public schools closings. *Chicago Tribune.* Chicago, Ill. Retrieved from http://articles.chicagotribune.com/2013-03-21/news/chi-cps-to-announce-school-closings-foes-say-they-will-target-minorities-20130320_1_cps-and-city-hall-school-district-clarice-berry

Akiva, T. (2012, March). *Involving youth in running youth programs: How common and what might it do for youth?* Paper presented at the biennial meeting of the Society for Research on Adolescence, Vancouver, B.C., Canada.

Allen, C. & Kirshner, B. (2012, November). *"Find a way or make one": A case study of youth participatory action research within No Excuses schools.* Paper presented at the annual meeting of the American Anthropological Association, San Francisco, Calif.

Al Jazeera (2013). Newark students walkout over cutbacks. Retrieved online from http://stream.aljazeera.com/story/201304102124-0022669

American Political Science Association (2004). *American democracy in an age of rising inequality* (pp. 1–22). American Political Science Association: Task Force on Inequality and American Democracy.

American Psychological Association (2014). *Undocumented Americans.* Retrieved online from http://www.apa.org/topics/immigration/undocumented-video.aspx

Anyon, J. (2005). *Radical possibilities: Public policy, urban education, and a new social movement.* New York: Routledge.

Apartheid Museum (n.d.). Permanent exhibit: The significance of 1976. Johannesburg, South Africa.

Balagna, R. M., Young, E. L., & Smith, T. B. (2013). School experiences of early adolescent Latinos/as at risk for emotional and behavioral disorders. *School Psychology Quarterly, 28*(2), 101–121. doi:10.1037/spq0000018

Baldridge, B. J. (2014). Relocating the deficit: Reimagining black youth in neoliberal times. *American Educational Research Journal, 51*(3), 440–472. doi:10.3102/0002831214532514

Baldwin, J. (1963/2008). A talk to teachers. *Yearbook of the National Society for the Study of Education, 107*(2), 15–20. doi:10.1111/j.1744-7984.2008.00154.x

Bamberg, M. (2007). Considering counter-narratives. In M. Bamberg & M. Andrews (eds.) *Considering counter-narratives: Narrating, resisting, making sense* (pp. 351–372). Herndon, Va.: John Benjamins Publishing Company.

Bandura, A. (1999). *Self-efficacy: The exercise of control.* New York: W. H. Freeman & Company.

Becker, E. (2001, February 9). As ex-theorist on young "superpredators," Bush aide has regrets. *New York Times.* Retrieved from http://www.nytimes.com

Becker, H. (1998). *Tricks of the trade: How to think about your research while you're doing it.* Chicago, Ill.: University of Chicago Press.

Benford, R., & Snow, D. (2000). Framing processes and social movements: An overview and assessment. *Annual Review of Sociology, 26,* 611–639.

Biko, S. (1980/2002). *I write what I like: Selected writings.* Chicago, Ill.: University of Chicago Press.

Bonilla-Silva, E. (2014). *Racism without racists: Color-blind racism and the persistence of racial inequality in the United States* (4th ed.). New York: Rowman & Littlefield.

Bourdieu, P. (1977). *Outline of a theory of practice.* Cambridge: Cambridge University Press.

Briscoe, F. M., & Khalifa, M. A. (2013). "That racism thing": A critical race discourse analysis of a conflict over the proposed closure of a black high school. *Race, ethnicity and education.* DOI: 10.1080/13613324.2013.792798

Brown, J. S., Collins, A., & Duguid, P. (1989). Situated cognition and the culture of learning. *Education Researcher, 18*(1), 32–42. doi:10.3102/0013189X018001032

Burton, L. M., Obeidallah, D. A., & Allison, K. (1996). Ethnographic insights on social context and adolescent development among inner-city African-American teens. In R.A. Shweder, A. Colby, & R. Jessor (eds.), *Ethnography and human development: Context and meaning in social inquiry* (pp. 396–418). Chicago, Ill.: University of Chicago Press.

Cahill, C. (2010). "Why do they hate us?" Reframing immigration through participatory action research. *Area, 42*(2), 152–161. doi:10.1111/j.1475-4762.2009.00929.x

Cahill, C., Rios-Moore, I., & Threatts, T. (2008). Different eyes/open eyes: Community-based participatory action research. In J. Cammarota & M. Fine (eds.), *Revolutionizing education: Youth participatory action research in motion* (pp. 89–124). New York: Routledge.

California Tomorrow (n.d.). Equity and diversity in after school and youth programs initiative. Retrieved from http://www.californiatomorrow.org/publications/print/index.php?cat_id=3

Camino, L. (2005). Pitfalls and promising practices of youth-adult partnerships: An evaluator's reflections. *Journal of Community Psychology, 33*(1), 75–85.

Cammarota, J. (2007). A social justice approach to achievement: Guiding Latina/o students toward educational attainment with a challenging, socially relevant curriculum. *Equity and Excellence in Education, 40,* 87–96. doi:10.1080/10665680601015153

Cammarota, J., & Fine, M. (eds.). (2008). *Revolutionizing education: Youth participatory action research in motion.* New York: Routledge.

Cammarota, J., & Romero, A. (eds.) (2014). *Raza studies: The public option for educational revolution.* Tucson: University of Arizona Press.

Campbell, D. & Erbstein, N. (2012). Engaging youth in community change: A comparative analysis of seven coalitions. *Community Development, 43*(1), 63–79.

Carter, P. L., & Welner, K. (eds.). (2013). *Closing the opportunity gap: What America must do to give every child an even chance.* New York: Oxford University Press. doi:10.1093/acprof:oso/9780199982981.001.0001

Carter, S. C. (2000). *No excuses: Lessons from 21 high-performing, high-poverty schools.* Washington, D.C.: Heritage Foundation.

Ceasar, S. (2011a, November 20). Arizona educators clash over Mexican American studies. *Los Angeles Times Articles.* Retrieved from http://articles.latimes.com/2011/nov/20/nation/la-na-ethnic-studies-20111120

Ceasar, S. (2011b, December 27). Tucson's ethnic-studies program violates Arizona law, judge rules. *Los Angeles Times Articles.* Retrieved from http://articles.latimes.com/2011/dec/27/nation/la-na-tucson-mexican-american-studies-20111228

Ceballo, R., Huerta, M., & Epstein-Ngo, Q. (2010). Parental and school influences promoting academic success among Latino students. In J. L. Meece and J. S. Eccles (eds.), *Handbook of research on schools, schooling, and human development* (pp. 6–21). New York: Routledge.

Center for Education in Law and Democracy (n.d.). *pARTicipation: A civic engagement curriculum.* Retrieved from http://www.lawanddemocracy.org/celebrate.html.

Cervone, B., & Cushman, K. (2002). Moving youth participation into the classroom: Students as allies. *New Directions for Youth Development, 2002*(96), 83–100. doi:10.1002/yd.28

Checkoway, B., & Richards-Schuster, K. (2006). Youth participation for educational reform in low-income communities of color. In S. Ginwright, P. Noguera, & J. Cammarota (eds.), *Beyond resistance: Youth activism and community change* (pp. 319–330). New York: Routledge.

CIRCLE (2012). *At least 80 electoral votes depended on youth.* Medford, Mass.: Center for Information and Research on Civic Learning and Engagement. Retrieved from http://www.civicyouth.org/at-least-80-electoral-votes-depended-on-youth/

Cloud, J. (2009, September 2). The teen brain: The more mature, the more reckless. *Time.* Retrieved from http://www.time.com/time/health/article/0,8599,1919663,00.html

Coates, T. N. (2014, August 18). Reparations for Ferguson: Total police control over black bodies has echoes in American history. *The Atlantic.* Retrieved from http://www.theatlantic.com/national/archive/2014/08/Reparations-For-Ferguson/376098/

Cohen, C. J. (2006). African American youth: Broadening our understanding of politics, civic engagement, and activism. *Youth Activism SSRC Web Forum.* Retrieved from http://ya.ssrc.org/african/Cohen/pf

Cohen, C. J. (2010). *Democracy remixed: Black youth and the future of American politics.* New York: Oxford University Press.

Cohen, M. (2013, October 23). Signs of a shift on immigration among G.O.P. rank-and-file. *New York Times.* Retrieved from http://fivethirtyeight.blogs.nytimes.com/2013/02/08/signs-of-a-shift-on-immigration-among-g-o-p-rank-and-file/

Cohn, D. (2010, February 24). A demographic portrait of the millennial generation. *Pew Research Center's Social & Demographic Trends Project.* Retrieved from http://www.pewsocialtrends.org/2010/02/24/a-demographic-portrait-of-the-millennial-generation/

Cole, M. (1996). *Cultural psychology: A once and future discipline.* Cambridge, Mass.: Harvard University Press.

Collaborative for Academic, Social, and Emotional Learning. (n.d.) *What is social and emotional learning?* Retrieved online from http://www.casel.org/social-and-emotional-learning/

Collatos, A., Morrell, E., Nuno, A., & Lara, R. (2004). Critical sociology in K-16 early intervention: Remaking Latino pathways to higher education. *Journal of Hispanic Higher Education, 3*(2), 164–179. doi:10.1177/1538192704262989

Commission on Youth Voting and Civic Knowledge. (2013). *All together now: Collaboration and innovation for youth engagement.* Medford, Mass.: CIRCLE. Retrieved from http://www.civicyouth.org/about-circle/commission-on-youth-voting-civic-knowledge/

Common Core State Standards Initiative (2014). *Key shifts in English Language Arts.* Retrieved from http://www.corestandards.org/other-resources/key-shifts-in-english-language-arts/

Cook-Sather, A. (2002). Authorizing students' perspectives: Toward trust, dialogue, and change in education. *Educational Researcher, 31*(4), 3–14.

Corrunker, L. (2012). "Coming out of the shadows": Dream Act activism in the context of global anti-deportation activism. *19 Indiana Journal of Global Legal Studies 143 (2012), 19*(1). Retrieved from http://www.repository.law.indiana.edu/ijgls/vol19/iss1/6

Creswell, J. W., & Plano-Clark, V. L. (2006). *Designing and conducting mixed methods research.* Thousand Oaks, Calif.: Sage Publications.

Creswell, J. W., & Tashakkori, A. (2007). Editorial: Developing publishable mixed methods manuscripts. *Journal of Mixed Methods Research, 1*(2), 107–111.

Croninger, R., & Lee, V. (2001). Social capital and dropping out of high school: Benefits to at-risk students of teachers' support and guidance. *Teachers College Record, 103*(4), 548–581. doi:10.1111/0161-4681.00127

Darling-Hammond, L. (2004). Inequality and the right to learn: Access to qualified teachers in California's public schools. *Teacher's College Record, 106*(10), 1936–1966. doi:10.1111/j.1467-9620.2004.00422.x

Delgado, M., & Staples, L. (2007). *Youth-led community organizing: Theory and action.* New York: Oxford University Press. doi:10.1093/acprof:oso/9780195182767.001.0001

DeMeulenaere, E. (2012). Toward a pedagogy of trust. In S. Michaels & C. Dudley-Martin (eds.), *High-expectation curricula: Helping all students succeed with powerful learning*. New York: Teachers College Press.

Deutsch, N., & Hirsch, B. (2002). A place to call home: Youth organizations in the lives of inner city adolescents. In T. Brinthaupt & R. Lipka (eds.) *Understanding early adolescent self and identity: Applications and interventions* (pp. 293–320). Albany, N.Y.: State University of New York Press.

Diemer, M. A., & Hsieh, C. (2008). Sociopolitical development and vocational expectations among lower-SES adolescents of color. *Career Development Quarterly, 56*(3), 257–267. doi:10.1002/j.2161-0045.2008.tb00040.x

Diemer, M. A., & Li, C. (2011). Critical consciousness and political engagement among marginalized youth. *Child Development, 82*(6), 1815–1833. doi:10.1111/j.1467-8624.2011.01650.x

Downey, M. (2009, November 3). Robert P. Moses: We tolerate a "sharecropper's education." *Atlanta Journal Constitution: Get Schooled Blog*. Retrieved from http://blogs.ajc.com/get-schooled-blog/2009/11/03/robert-p-moses-we-tolerate-a sharecroppers-education/?cxntfid=blogs_get_schooled_blog

Duckworth, A. L. (2013). *Research statement*. Retrieved from https://sites.sas.upenn .edu/duckworth/pages/research-statement

Duckworth, A. L., & Eskreis-Wingler, L. (2013). True Grit. *Observer: Association for Psychological Science, 26*(4). Retrieved from http://www.psychologicalscience.org/ index.php/publications/observer/2013/april-13/true-grit.html

Duncan-Andrade, J. (2007). Gangstas, Wankstas, and Ridas: Defining, developing, and supporting effective teachers in urban schools. *International Journal of Qualitative Studies in Education, 20*(6), 617–638. doi:10.1080/09518390701630767

Duncan-Andrade, J., & Morrell, E. (2010). *The art of critical pedagogy: Possibilities for moving from theory to practice in urban schools*. New York: Peter Lang.

Durlak, J. A., & Weissberg, R. P. (2011). Promoting social and emotional development is an essential part of students' education. *Human Development, 54*(1), 1–3. doi:10.1159/000324337

Eccles, J. S., Wigfield, A., & Schiefele, U. (1998). Motivation to succeed. In W. Damon & N. Eisenberg (eds.), *Handbook of child psychology*, 5th ed.: Vol. 3. *Social, emotional, and personality development* (pp. 1017–1095). Hoboken, N.J.: John Wiley & Sons.

Ellis, S., & Sechaba, T. (1992). *Comrades against apartheid: The ANC and the South African Communist Party in exile*. Bloomington: Indiana University Press.

Engdhal, T. (2012, May 9). Key bills rescued as session ends. *Chalkbeat Colorado*. Retrieved from http://co.chalkbeat.org/2012/05/09/four-orphaned-ed-bills-find -homes/

Fielding, M. (2004). Transformative approaches to student voice: Theoretical underpinnings, recalcitrant realities. *British Educational Research Journal, 30*(2), 295–311. doi:10.1080/0141192042000195236

Flanagan, C. A. (2013). *Teenage citizens: The political theories of the young*. Cambridge, Mass.: Harvard University Press.

Flanagan, C., & Faison, N. (2001). *Youth civic development: Implications of research for social policy and programs.* Ann Arbor, Mich.: Society for Research in Child Development.

Flanagan, C., & Levine, P. (2010). Civic engagement and the transition to adulthood. *The Future of Children, 20*(1), 159–179. doi:10.1353/foc.0.0043

Flanagan, C., Levine, P., & Settersten, R. (2009). *Civic engagement and the changing transition to adulthood.* Medford, Mass.: Center for Information and Research on Civic Learning and Engagement.

Flanagan, C. A., Syvertsen, A. K., & Stout, M. D. (2007, May). *Civic measurement models: Tapping adolescents' civic engagement* (Working Paper 55). College Park, Md.: Center for Information & Research on Civic Learning & Engagement.

Flynn, B. (2012). *What's wrong with Congress? It's not big enough. CNN.* Retrieved July 3, 2014, from http://www.cnn.com/2012/03/09/opinion/flynn-expand-congress/index.html

Freire, P. (1970/2002). *Pedagogy of the oppressed.* New York: Continuum.

Friedman, R. A. (2014, June 28). Why teenagers act crazy. *New York Times.* Retrieved from http://www.nytimes.com/2014/06/29/opinion/sunday/why-teenagers-act-crazy.html

Frontline (n.d.). Do your teens seem like aliens? *Inside the teenage brain, Frontline, PBS.* Retrieved from http://www.pbs.org/wgbh/pages/frontline/shows/teenbrain/etc/aliens.html

Fung, A. (2007). Democratic theory and political science: A pragmatic method of constructive engagement. *American Political Science Review, 101*(3), 443–458. doi:10.1017/S000305540707030X

Gabrielson, R., Jones, R. G., & Sagara, E. (2014, October 10). Deadly force, in black and white. *ProPublica.* Retrieved from http://www.propublica.org/article/deadly-force-in-black-and-white

Galletta, A. (2012). Participatory action research. *Cleveland State University.* Retrieved from http://www.csuohio.edu/cehs/departments/C_F/participatory_action/Participation_action_research.html

Gilman, H. R. (2014, June 26). What happened when the city of Boston asked teenagers for help with the budget. *Next City.* Retrieved from http://nextcity.org/daily/entry/boston-young-people-participatory-budgeting-winners-youth-lead-change

Ginwright, S. (2003). *Youth organizing: Expanding possibilities for youth development* (Occasional paper No. 3). New York: Funders Collaborative on Youth Organizing.

Ginwright, S., & Cammarota, J. (2002). New terrain in youth development: The promise of a social justice approach. *Social Justice, 29*(4), 82–95.

Ginwright, S., & James, T. (2002). From assets to agents of change: Social justice, organizing, and youth development. *New Directions for Youth Development, 96,* 27–46. doi:10.1002/yd.25

Ginwright, S. A. (2010). *Black youth rising: Activism and radical healing in urban America.* New York: Teachers College Press.

Ginwright, S., Noguera, P., & Cammarota, J. (eds.) (2005). *Beyond resistance: Youth activism and community change: New democratic possibilities for policy and practice for America's youth.* Oxford, U.K.: Routledge.

Goffman, E. (1974). *Frame analysis: An essay on the organization of experience.* London: Harper and Row.

Gonzales, R. G. (2008). Left out but not shut down: Political activism and the undocumented student movement. *Northwestern Journal of Law and Social Policy, 3*(2), 219–239.

Gonzales, R. G. (2011). Learning to be illegal. *American Sociological Review, 76*(4), 602–619. doi:10.1177/0003122411411901

Gordon, H. (2010). *We fight to win: Inequality and the politics of youth activism.* New Brunswick, N.J.: Rutgers University Press.

Gramsci, A. (2010). *Prison notebooks.* New York: Columbia University Press.

Greenberg, M. T. et al. (2003). Enhancing school-based prevention and youth development through coordinated social, emotional, and academic learning. *American Psychologist, 58*(6–7), 466–474. doi:10.1037/0003-066X.58.6-7.466

Gregory, A. (2014). *Transforming schools and classrooms to reduce disparities in school discipline.* Presentation at the biennial meeting of the Society for Research on Adolescence, Austin, Texas.

Griffin-El, N. (2014). *The pedagogy of inclusive innovation through dreaming.* Unpublished manuscript. Retrieved from https://www.academia.edu/7540491/The_Pedagogy_of_Inclusive_Innovation_through_Dreaming

Gutiérrez, K. (2008). Developing a sociocritical literacy in the Third Space. *Reading Research Quarterly, 43*(2), 148–164. doi:10.1598/RRQ.43.2.3

Hall, G. S. (1904). *Adolescence: Its psychology and its relations to physiology, anthropology, sociology, sex, crime, religion and education.* New York: D. Appleton and Company.

Hand, V., Penuel, W. R., & Gutiérrez, K. D. (2012, April). *Framing to disrupt and expand opportunities to learn in multilevel educational systems.* Paper presented in April 2012 at the annual meeting of the American Educational Research Association, Vancouver, B.C.

Hanson, J. (2013). *In defense of a deliberative democratic civics education.* (Unpublished doctoral dissertation.) University of Colorado: Boulder.

Harper, S. R., & Associates (2014). *Succeeding in the city. A report from the New York City Black and Latino male high school achievement study.* Philadelphia: University of Pennsylvania, Center for the Study of Race and Equity in Education.

Hart, D. et al. (2007). High school community service as a predictor of adult voting and volunteering. *American Educational Research Journal, 44*(1), 197–219. doi:10.3102/0002831206298173

Heck, K. E., & Subramaniam, A. (2009). *Youth development frameworks.* 4-H Center for Youth Development, University of California, Davis.

Herold, B. (2011, March 31). Urban activists: School closures hurt our communities. *Education Week.* Retrieved from http://www.edweek.org/ew/articles/2011/03/31/27pnbk_schoolclosures.h30.html

Hipolito-Delgado, C. P., Gallegos Payan, S., & Baca, T. (2014). Self-hatred, self-doubt, and assimilation: Las consecuencias de colonización y opresión. In E. J. R. David (ed.). *Internalized oppression: The psychology of marginalized groups* (pp. 109–136). New York: Springer.

Hogan, K. (2002). Pitfalls of community-based learning: How power dynamics limit adolescents' trajectories of growth and participation. *Teachers College Record, 104*(3), 586–624.

Holland, D. et al. (1998). *Identity and agency in cultural worlds.* Cambridge, Mass.: Harvard University Press.

Horton, M. (with Kohl, H. & Kohl, J.). (1990). *The long haul: An autobiography.* New York: Doubleday.

Howard, T. C. (2008). Who really cares? The disenfranchisement of African American males in preK-12 schools: A critical race theory perspective. *Teachers College Record, 110*(5), 954–985.

Howe, K., & Meens, D. (2012). *Democracy left behind: How recent education reforms undermine local governance and democratic education.* Boulder, Colo.: National Education Policy Center.

Hoytt, E. H., Schiraldi, V., Smith, B. V., & Ziedenberg, J. (2002). *Reducing racial disparities in detention.* Baltimore, Md.: Annie E. Casey Foundation.

Huisenga, S. (2011, December 1). Newt Gingrich: Poor kids don't work "unless it's illegal." *CBS News.* Retrieved online February 2, 2012 from http://www.cbsnews.com/news/newt-gingrich-poor-kids-dont-work-unless-its-illegal/

Hunt, S. A., Benford, R. D., & Snow, D. A. (1994). Identity fields: Framing processes and the social construction of movement identities. In H. J. E. Larana, & J. R. Gusfield (eds.), *New social movements: From ideology to identity* (pp. 185–207). Philadelphia: Temple University Press.

Huron, A. (2013). DC schools slated for closure. Retrieved online May 3, 2013 from http://www.washingtoncitypaper.com/blogs/housingcomplex/2013/05/14/map-closing-schools-are-overwhelmingly-in-minority-neighborhoods/

Hursh, D. (2006). The crisis in urban education: Resisting neoliberal policies and forging democratic possibilities. *Educational Researcher, 35*(4), 19–25.

Hyman, J. B., & Levine, P. (2008). *Civic engagement and the disadvantaged: Challenges, opportunities, and recommendations* (CIRCLE Working Paper No. 63) (p. 20). Medford, Mass.: Center for Information and Research on Civic Learning and Engagement.

INCITE. (2007). *The revolution will not be funded: Beyond the non-profit industrial complex.* Boston, Mass.: South End Press.

Irizarry, J. (2011). Buscando la libertad: Latino youths in search of freedom in school. *Democracy and Education, 19*(1), 1–10. Retrieved from http://democracyeducation-journal.org/home/vol19/iss1/4

Ito, M. et al. (2013). *Connected learning: An agenda for research and design.* Irvine, Calif.: Connected Learning Research Network.

James, T., & McGillicuddy, K. (2001). Building youth movements for community change. *Non-Profit Quarterly, 8*(4), 1–3.

Jean, C., & Zion, S. (in preparation). *"I can't go back": The sociopolitical development of teachers in urban schools.* Denver: University of Colorado.

Jenkins, H. et al. (2005). Confronting the challenges of participatory culture: Media education for the 21st century. Retrieved from http://www.newmedialiteracies.org/wp-content/uploads/pdfs/NMLWhitePaper.pdf

John W. Gardner Center for Youth and Their Communities (2014). *Youth engaged in leadership and learning.* Stanford, Calif.: Stanford University. Retrieved from http://jgc.stanford.edu/our_work/yell.html

Jurow, S., Teeters, L., Shea, M., & Severance, S. (2014). *Transforming the scale of community advocacy in the movement for food justice.* Paper presented at the biennial meeting of the International Society of the Learning Sciences, Boulder, Colo.

Kahne, J., & Middaugh, E. (2009). Democracy for some: The unequal provision of civic learning opportunities in U.S. high schools. In J. Youniss & P. Levine (eds.), *Constructive policy for youth civic engagement* (pp. 29–58). Nashville, Tenn.: Vanderbilt University Press.

Kahne, J., & Westheimer, J. (1996). In the service of what? The politics of service learning. *Phi Delta Kappan, 77*(9), 593–599.

Kilgore, D. W. (1999). Understanding learning in social movements: A theory of collective learning. *International Journal of Lifelong Education, 18*(3), 191–202.

Kirshner, B. (2008). Guided participation in three youth activism organizations: Facilitation, apprenticeship, and joint work. *Journal of the Learning Sciences, 17*(1), 60–101. doi:10.1080/10508400701793190

Kirshner, B. (2010). Productive dilemmas in youth participatory action research. In W. R. Penuel & K. O'Connor (eds.), *Learning research as a human science* (pp. 238–251). *National Society for the Study of Education Yearbook, 109* (1).

Kirshner, B. (2014). *Every generation has its struggle.* Paper presented at the biennial meeting of the International Society of the Learning Sciences, Boulder, Colo.

Kirshner, B., & Jefferson, A. (in press). Participatory democracy and struggling schools: Making space for youth in school turnarounds. *Teachers College Record.*

Kirshner, B., & Pozzoboni, K. (2011). Student interpretations of a school closure: Implications for student voice in equity-based reform. *Teachers College Record, 113*(8), 1633–1667.

Kirshner, B., Gaertner, M., & Pozzoboni, K. (2010). Tracing transitions: Understanding the impact of a school closure on displaced students. *Educational Evaluation and Policy Analysis, 32*(30), 407–429. doi:10.3102/0162373710376823

Kirshner, B., Hipolito-Delgado, C., & Zion, S. (2014). *PAR as classroom pedagogy: Evidence of positive impact on youth development and school climate.* Paper presented at the annual meeting of the American Educational Research Association, Philadelphia, Pa.

Kirshner, B., Mendoza, E., & Allen, C. (2012, April). *Mapping disruptions of common sense: Place-making with students at Roosevelt High School.* Paper presented at the annual meeting of the American Education Research Association, Vancouver, B.C.

Kirshner, B., Pozzoboni, K., & Jones, H. (2011). Learning how to manage bias: A case study of youth participatory action research. *Applied Developmental Science, 15*(3), 140–155.

Klem, A., & Connell, J. (2004). Relationships matter: Linking teacher support to student engagement and achievement. *Journal of School Health, 74*(7), 262–274. doi:10.1111/j.1746-1561.2004.tb08283.x

Knox, R. (2010). The teen brain: It's just not grown up yet. NPR. *NPR.org.* Retrieved from http://www.npr.org/templates/story/story.php?storyId=124119468

Kuhn, D., & Franklin, S. (2006). The second decade: What develops (and how). In W. Damon et al. (eds.), *Handbook of child psychology, volume 2, cognition, perception, and language, 6th edition* (pp. 953–993). Hoboken, N.J.: John Wiley and Sons.

Kurtz, H. (2003). Scale frames and counter-scale frames: Constructing the problem of environmental injustice. *Political Geography, 22,* 887–916.

Kwon, S. A. (2006). Youth of color organizing for juvenile justice. In S. Ginwright, P. Noguera, & J. Cammarota (eds.), *Beyond resistance: Youth activism and community change: New democratic possibilities for policy and practice for America's youth* (pp. 215–228). Oxford, U.K.: Routledge.

Kwon, S. A. (2013). *Uncivil youth: Race, activism, and affirmative governmentality.* Durham, N.C.: Duke University Press. doi:10.1215/9780822399094

Ladson-Billings, G. (1997). *The dreamkeepers: Successful teachers of African-American children.* San Francisco, Calif.: Jossey-Bass Publishers.

Larson, R. W. (2000). Toward a psychology of positive youth development. *American Psychologist, 55*(1), 170–183. doi:10.1037/0003-066X.55.1.170

Larson, R., & Hansen, D. (2005). The development of strategic thinking: Learning to impact human systems in a youth activism program. *Human Development, 48*(6), 327–349. doi:10.1159/000088251

Lattanzio, V. (2013, May 18). Thousands of students walk out, protest budget cuts. *NBC 10 Philadelphia.* Philadelphia: NBC. Retrieved from http://www.nbc philadelphia.com/news/local/Philly-Teachers-Protest-Budget-Cuts-Student-Walkouts-207850051.html

Lave, J., & Wenger, E. (1991). *Situated learning: Legitimate peripheral participation.* Cambridge, U.K.: Cambridge University Press. doi:10.1017/CBO9780511815355

Lederman, D. (2009). College for all. *Inside Higher Ed.* Retrieved from http://www.insidehighered.com/news/2009/02/25/obama#ixzz2kPX8H6qN.

Lee, C. (2006). *Denver public schools: Resegregation, Latino style.* Cambridge, Mass.: Civil Rights Project.

Lee, V., & Smith, J. B. (1999). Social support and achievement for young adolescents in Chicago: The role of school academic press. *American Educational Research Journal, 36*(4), 907–945. doi:10.3102/00028312036004907

Lerner, R. M., Almerigi, J. B., Theokas, C., & Lerner, J. V. (2005). Positive youth development: A view of the issues. *Journal of Early Adolescence, 25*(1), 10–16.

Lerner, R. M., Brentano, C., Dowling, E. M., & Anderson, P. M. (2002). Positive youth development: Thriving as the basis of personhood and civil society. *New Directions for Youth Development, 95*(Fall), 11–36. doi:10.1002/yd.14

Lesko, N. (1996). Denaturalizing adolescence: The politics of contemporary representations. *Youth & Society, 28*(2), 139–161. doi:10.1177/0044118X96028002001

Levine, P. (2013). *We are the ones we have been waiting for: The promise of civic renewal in America.* New York: Oxford University Press.

Levine, P., & Nierras, R. M. (2007). Activists' views of deliberation. *Journal of Public Deliberation, 3*(1). Retrieved from http://www.publicdeliberation.net/jpd/vol3/iss1/art4

Levinson, M. (2012). *No citizen left behind.* Cambridge, Mass.: Harvard University Press. doi:10.4159/harvard.9780674065291

Li, J., & Julian, M. M. (2012). Developmental relationships as the active ingredient: A unifying working hypothesis of "what works" across intervention settings. *American Journal of Orthopsychiatry, 82*(2), 157–166. doi:10.1111/j.1939-0025.2012.01151.x

Library of Congress (2004). Exhibit: *Brown v. Board of Education of Topeka, Kansas— Brown v. Board at Fifty.* Retrieved online from http://www.loc.gov/exhibits/brown/brown-brown.html

Lipman, P. (2004). *High stakes education: Inequality, globalization, and urban school reform.* New York: RoutledgeFalmer. doi:10.4324/9780203465509

Lipman, P., & Haines, N. (2007). From accountability to privatization and African American exclusion: Chicago's "Renaissance 2010." *Educational Policy, 21*(3), 471–502. doi:10.1177/0895904806297734

Lopez, M. H., & Marcelo, K. B. (2008). The civic engagement of immigrant youth: New evidence from the "2006 Civic and Political Health of the Nation Survey." *Applied Developmental Science 12*(2), 66–73.

MacLeod, J. (1987). *Ain't no makin' it: Aspirations and attainment in a low income neighborhood.* Boulder, Colo.: Westview Press.

Margolick, D. (2011). Elizabeth Eckford and Hazel Bryan: The story behind the photograph that shamed America. *U.K. Telegraph.* Retrieved from http://www.telegraph.co.uk/news/worldnews/northamerica/8813134/Elizabeth-Eckford-and-Hazel-Bryan-the-story-behind-the-photograph-that-shamed-America.html

Maxwell, L. A. (2006, March 15). City districts tackle round of school closings. *Education Week, 25,* 7.

McDermott, R. (2010). The passions of learning in tight circumstances: Toward a political economy of the mind. *Yearbook of the National Society for the Study of Education, 109*(1), 144–159.

McDevitt, M. J., & Caton-Rosser, M. S. (2009). Deliberative barbarians: Reconciling the civic and the agonistic in democratic education. *InterActions: UCLA Journal of Education and Information Studies, 5*(2), 1–22. Retrieved from http://escholarship.org/uc/item/8qh731nz

McFarland, D., & Starmanns, C. E. (2009). Inside student government: The variable organization of high school student councils. *Teachers College Record, 111*(1), 27–54. Retrieved from http://www.tcrecord.org.

McLaughlin, M. (2000). *Community counts: How youth organizations matter for youth development.* Washington, D.C.: Public Education Network.

Mead, M. (1928). *Coming of age in Samoa.* New York: HarperCollins.

Metz, E. C., & Youniss, J. (2005). Longitudinal gains in civic development through school-based required service. *Political Psychology 26*(3), 413–437. doi:10.1111/j.1467 -9221.2005.00424.x

Midgley, C., et al. (2000). *Manual for the patterns of adaptive learning scales.* Ann Arbor, Mich.: University of Michigan, School of Education.

Mitra, D. L. (2008). *Student voice in school reform: Building youth-adult partnerships that strengthen schools and empower youth.* Albany, N.Y.: State University of New York Press.

Morrell, E. (2008). Six summers of YPAR: Learning, action, and change in urban education. In J. Cammarota & M. Fine (eds.), *Revolutionizing education: Youth participatory action research in motion* (pp. 155–183). New York: Routledge.

Nakkula, M. J., & Toshalis, E. (2006). *Understanding youth: Adolescent development for educators.* Cambridge, Mass.: Harvard Education Press.

Nasir, N. S. et al. (2006). Learning as a cultural process: Achieving equity through diversity. In R. K. Sawyer (ed.), *The Cambridge handbook of the learning sciences* (pp. 491–504). New York: Cambridge University Press.

National Immigrant Youth Alliance. (2010). *Facebook page.* Retrieved March 26, 2014, from https://www.facebook.com/NationalImmigrantYouthAlliance?sk=info

National Public Radio (2008, June 3). Vandals forced to study poetry of Frost. *NPR.org.* Retrieved from http://www.npr.org/templates/story/story.php?storyId=91126248

National Research Council (1999). *How people learn: Mind, brain, experience, and school.* Washington, D.C.: National Academies Press.

National Research Council (2002). *Community programs to promote youth development.* Washington, D.C.: National Academies Press.

National Research Council (2003). *Engaging schools: Fostering high school students' motivation to learn.* Washington, D.C.: National Academies Press.

Ndlovu, S. M. (2010). The Soweto uprising. In *The road to democracy* (pp. 317–368). Pretoria: Unisa Press. Retrieved from http://www.sadet.co.za/road_democracy_vol2.html

Nespor, J. (2008). Education and place. *Educational Theory, 58,* 475–489.

New York Times Editorial Board (2010, November 29). Dreaming of reform. Retrieved from http://www.nytimes.com/2010/11/30/opinion/30tue2.html?module=Search& mabReward=relbias%3As

Nicholls, W. (2013). *The DREAMers: How the undocumented youth movement transformed the immigrant rights debate.* Stanford: Stanford University Press. Kindle Edition.

Noguera, P. A. (2003). *City schools and the American dream: Reclaiming the promise of public education.* New York: Teachers College Press.

Noguera, P. A. (2008). *The trouble with black boys . . . and other reflections on race, equity, and the future of public education.* San Francisco, Calif.: Jossey-Bass.

O'Connor, K., Hanny, C., & Lewis, C. (2011). Doing "business as usual": Dynamics of voice in community organizing talk. *Anthropology & Education Quarterly, 42*(2), 154–171. doi:10.1111/j.1548-1492.2011.01122.x

O'Donoghue, J., & Strobel, K. (2006). *Directivity and freedom: The role of adults in empowering youth activists.* Paper presented at the biennial conference of the Society for Research on Adolescence, San Francisco, Calif.

Oakes, J. (2004). Investigating the claims in Williams v. State of California: An unconstitutional denial of education's basic tools? *Teachers College Record, 106*(10), 1889–1906. doi:10.1111/j.1467-9620.2004.00420.x

Oakes, J., & Lipton, M. (2002). Struggling for educational equity in diverse communities: School reform as social movement. *Journal of Educational Change, 3*(3–4), 383–406. doi:10.1023/A:1021225728762

Oakes, J., & Rogers, J. (2006). *Learning power: Organizing for education and justice.* New York: Teachers College Press.

Olson, L. (2006, September 20). As AYP bar rises, more schools fail: Percent missing NCLB goals climbs amid greater testing. *Education Week.* Retrieved from http://www.edweek.org/ew/toc/2006/09/20/index.html.

Orellana, M. F. et al. (2003). In other words: Translating or "para-phrasing" as a family literacy practice in immigrant households. *Reading Research Quarterly, 38*(1), 12–34. doi:10.1598/RRQ.38.1.2

Ozer, E. J., & Schotland, M. (2011). Psychological empowerment among urban youth: Measure development and relationship to psychosocial functioning. *Health Education & Behavior, 38*(4), 348–356. doi:10.1177/1090198110373734

Ozer, E. J., & Wright, D. (2012). Beyond school spirit: The effects of youth-led participatory action research in two urban high schools. *Journal of Research on Adolescence, 22*(2), 267–283. doi:10.1111/j.1532-7795.2012.00780.x

Pacheco, M. (2012). Learning in/through everyday resistance: A cultural-historical perspective on community resources and curriculum. *Educational Researcher, 41*(4), 121–132. doi:10.3102/0013189X12442982

Packer, M. J., & Goicoechea, G. (2000). Sociocultural and constructivist theories of learning: Ontology, not just epistemology. *Educational Psychologist, 35*(4), 227–241.

Paris, D., & Alim H. S. (2014). What are we seeking to sustain through culturally sustaining pedagogy? A loving critique forward. *Harvard Educational Review.* Retrieved online from http://her.hepg.org/content/982l873k2ht16m77/?p=eecc5274 f02b4c3cad1352855771b6c5&pi=5

Payton, J. et al. (2008). *The positive impact of social and emotional learning for kindergarten to eighth-grade students: Findings from three scientific reviews.* Chicago, Ill.: Collaborative for Academic, Social, and Emotional Learning.

Pease, R. (2012). *Padres y Jóvenes Unidos help win the smart school discipline law, overturning extreme post-Columbine approach. Public Interests Projects.* Retrieved July 3, 2014, from http://www.publicinterestprojects.org/featured/padres-y-jovenes-unidos-help-win-the-smart-school-discipline-law-overturning-extreme-post-columbine-approach/

Perez, W. (2009). *We ARE Americans; Undocumented students pursuing the American Dream.* Sterling, Va.: Stylus.

Perez, W. et al. (2010). Civic engagement patterns of undocumented Mexican students. *Journal of Hispanic Higher Education, 9*(3), 245–265. doi:10.1177/1538192710371007

Perlstein, D. (2002). Minds stayed on freedom: Politics and pedagogy in the African American freedom struggle. *American Educational Research Journal, 39*(2), 249–277. doi:10.3102/00028312039002249

Piaget, J. (1965). *The moral judgment of the child.* New York: Free Press.

Pollock, M. (2005). Race-bending. In S. Maira & E. Soep (eds.), *Youthscapes: The popular, the national, the global* (pp. 43–63). Philadelphia, Pa.: University of Pennsylvania Press.

Pollock, M. (2008). *Everyday antiracism.* New York: New Press.

Pope, A., Stolte, L., & Cohen, A. K. (2011). Closing the civic engagement gap: The potential of action civics. *Social Education, 75*(5), 267–270.

Prilleltensky I. (2008). The role of power in wellness, oppression, and liberation: The promise of psychopolitical validity. *Journal of Community Psychology, 36*(2), 116–136. doi:10.1002/jcop.20225

Prout, A. (2005). *The future of childhood: Towards the interdisciplinary study of children.* London: RoutledgeFalmer.

Purcell, R. (2012). Community development and everyday life. *Community Development Journal, 47*(2), 266-281. doi:10.1093/cdj/bsq058

Quaid, L. (2009, May 11). Obama wants to turn around 5000 failing schools. *Associated Press.* Retrieved from http://www.google.com/hostednews/ap/article/ALeqM5jEfL zvCMhD6B_TFxCPZ5GHU_O-4QD984AL6Go.

Reardon, S. (2011). The widening academic achievement gap between the rich and the poor: New evidence and possible explanations. In R. Murnane & G. Duncan (eds.), *Whither opportunity? Rising inequality and the uncertain life chances of low-income children* (pp. 91–115). New York: Russell Sage Foundation Press.

Reardon, S. (2013, November 12). No rich child left behind. *New York Times.* Retrieved from http://opinionator.blogs.nytimes.com/2013/04/27/no-rich-child-left-behind/

Renee, M., Welner, K. G., & Oakes, J. (2010). Social movement organizing and equity-focused educational change: Shifting the zone of mediation. In A. Hargreaves et al. (eds.) *International Handbook of Educational Change, second edition* (pp. 153–168). New York: Springer Netherlands.

Rice, M. (2013, October 29). ASSET bill becomes law—opens doors, raises questions. *Metro Post-Telegraph.* Retrieved October 29, 2013, from http://www.post-telegraph .com/news/education/asset-bill-becomes-law-opens-doors-raises-questions/

Robbins, C. G. (2005). Zero tolerance and the politics of racial injustice. *Journal of Negro Education, 74*(1), 2–17.

Robillard, K. (2012, November 7). Election 2012: Study: Youth vote was decisive. *POLITICO.* Retrieved from http://www.politico.com/news/stories/1112/83510.html

Rogers, J., Morrell, E., & Enyedy, N. (2007). Studying the struggle: Contexts for learning and identity development for urban youth. *American Behavioral Scientist, 51*(3), 419–443. doi:10.1177/0002764207306069

Rogoff, B. (1997). Evaluating development in the process of participation: Theory, methods, and practice building on each other. In E. Amsel and K. A. Renninger (eds.), *Change and development: Issues of theory, method, and application* (pp. 266–286). Mahwah, N.J.: Lawrence Erlbaum Associates.

Rogoff, B. (2003). *The cultural nature of human development.* New York: Oxford University Press.

Rogoff, B. et al. (2003). Firsthand learning through intent participation. *Annual Review of Psychology, 54*, 175–203. doi:10.1146/annurev.psych.54.101601.145118

Rosales, F. A. (1997). *Chicano! The history of the Mexican American civil rights movement.* Houston: Arte Publico Press.

Rose, M. (2004). *The mind at work: Valuing the intelligence of the American worker.* New York: Penguin Books.

Rose, M. (2013, January 23). Character education is not enough to help poor kids. *Christian Science Monitor.* Retrieved from http://www.csmonitor.com/Commentary

Rothstein, R. (2013). *For public schools, segregation then, segregation since: Education and the unfinished march.* Economic Policy Institute. Retrieved from http://www.epi.org/files/2013/Unfinished-March-School-Segregation.pdf

Rubin, B. C. (2007). "There's still not justice": Youth civic identity development amid distinct school and community contexts. *Teachers College Record, 109*(2), 449–481.

Rubin, B. C. (2011). *Making citizens: Transforming civic learning for diverse social studies classrooms* (1st ed.). London: Routledge.

Rubin, B. C., & Silva, E. M. (eds.). (2003). *Critical voices in school reform.* Oxford, U.K.: RoutledgeFalmer.

Rubin, B., & Jones, M. (2007). Student action research: Reaping the benefits for students and school leaders. *National Association of Secondary School Principals Bulletin, 91*(4), 363–378.

Rumberger, R. W. (2003). The causes and consequences of student mobility. *Journal of Negro Education, 72*(1), 6–21.

Sabo Flores, K. (2008). *Youth participatory evaluation: Strategies for engaging young people.* San Francisco, Calif.: John Wiley and Sons.

Sandoval, W. A., & Bell, P. (2004). Design-based research methods for studying learning in context: Introduction. *Educational Psychologist, 39*(4), 199–201. doi:10.1207/s15326985ep3904_1

Schiff, M. (2013). *Dignity, disparity, and desistance: Effective restorative justice strategies to plug the "school-to-prison" pipeline.* Prepared for the Center for Civil Rights Remedies and the Research-to-Practice Collaborative, National Conference on Race and Gender Disparities in Discipline. Boca Raton, Fla.: Florida International University.

Schneider, A., & Ingram, H. (1993). How the social construction of target populations contributes to problems in policy design. *Policy Currents, 3*(1). Retrieved from http://www.fsu.edu/~spap/orgs/apsa/vol3_no1/

Schollenberger, T. (2013). *Racial disparities in school suspension and subsequent outcomes: Evidence from the National Longitudinal Survey of Youth 1997.* Los Angeles: Civil Rights Project, Proyecto Derechos Civiles.

Schott Foundation (2013). *The color of school closures*. Infographic retrieved online from http://www.otlcampaign.org/sites/default/files/school-closings.jpg

Schultz, B. D. (2008). *Spectacular things happen along the way: Lessons from an urban classroom*. New York: Teachers College Press.

Schutz, A., & Sandy, M. (2011). *Collective action for social change: An introduction to community organizing*. New York: Palgrave, Macmillan. doi:10.1057/9780230118539

Seif, H. (2004). "Wise Up!" Undocumented Latino youth, Mexican-American legislators, and the struggle for higher education access. *Latino Studies, 2*(2), 210–230. doi:10.1057/palgrave.lst.8600080

Seif, H. (2009). The civic education and engagement of Latina/o immigrant youth: Challenging boundaries and creating safe spaces. Research paper series on Latino immigrant and civic participation: No. 5. Washington, D.C.: Woodrow Wilson International Center for Scholars. Retrieved from http://www.wilsoncenter.org/sites/default/files/Seif%20-%20Challenging%20Boundaries%20and%20Creating%20Safe%20Spaces.pdf

Sharkey, P. (2009). *Neighborhoods and the black-white mobility gap*. Economic Mobility Project, an Initiative of the Pew Charitable Trusts.

Sirriani, C. (2005). Youth civic engagement: Systems change and culture change in Hampton, Virginia. (*CIRCLE Working Paper 31*.) Medford, Mass.: Center for Information and Research on Civic Learning and Engagement.

Skiba, R. J. (2010). *Zero tolerance and alternative discipline strategies*. Bethesda, Md.: National Association of School Psychologists.

Skiba, R. J., & Knesting, K. (2001). Zero tolerance, zero evidence: An analysis of school disciplinary practice. *New Directions for Mental Health Services, 2001*(92), 17–43. doi:10.1002/yd.23320019204

Soep, E., & Chávez, V. (2010). *Drop that knowledge: Youth radio stories*. Berkeley, Calif.: University of California Press.

Solorzano, D. G., & Bernal, D. D. (2001). Examining transformational resistance through a critical race and Latcrit theory framework: Chicana and Chicano students in an urban context. *Urban Education, 36*(3), 308–342. doi:10.1177/0042085901363002

Solorzano, D. G., Ceja, M., & Yosso, T. J. (2000). Critical race theory, racial microaggressions, and campus racial climate: The experiences of African American college students. *Journal of Negro Education, 69*(1/2), 60–73.

Spradley, J. 1979. *The ethnographic interview*. Fort Worth, Tex.: Harcourt Brace Jovanovich.

Stanley, J., & Weaver, V. (2014, January 12). Is the United States a "racial democracy"? *New York Times: Opinionator*. Retrieved from http://opinionator.blogs.nytimes.com/2014/01/12/is-the-united-states-a-racial-democracy/

Stone, B, & Rennekamp, R. (2004). *New foundations for the 4-H youth development profession: 4-H professional research, knowledge, and competencies study, 2004*. Conducted in cooperation with the National 4-H Professional Development Task Force. National 4-H Headquarters, CSREES, USDA.

Stovall, D. (2006). We can relate: Hip-hop culture, critical pedagogy, and the secondary classroom. *Urban Education, 41*(6), 585–602. doi:10.1177/0042085906292513

Su, C. (2009). *Streetwise for book smarts: Grassroots organizing and education reform in the Bronx.* Ithaca, N.Y.: Cornell University Press.

Su, C. (2010). Marginalized stakeholders and performative politics: Dueling discourses in edution policymaking. *Critical Policy Studies, 4*(4), 362–383.

Sue, D. W. et al. (2007). Racial microaggressions in everyday life: Implications for clinical practice. *American Psychologist, 62*(4), 271–286. doi:10.1037/0003-066X .62.4.271

Sukarieh, M., & Tannock, S. (2011). The positivity imperative: A critical look at the "new" youth development movement. *Journal of Youth Studies, 14*(6), 675–691. doi: 10.1080/13676261.2011.571663

Sullivan, F. (2014). *Electoral engagement among African Americans.* Medford, Mass.: Center for Information and Research on Civic Learning and Engagement. Retrieved from http://www.civicyouth.org/wp-content/uploads/2014/09/CIRCLE_ FS2014_EngagementByEthnicity-AfricanAmerican.pdf

Swanson, C. B. (2009). *Closing the graduation gap: Educational and economic conditions in America's largest cities.* Bethesda, Md.: Editorial Projects in Education Research Center. Retrieved from http://www.americaspromise.org/cities-crisis

Task Force on Youth Development and Community Programs (1992). *A matter of time: Risk and opportunity in the nonschool hours.* Washington, D.C.: Carnegie Council on Adolescent Development.

Tejeda, C., Espinoza, M., & Gutierrez, K. (2003). Toward a decolonizing pedagogy: Social justice reconsidered. In *Pedagogies of difference: Rethinking education for social change* (pp. 10–40). New York: RoutledgeFalmer.

Thomas, V. (2012, May 3). Detroit students suspended after walkout return to school. *CBS Detroit.* Retrieved from http://detroit.cbslocal.com/2012/05/03/detroit-students -suspended-after-walkout-return-to-school/

Torre, M. E., & Fine, M. (2006). Researching and resisting: Democratic policy research by and for youth. In S. Ginwright, P. Noguera, & J. Cammarota (eds.), *Beyond resistance: Youth activism and community change: New democratic possibilities for policy and practice for America's youth* (pp. 269–285). Oxford, U.K.: Routledge.

Torre, M. E., & Fine, M. (2008). Engaging youth in participatory inquiry for social justice. In M. Pollock (ed.), *Everyday anti-racism: Getting real about race in school* (pp. 165–171). New York: New Press.

Torres-Fleming, A., Valdes, P., & Pillai, S. (2010). *Youth organizing field scan.* New York: Funders' Collaborative on Youth Organizing.

Tough, P. (2006, November 26). What it takes to make a student. *New York Times.* Retrieved from http://www.nytimes.com/2006/11/26/magazine/26tough.html

Tough, P. (2012). *How children succeed: Grit, curiosity, and the hidden power of character.* New York: Houghton Mifflin.

Tracy, R., Coronel, I., & Martinez, M. (2010). *Powerful yet small moves: What educators can do to support undocumented students.* Unpublished manuscript.

Tuck, E., & Yang, K. W. (2014). *Youth resistance research and theories of change.* New York: Routledge.

U.S. Department of Education (2014). U.S. Departments of Education and Justice release school discipline guidance package to enhance school climate and improve school discipline policies/practices. Press Release. Retrieved March 17, 2014, from https://www.ed.gov/news/press-releases/us-departments-education-and-justice -release-school-discipline-guidance-package-

UCLA/IDEA(n.d.): *The Williams settlement: What does it mean for California communities?* Los Angeles, Calif.: UCLA's Institute for Democracy, Equity, and Access. Retrieved from: http://justschools.gseis.ucla.edu/news/williams/

United Nations (1990). *Convention on the Rights of the Child.* Retrieved from http:// www2.ohchr.org/english/law/crc.htm

Urie, H. (2010, December 14). Boulder DA: Police should step back from school discipline. *Daily Camera.* Retrieved from http://www.dailycamera.com/news/ ci_16851028.

Vadeboncoeur, J. A. (2005). Naturalised, restricted, packaged, and sold: Reifying the fictions of "adolescent" and "adolescence." In J. A. Vadeboncoeur & L. P. Stevens (eds.), *Re/constructing "the adolescent": Sign, symbol, and body* (pp. 1–24). New York: Peter Lang.

Valencia, R. R. (2008). *Chicano students and the courts: The Mexican American legal struggle for educational equality.* New York: NYU Press.

Valencia, R. R. (2010). *Dismantling contemporary deficit thinking: Educational thought and practice.* New York: Routledge.

Valenzuela, A. (2005). Subtractive schooling, caring relations, and social capital in the schooling of U.S.-Mexican youth. In L. Weis & M. Fine (eds.), *Beyond silenced voices: Class, race, and gender in United States schools* (pp. 83–94). Albany, N.Y.: State University of New York Press.

Vance, F. (2012). An emerging model of knowledge for youth development professionals. *Positive Youth Development: Bridging Research And Practice, 7*(1), 36–55.

Vargas, J. A. (2012, June 25). We are Americans, just not legally. *Time Magazine.* Retrieved from time.com/2987974/jose-vargas-detained-time-cover-story/

Vossoughi, S. et al. (2013). Tinkering, learning, and equity in the after-school setting. *FabLearn 2013.* Retrieved from http://fablearn.stanford.edu/2013/papers/

Vygotsky, L. S. (1978). *Mind in society: The development of higher psychological processes.* Cambridge, Mass.: Harvard University Press.

Warren, M. R., & Mapp, K. L. (2010). *A match on dry grass: Community organizing as a catalyst for school reform.* New York: Oxford University Press.

Warren, M. R., Mira, M., & Nikundiwe, T. (2008). Youth organizing: From youth development to school reform. *New Directions for Youth Development, 2008*(117), 27–42. doi:10.1002/yd.245

Watts, R., & Flanagan, C. (2007). Pushing the envelope on civic engagement: A developmental and liberation psychology perspective. *Journal of Community Psychology, 35*(6), 779–792.

Watts, R. J., Williams, N. C., & Jagers, R. J. (2003). Sociopolitical development. *American Journal of Community Psychology, 31*(1), 185–194. doi:10.1023/A:1023091024140

Way, N. (1998). *Everyday courage: The lives and stories of urban teenagers.* New York: NYU Press.

Weis, L., & Fine, M. (2012). Critical bifocality and circuits of privilege: Expanding critical ethnographic theory and design. *Harvard Educational Review, 82*(2), 173–201.

Weisner, T. (1998). Human development, child well-being, and the cultural project of development. *New Directions for Child Development, 81*(Fall), 69–85. doi:10.1002/cd.23219988006

Welner, K. G. (2001). *Legal rights, local wrongs: When community control collides with educational equity*: Albany, N.Y.: State University of New York Press.

Wertsch, J. (1998). *Mind as action.* New York: Oxford University Press.

Wertsch, J. V. (1991). *Voices of the mind: A sociocultural approach to mediated action.* Cambridge, Mass.: Harvard University Press.

Westheimer, J., & Kahne, J. (2004). What kind of citizen? The politics of educating for democracy. *American Educational Research Journal, 41*(2), 237–269. doi:10.3102/00028312041002237

Wexler Love, E. (2010). *Aspirations, involvement, and survival: Immigrant Latino youth navigating school and community.* (Unpublished doctoral dissertation.) Boulder, Colo.: University of Colorado.

Wilson, L. (2012). *Steve Biko.* Athens, Ohio: Ohio University Press.

Winship, S. (2011). Is U.S. upward economic mobility impaired? *Brookings Institution.* Retrieved from http://www.brookings.edu/research/articles/2011/11/09-economic-mobility-winship

Wortham, S. (2005). *Learning identity: The joint emergence of social identity and academic learning.* New York: Cambridge University Press. doi:10.1017/CBO9780511810015

Youniss, J., & Hart, D. (2005). Intersection of social institutions with civic development. *New Directions for Child and Adolescent Development, 109*(Fall), 73–82. doi:10.1002/cd.139

Youniss, J., & Yates, M. (1997). *Community service and social responsibility in youth.* Chicago: University of Chicago Press.

Zeldin, S., Camino, L., & Calvert, M. (2003). *Toward an understanding of youth in community governance: Policy priorities and research directions.* Ann Arbor, Mich.: Society for Research in Child Development (Social Policy Report series).

Zeldin, S., Christens, B. D., & Powers, J. L. (2012). The psychology and practice of youth-adult partnership: Bridging generations for youth development and community change. *American Journal of Community Psychology, 51*(3–4), 385–397. doi:10.1007/s10464-012-9558-y

Zeldin, S. et al. (2000). *Youth in decision-making: A study of the impacts of youth on adults and organizations.* Chevy Chase, Md.: National 4-H Council.

Zimmerman, A. (2012). *Documenting DREAMs: New media, undocumented youth and the immigrant rights movement.* Presented at the A Case Study Report Working

Paper: Media, Activism and Participatory Politics Project. Los Angeles: University of Southern California.

Zion S., & Petty, S. (2014). Student voices in urban school and district improvement: Creating youth-adult partnerships for student success and social justice. In E. E. Kozleski & K. K. Thorius (eds.), *Ability, equity and culture: Sustaining inclusive urban education reform* (pp. 35–62). New York: Teachers College Press.

Zuckerman, E. (2013a, March 14). *Beyond the crisis in civics.* Presentation delivered at the annual conference of Digital Media & Learning, Chicago, Ill.

Zuckerman, E. (2013b, October 15). Political activism is as strong as ever, but now it's digital—and passionate. *Guardian.* Retrieved October 16, 2013 from http://www.theguardian.com/commentisfree/2013/oct/15/political-activism-on-digital-platform

INDEX

Action civics, 6, 136, 141, 156, 162, 176–177, 199
Adolescent brain, 11–12, 13
Advancement Project, the, 70, 72, 75
Alexander, Michelle, 71
Arab Spring, 170

Baldwin, James, 167
Biko, Steven, 53
Black Consciousness, 53, 81

California Propositions, 2; Proposition 21, 2, 70
Cammarota, Julio, 30
Civic engagement, 55; Critical Civic Inquiry and, 144, 161; among millennial youth, 56–62; philanthropy and, 182; theories of, 27, 60, 170, 181; the study of, 17–18, 199; trends in the United States, 55–62; among undocumented youth, 205
Collective agency, 18, 23, 24, 33, 47, 51, 110, 135, 162, 169
Community organizing, 3, 5, 62, 78, 116, 171
Critical Civic Inquiry (CCI), 6, 19, 34, 180; about, 135–137; challenges to CCI in year two, 141–162; class project addressing racism, 40–46; key practices of, 35; 138–139; literacy class project, 177; special education class project, 179; student outcomes, 35, 50–51; teacher strategies, 156–162

Deficit views of youth of color, 164–167, 172, 174, 180

Deliberative democracy, 80–82, 109; deliberation with students, 85, 177–179, 183; participatory budgeting as example of, 179
Dignity, 33, 52, 133, 172; activism and, 163; of youth of color, 135, 164–165; youth voice and, 5; in media representations of youth of color, 6; rights and, 59

Eckford, Elizabeth, 134
Educational inequality, 3, 6–11, 17, 20, 25, 30, 32, 136, 180, 183; dispossession contributing to, 9–11, 20, 25, 52, 183; inequity versus inequality, 201; race and, 14–16, 164, 174, 180; school closures in context of, 13–14; segregation, 10; Williams v. California, 9

Fine, Michelle, 8, 32,
Frames and framing, 108; activism campaigns and, 116–119, 132, 155–156; school closures and 86; social constructions of youth and, 165
Freire, Paolo, 5, 31–32, 168, 172, 177; banking model of education, 33; critical consciousness, 32–33; praxis, 32, 33

Gay Straight Alliance (GSA), 59, 60
Gilligan, Carol, 168
Ginwright, Shawn, 16, 30
Gonzales, Roberto, 62

Hall, G. Stanley, 11
Hipolito-Delgado, Carlos, 6, 35, 136, 197, 198

ABOUT THE AUTHOR

Ben Kirshner is Associate Professor of Education at the University of Colorado Boulder, specializing in youth development and learning sciences. He directs *CU Engage: Center for Community-Based Learning and Research*, whose mission is to work collaboratively with students, staff, faculty, and community groups to address complex public challenges. Ben lives with his family in Boulder, Colorado.